REPORTS
FROM
AMERICA

REPORTS
FROM
AMERICA

William Howard Russell and the Civil War

ILANA D. MILLER

SUTTON PUBLISHING

First published in 2001 by
Sutton Publishing Limited · Phoenix Mill
Thrupp · Stroud · Gloucestershire · GL5 2BU

British Library Cataloguing in Publication Data
A catalogue record for this book is available from the British Library

ISBN 0 7509 2557 4

Typeset in 11.5/15 Adobe Garamond
Book design and typography by Dean Bornstein
Printed in Great Britain by
J.H. Haynes and Co. Ltd, Sparkford, Somerset.

To My Dear Parents
and
The Darling "M"s

Contents

Part Three: The North. June, 1861 – April, 1862

→ ←

→ ←

Acknowledgments

William Howard Russell is a dream subject. His writing is so vivid and his personality so strong that he virtually leaps off the page. I just tagged along with him on his adventures, easily slipping into his exciting world. My biggest "thank you", therefore, goes to him for making this project such a pleasure.

My thanks also go to:

My mentors in American History, Dr. John McClung and Dr. Stephen Sale of Pepperdine University, Malibu, California, and my mentor in Civil War History, Dr. James L. McDonough.

The Readers Service, the Photography and Rare Books Departments at the Huntington Library, San Marino, California, and all the helpful librarians at Pepperdine University, the University Research Library at UCLA, and Santa Monica Public Library. For help in locating certain photographs, Mike Standifer, Kate Carr, and, for their patience, everyone else at the Elizabeth Glaser Pediatric AIDS Foundation.

To Mindy Paskil for her beautiful map and artistic imaginings.

For their continued inspiration over the years, my dear parents, Sherman and Gloria Miller, as well as my brother, Scott, Lisa, their wonderful family, and my entire family.

For their unwavering support, my fellow writers: Sue Woolmans, Baroness Sheri de Borchgrave, Judy O'Brien, Teresa Basinski Eckford, Tonyia Gray, Arturo Beéche, and Norman T. Herman.

To my editor at Sutton, Jane Crompton, for her cheerful attitude and encouragement.

And lastly, to Elizabeth Mary Hickey and Sister Mary Aloysia Hickey of the Nazareth House, Liverpool for their constant prayers and thoughts.

PART I

The North

SPRING, 1861

Chapter One

"The Gentleman from *The Times*"

WILLIAM HOWARD RUSSELL arrived in New York Harbor on a cold, snowy day in March of 1861. Despite the inclement weather, the celebrated war correspondent for *The Times* of London was eager to report what was then a foregone conclusion—the impending American Civil War.

The British found the contentious questions of the Civil War both puzzling and obscure. Nevertheless, they delighted in news from America because the United States was the country of the future. But more importantly, the average Briton found the Americans fascinatingly "awful." To this end, Billy Russell was sent over to interpret this new and incomprehensible conflict. Since it was based primarily on the peculiar doctrine of States Rights, which to most people's minds meant slavery, it was quite mystifying to the British.

Aboard the paddle steamer *Arabia*, slowly making her way up the Hudson into New York Harbor, the "gentleman of *The Times*" was able to swiftly assess the Northern city's naval defenses. In his diary entry, Russell wrote ". . . against a wooden fleet New York is now all but secure. . . ."[1] With these words, the first professional war correspondent[2] began his frenzied observations that initially made his sojourn in the civil war-torn United States regrettably notorious; and, in the end, regrettably too short.

It was obvious to *The Times* editor, John Thaddeus Delane, that there was a catastrophe brewing in England's former colonies. Though the country was less than one hundred years old, the occurrences could easily be interpreted as the final death throes of the Union. To that end, Delane knew that he needed someone who "knew the military business on the job."[3] For such a position, it was inevitable that Billy Russell would be chosen. There was no one with broader experience, or a finer reputation, to report and evaluate the intricate points of the coming conflict. Especially so since his previous Letters* from the Schleswig-Holstein confrontation of 1850, the Crimean War, and the Indian Mutiny of 1858 had made him one of the most respected, famous and, more importantly, credible newspapermen of his time. Indeed, his reputation was such that his arrival in the United States, though several months before the outbreak of the conflict, was judged by Americans to be an ominous sign. His notable presence confirmed to the British that war between the North and South was inevitable. Because of his prodigious body of excellent reporting, it was natural that *The Times* relied "very largely on Russell for its reputation as a purveyor of foreign news. . . ."[4] It was generally accepted that the all-encompassing watch-phrase after a major conflict, or even a minor one, was "What will Russell say?" Therefore, it was no surprise that Russell's presence was demanded at this crucial time.

William Howard Russell, journalist and personification of the Victorian English gentleman, was actually born in Lily Vale, in the parish of Tallaght, County Dublin, Ireland, on March 28, 1819. Until his later years, he insisted that he was *not* born in the same year as his sovereign, Queen Victoria, but one year after. According to a small biographical sketch he did, entitled *Retrospect*, he had always thought it was 1820 until he was sent an abstract of the Register, which said 1819.[5] Eventually, however, he acknowledged the additional year.

His parents, who moved to Liverpool to seek better economic opportunities, left young Russell in the care of his maternal grandfather, Captain John Kelly, a retired army officer.[6] Like many couples in Ire-

---

* A capital "L" will be used to differentiate between private letters and correspondence written to *The Times*.

land of that day, Russell's father was Protestant and his mother was a Roman Catholic. An agreement was made to raise the boys of the family in the father's religion and the girls in the mother's. However, for the time that little Billy lived with Captain Kelly, he was indoctrinated in Catholicism. Several years later, at the death of his grandfather, the young boy was sent to Dublin to live with his paternal grandparents. With this change in grandparents, Russell's indoctrination also changed. He was now living in a Protestant, "Orange" household.

Perhaps to enhance his grandson's opportunities for a worthwhile career, and certainly because of his own prejudices, Russell's grandfather converted the boy from Roman Catholicism to Protestantism.[7] No doubt, this was a first step in his becoming a full-fledged "John Bull" Englishman. Afterwards, the young man took the entrance examinations for Trinity College in Dublin. Though he passed, and eventually attended, his failure to obtain a scholarship from the institution proved a major disappointment to his grandparents.

According to his biographer, even with a religiously divided family, absent parents and financial insecurity, Russell nevertheless managed to grow up balanced and secure. He was affable, direct, cheerful, good-natured and generous; a tribute to those who brought him up, no matter the circumstances.[8]

Russell's first experience in journalism took place at the youthful age of sixteen. After shooting a very rare bird, he wrote a detailed article about the fowl. Because of the uniqueness of the creature, Russell came to be considered an authority and was later quoted in books about birds of Ireland. After a rather unremarkable college career, from which he left minus a degree, William Russell, at twenty-one still undecided about his future career, met his cousin Robert Russell, who had arrived in Ireland as special correspondent for *The Times*. Robert Russell had been sent to Dublin to cover the Irish elections. Feeling, perhaps, less than qualified to report solely on his own, Robert organized some of the graduates of Trinity to write under his supervision. He paid William one guinea a day and his hotel expenses.[9]

Afterward the elections, Russell continued to contribute articles to *The Times*. Through his vivid accounts of the Irish famine and discontent, he eventually came to the notice of the editor, John Delane, who suggested that he come to London and read for the English bar. Taking the good editor's advice, Russell arrived with a glowing, yet understated, reference from his former schoolmaster, the Reverend Geoghegan: "I believe you to possess the very qualities requisite to form a good reporter."[10] He was promptly engaged to write exclusive reports on events and issues in Ireland. Since he was a special reporter, Russell was not on retainer and, therefore, was obliged to take a full-time position as a junior schoolmaster in Kensington.

In 1842, the position became redundant at the school, and Russell was dismissed. Now, he needed to find a practical career. Just when he had decided he would work as a freelance journalist, Delane offered him a permanent position as parliamentary reporter. Although he accepted, his main interest was Ireland, its problems and unrest, including the trial of Daniel O'Connell and his followers. His reporting of this trial should have marked his first distinguished and exclusive story. Unfortunately, this was not the case. At the door of Printing House Square, where *The Times* was published, a lethargic-looking young man was loitering. He engaged young Russell, who had returned from the O'Connell trial, in lengthy conversation about that subject—Russell saw his "exclusive" in the *Morning Herald* the next day. The inexperienced reporter learned the difficult but valuable lesson of not idly giving out information.[11]

Russell continued his studies for the bar while pursuing a writing career with *The Times*. In 1845, offered a more substantial salary, he moved to the *Morning Chronicle*. Once more, his assignment was parliamentary proceedings.

In 1846, he returned to Ireland to marry his fiancée, Mary Burrowes, a young lady he had known for three years. She was the daughter of a prominent Roman Catholic family, who were diametrically opposed to Russell politically. She was, according to one of Russell's biographers, one of those "pretty, unassertive, rather helpless young women that men of vigor often find attractive."[12] The following year, their first child, Alice, was born. Russell continued his work in Ireland, reporting its myriad problems. In 1847, the *Morning Chronicle*, experiencing financial difficulties, reduced the salaries of its reporters. Russell, who was now ill as well as newly-married, was given the ultimatum to get up and work, or leave the paper.[13] He decided to return to London in order to continue his studies for the bar. To support himself and his bride, he once again turned to freelance writing.

In 1848, Russell returned to *The Times*, this time permanently. For several years, he covered state trials and his preferred interest, Irish problems. In 1850, he was assigned to the Schleswig-Holstein War, providing him with his first major opportunity. Exciting Letters flowed back to *The Times*, recounting, first-hand, the decisive Battle of Idstedt. In his zeal to get the story, the reporter was wounded in the fray, perhaps the first of such wounded reporters in history, doing their all for their readers; this would be only the first of several wounds that Billy Russell would sustain in the heat of battle.

In June of that year, he was finally called to the bar at Middle Temple. Russell never actively practiced law, but for many years took the infrequent case.

Following his journalistic success at Idstedt, Russell rapidly became a popular war correspondent. To the Victorian readers of his Letters, ". . . war ceased to be an objective undertaking taking place in some far-off field. Russell brought war to the fireside, . . . [and] . . . the breakfast table. . . ."[14] He was innately gifted with foresight, and had the painter's and naturalist's eye for vivid description. More importantly, he wrote things down in a readable manner that was accessible to all.[15]

The young reporter also became enormously popular with literary figures, such as William Makepeace Thackeray and Charles Dickens, who elected him to their very insulated and exclusive Garrick Club. Not only was he now known for his fledgling fame as a war correspondent, but also as a man with a tremendous aptitude for friend-ship,[16] one well-known for his wit and ability as a raconteur, as well as a trencherman, a drinker and a gambler. He was a congenial man, ex-cellent company and constantly sought after as a dinner companion.[17]

In 1852, Russell covered the funeral of the Duke of Wellington. One fateful passage finished with the words: ". . . should days of darkness again come and this land of freedom be once more threatened, God may grant us another Wellesley to lead our armies and win our bat-tles."[18]

Two years later, Russell was sent, as special correspondent, to cover the Crimean War. The conflict may not have had the magnitude of a Trafalgar, but it changed the face of the British armed forces forever. That April, Russell found himself in Gallipoli, Turkey, and remained in the Crimea for nearly two years. He was in a quandary, for he had no real precedents regarding what to report. Before, he had written Letters on two combatants, about whom he could easily and objec-tively comment. This time, however, it was his own army whose suf-ferings he was forced to witness. He queried himself endlessly as to what an honest man could report regarding the ". . . obvious utter in-competence . . ."[19] of the British Army. As a result, the misery of the Crimea was told truthfully. When he found abuses and mismanage-ment in the commissariat and the medical departments, he wrote about them. He saw an army that lacked sufficient amounts of every-thing: food, water, clothing, guns, munitions; one mired in unneces-sary hardship, and he wrote about that, too.[20] He was no less honest in his criticism of Lord Raglan, Commander-in-Chief of the armies of the Crimea. Raglan had the dubious distinction of being ". . . the first general to conduct a war under the eyes of newspaper corespondents."[21]

Russell ". . . related what he saw and reported what he heard hon-estly, and with a vigor and vividness that earned him unquestioned right to the reputation he gained."[22] The most famous and hard-hit-ting of his Letters were written about the suffering of the army in the miserably cold winter of 1854/55, including the thoroughly "botched-up" Battle of Balaclava. It is reputed to have inspired Alfred, Lord Tennyson to compose "The Charge of the Light Brigade." Later, it no doubt inspired Rudyard Kipling, in his poem of 1902, "Tommy", since Russell was the man who coined the term "the thin red line."

Inspiring as these accounts were, they did not endear Russell to the headquarters staff who, meanly, prevented him from drawing rations. Luckily, Russell's well-known charm prevailed, and he was able to depend on friends and acquaintances for food and clothing.

His greatest contribution, and one long remembered, was his appeal for nursing aid. Disease was rampant in the soldiers' camp, the result of a deplorable lack of sanitation. These pleas inspired the indefatigable Florence Nightingale to organize a hearty band of nurses to relieve the graphically described wretchedness at Scutari.[23] Additionally, his Letters were said to have caused the fall of Lord Aberdeen's government; if so, this would be the first time a correspondent had caused such a government upheaval.[24] Russell, however, never felt like a casual observer. In a letter, filled with pain, he told his wife Mary of ". . . the kind good friends I have lost, the dear companions of many a ride and walk and lonely hour."[25] An emotional man, who often wrote in the heat of moral indignation, he cursed all who delighted in war.

It is interesting to note that George Washburn Smalley of the *New York Tribune*, another great war correspondent and writer, described Russell's Crimean accomplishments in this way:

> The one great triumph of English journalism in the Crimea . . . was due to the genius and courage of one man, Dr. Russell.[*] . . . It never will be, till another Russell appears to rescue another British Army. . . . That great exploit was not primarily journalistic but personal.[26]

Russell, however, was not so self-laudatory as others might have been

---

[*] On return from the Crimea, Russell was created an honorary LL.D. of Trinity College in Dublin.

in these circumstances. In some agitation, he wrote to his foreign manager, Mowbray Morris:

> I have incurred the hostility of powerful classes in England who have never forgiven and never will forgive the course I took during the war in the Crimea. And I have reason to know that among them was poor Prince Albert and no doubt the Queen herself.[27]

There was little doubt that *The Times* and Russell made history, since it was in the paper itself that the British government learned of the Russian peace proposals that ended that war.

Doubts and censure notwithstanding, by the time of the Indian Mutiny of 1858, Russell was world-famous and treated with deference wherever he went. The mutiny became his next major assignment. In his capacity as an experienced military observer, he was asked to judge the truthfulness of the accounts of the horrible massacres that were "'raising the ire' of the country."[28] For this assignment, he was asked to accompany Colin Campbell, Lord Clyde, whose object was to put down the mutineers. During this campaign, Russell was, again, wounded and, because of the injury, he had to be carried in a litter for several weeks. However, despite his infirmity, he continued to send home his dispatches. It is to these dispatches that Delane, Russell's editor, attributes the cessation of indiscriminate executions. Russell wrote:

> For the Sepoy let there be justice, and, if justice be death, let execution be done, but let us cease to disgrace ourselves by indiscriminate clamouring for "more heads"....[29]

Delane replied to him saying: "I feel myself, and hear everybody saying, that we are at last beginning to learn something about India...."[30] Russell, his task completed, left India in 1859.

That summer, wishing to take a well-deserved break and to restore the general health of their family, the Russells traveled to Switzerland for a holiday. Mary was frequently ill, and had lost a fifth child when

Russell was in India. She miscarried a sixth when they returned from Switzerland. It was there, however, that he met a friend, John Bigelow, who piqued his curiosity about America.[31]

Upon his return to Great Britain, Russell became editor and chief partner of the *Army and Navy Gazette*. He and a group of friends felt that there was sufficient interest in the imperial defenses to publish a magazine, devoted exclusively to this subject. The publishers, Bradbury and Evans, consented to publish the journal on the condition that Russell remain at the helm. This he did for the next forty-one years.In addition, they promised to publish any books that Russell might write about his various experiences. This proved to be a lucrative opportunity for the journalist, who was constantly worried about his sickly wife and endlessly concerned about leaving her for long periods of time. As editor of the *Gazette*, he also arranged that he be allowed to freelance for *The Times* whenever an assignment of importance became available . . . and so it happened in 1860.

At about this time, Russell began to develop friendships with several Americans, which would prove useful during his eventual sojourn in the States. Of particular note were Mr. John Bigelow and his family, who were visiting London that year. Thus a correspondence began between the two men, in which each expressed his opinion of the events taking place in the United States.

The Times already had a correspondent in New York. Since 1854, J.C. Bancroft Davis, a lawyer with Northern sensibilities, had been sending Letters back to England. *The Times* manager Mowbray Morris called him "a remarkably good specimen of an American."[32] Delane reasoned that, with the coming conflicts, another point of view, especially a Southern one, would prove invaluable. Russell, the natural choice, was told by his friend Thackeray: "You must go. It will be a great opportunity."[33]

In a letter to John Bigelow, just before his arrival in New York, Russell wrote:

. . . every friend of despotism rejoices at your misfortune; . . . it is the shame of them who have perhaps over zealously advocated the absolute perfection of the great Republic; it is assuredly a grave and serious obstacle to the march of constitutional liberty.[34]

In the same letter, he further stated that any good Englishman felt ". . . intense respect and great sympathy . . ." for said republic.

With all the respect and sympathy that Russell most sincerely professed, he was, nevertheless, quite clear in his conviction that the Union was permanently divided. It was unfortunate for his readers that for the year Russell spent in America, nothing convinced him otherwise. Perhaps it was because he saw a North indifferent and divisive, and a South cohesive and strongly unified.

Russell's Letters from various Southern cities reflect conclusions formed by objectively reasoned observation. From Charleston, South Carolina, he commented: "I am more satisfied than ever that the Union can never be restored as it was. . . ." From Montgomery, Alabama, he wrote: "I am convinced that the South can only be forced back by such a conquest as that which laid Poland prostrate at the feet of Russia." From New Orleans: "Now that the separation has come, there is not, in the constitution, or out of it, power to cement the broken fragments together." Finally, from Washington: "I remain faithful to my original belief that it's all up with the United States, but of course no real U.S. man will believe it."

In addition to this firm conviction that the Union could not be saved, Russell believed that the United States government would give up neither power nor possession. Nevertheless, if Russell made his trip with one mistaken preconceived notion, and, incidentally, most of the Fourth Estate agreed with him, in all other things he ". . . strove to write the truth as he knew it, put the event in historical context, and . . . [assess] . . . its significance and the lesson learned."[35] He felt very strongly that it was a reporter's duty to be as objective as humanly possible. In his introduction to the diaries from America he wrote:

No man ever set foot on the soil of the United States with a stronger and sincerer desire to ascertain and to tell the truth. . . . I have no theories to uphold, no prejudices to subserve, no interests to advance, no instructions to fulfil; I was a free agent, bound to communicate to the powerful organ of public opinion represented, my own daily impressions of the men, scenes and actions around me. . . .[6]

Further, in a letter to Bigelow, he modestly expressed doubts about his competence in American affairs: "I felt I had few qualifications for the post, though I had read *Uncle Tom's Cabin*, . . . and read extracts from fiery speeches of Calhoun. . . ."[37] Despite these scrupulous admissions of a certain lack of background, Russell became ". . . the most influential source . . ." of American affairs in Great Britain.[38]

Undoubtedly, a man with such a careful approach to the profession of journalism found it difficult to work with a newspaper whose pro-Southern sympathies, like most other papers in England, were quite marked. If preconceived notions abounded, then editor Delane, who wrote that ". . . the South threatens to secede . . . [but] . . . the quarrel will be patched up; for the North cannot live without the South, and lives, indeed, a good deal on and by it . . . ,"[39] was certainly more guilty of such prejudice than was Russell.

Despite all of Russell's good intentions, there were those who expressed doubts regarding his objectivity. Mary Chestnut, the famous Southern diarist, wrote that one of his Letters was ". . . very well done for a stranger who comes and in his haste unpacks his three p's—pen, paper, and prejudices. . . ."[40]

As Russell's ship made its way slowly into New York Harbor, much had already happened to divide the states.

* * * *

Russell had admitted that his knowledge of the conflict between the Northern and Southern sections of the United States was encapsulated in a reading of *Uncle Tom's Cabin* and attendance at several abolitionist meetings in London. He, no doubt, underestimated himself. Like most well-educated people of the day, he eagerly followed events in America, and certainly had some idea of how the country had come to this strange and desperate hour.

Interestingly enough, when a Dutch ship let the first Africans off the boat in 1619, the fledgling colonies had no codes under which they could legally enslave them. It was only by the mid-century that the colonies, needing cheap labor for their labor-intensive crops of tobacco and cotton, began writing the slave codes. Now men, who had been indentured servants and theoretically would work off their terms just as their white counterparts had done, were enslaved for life. There were always objections to this on biblical and moral grounds, and, eventually, the institution became peculiar to the agrarian southern part of the colonies.

After the end of the Revolutionary War, and a short period of Confederation, the American Founding Fathers sat down to write a Constitution—laws under which the United States would exist as a republic. Many disagreements were indeed resolved, but the one issue that seemed never to find a resolution was the issue of slavery. Debates about the morality of enslaving one's fellow man gave way to arguments about representation in Congress. Since in the lower house, the House of Representatives, representation was determined by population, the Southerners felt strongly that their slaves should be counted for that representation. Naturally, many in the North disagreed.

Eventually, after much wrangling, a compromise was reached that was called the "Three-Fifths" Compromise. This provided for a slave to be counted as three-fifths of a man. Therefore, when a census was taken for popular representation in Congress, three-fifths of the Southern slave population was also counted.

As compromises often go, this made very few people happy. Indeed, it is bewildering to speculate on how they arrived at this figure and as repugnant as slavery was to many of the signers, the thought of disunion was more abhorrent. This concession continued, so that guarantees for slavery and capture of fugitive slaves were included in the Constitution, though the word "slave" appeared nowhere in the document. And so, the United States, with a written Constitution, joined the nations of the world, partly slave and partly free.

However, this situation was not to last. As America began its expansions in the nineteenth century, the questions of free and slave arose repeatedly. In 1803, President Thomas Jefferson purchased the territory of Louisiana from Napoleon. The country doubled in size. When the land was divided into territories, and the territories into states, Missouri was the first to request entrance into the Union. At that time, 1819, there was a balance of eleven free and eleven slave states—an equilibrium that had proven somehow liveable.

With this new request for statehood, a fierce debate ensued. Luckily, Maine picked this time to ask for entrance into the Union, and a compromise was reached. The proposer was Henry Clay; a great senator, orator and five-time presidential candidate. He was called, for reasons that will become obvious, the Great Compromiser. The provisions were simple: Maine would come in as a free state, Missouri would come in slave, and all states north of the longitude and latitude of 36°30' would be free.

In 1828, Senator John C. Calhoun of South Carolina, his eye on national office, introduced the Doctrine of Nullification. This doctrine stated that if a state did not agree with a law passed by the Federal government, it could hold a state convention and declare the law to be null and void. This was tested in 1832, during the so-called "Nullification Crisis." Congress passed a tariff that South Carolina felt was unfair. They decided to nullify the law. President Andrew Jackson, a Southerner himself, threatened force and fortified some Federal forts in the area. The debate had reached boiling point when Henry Clay, again, proposed a compromise. Luckily, this compromise was accepted by the Federal and State governments—both parties stood down, and a lesson was learned: "No state could defy the Federal government alone."[41]

By this time, American nationalism was characterized by, among other things, her Manifest Destiny to settle the entire continent, from the east to the west coasts. To this end, the country continued expanding westward. In the 1840s, more territories, Texas and Oregon, were acquired. Texas, through a great deal of debate, became a state in 1845. Oregon, however, was another matter.

Britain and the United States had jointly occupied the Oregon Territory since the early part of the century. In 1845, President James K. Polk called for an end to this joint tenancy. A compromise was reached with England that the United States territory would reach only to the forty-ninth parallel, not 54°40', as the battle cry went, and a treaty was signed—not for the last time—averting war between the two countries.

After the Mexican War of 1846–48, the Treaty of Guadalupe Hidalgo was promulgated, ceding even more land to the United States. The Mexican Cession, as it was called, encompassed much of what is today the southwestern states, as well as California, Colorado and parts of Wyoming and Oklahoma. With such an enormous acquisition of land, more debates developed about whether their status would be slave or free. More compromises were needed.

The Wilmot Proviso, proposed by Pennsylvanian Congressman David Wilmot, stated that slavery should not exist in the Mexican Cession. This was never passed, though it was debated in Congress more than forty times. It was only one of the many solutions that were proposed. President Polk called for a bill that would provide free states north of 36°30', all the way to the Pacific Ocean. South of the parallel would be slave. This proposal satisfied no one.

By the time of Zachary Taylor's election in 1848, news of the discovery of gold in California was telegraphed across the nation and throughout the world. "Forty-niners" from every known country on earth were flocking to California to make their fortunes. Calls for organization of the Mexican Cession were heard urgently throughout the country.

Debate once again raged in Congress about the admission of the states, with an eye to keeping the balance between free and slave states. Henry Clay, for the last time, stepped in with what was later termed the Compromise of 1850. It was during this debate that William H. Seward, later Secretary of State during the Civil War, made his famous "Higher Law" speech. He said that there was "a higher law than the Constitution . . ." and that the crisis depended on whether ". . . the Union shall stand, and slavery removed by gradual voluntary effort . . . whether the Union shall be dissolved and civil war ensue, bringing on violent but complete and immediate emancipation."[42]

The Compromise of 1850 admitted California as a free state, and the Mexican Cession would be organized as territories, the terms of servitude to be decided later by the population. This pleased very few people, but staved off violent conflict for another decade.

The 1850s were full of expansionist dreams. Slave holders dreamed of empires in Mexico, Cuba and even Canada, while abolitionists pondered a country where everyone, black and white, would be equal under the law. Harriet Beecher Stowe, the daughter, sister and wife of Protestant clergymen, wrote *Uncle Tom's Cabin*, motivated by her heartache over the Fugitive Slave Act, another part of the Compromise of 1850. This section of the bill made it more difficult for fugitive slaves to obtain their freedom and easier for their masters to regain their so-called property. Mrs. Stowe's book personalized the issue of slavery and the horrendous condition of the black man. Queen Victoria wept when she read the book. The South was alarmed by its popularity.

In 1854, the Republican Party was formed, made up of anti-slavery elements of the Democratic Party and the Whig Party (the previous second party). Included were racist elements — those who didn't want slavery to expand to the territories because they could not envision blacks living there; included also were moral elements — the abolitionists who abhorred slavery, though they were often called radical Republicans; lastly, there were people like Abraham Lincoln, who, though he disliked slavery, hoped that it would die a gradual death and that the country would not take up arms because of it.

Events escalated when Kansas applied for statehood. Proponents of slave and free flooded the territory, hoping to gain a majority. John Brown, the radical abolitionist, and his sons arrived to fight the pro-slavery elements. Violence soon erupted, and the new Republican Party grabbed this issue and went overboard, calling for the relief of "bleeding Kansas."

Events weren't much more civilized on the floor of Congress. In 1855, Senator Charles Sumner made a speech enumerating the crimes of Kansas and all the killing that had taken place in the name of both sides. This so enraged a Southern congressman, Preston Brooks, that he tried to cane the senator to death. He nearly succeeded. The Brooks-Sumner confrontation was soon front-page news. Brooks was hailed as a hero in his native South Carolina and below the Mason-Dixon line, but the North was horrified. Indeed, the two sections of the country were becoming so polarized that the North looked at the South as something dark and evil, while the South saw the North as wanting to take away their basic freedoms and God-given rights.

The election of 1856 only illustrated further the separation of North and South. The Democrats ran a stately and slightly infirm old gentleman, a former Ambassador to Great Britain, James Buchanan. Since Buchanan had been in Britain a good deal of the early 1850s, he wasn't identified as being involved with the sectional crisis. In short, he offended nobody. The Republicans ran the so-called "Pathfinder", John C. Fremont, who had no particular record to embarrass the party. His slogan was "Free soil, free men, Fremont."

The result of the contest bode ill for the future, at least in the eyes of the South. Fremont won in eleven out of the sixteen free states, but, nevertheless, the sixty-five-year-old Buchanan, taking the South, triumphed. This election dismayed the South because they realized that a candidate who managed to carry all the free states, though he carried no slave states, could win the election. What was worse, this candidate could be anti-slavery.

Two days after Buchanan took office, the Dred Scott Decision was handed down by the Supreme Court. The issue before the Court was whether Scott, a slave living in the free territory of the Louisiana Purchase (later Minnesota), was able to sue for, and win his freedom. The grounds were that since he lived in free territory, he was a free man. The decision, written by Chief Justice Roger B. Taney of Maryland, did not agree. He wrote that Scott was a slave and property, and therefore he was not a citizen. Since he was not a citizen, he could not sue in Federal Court. Lastly, people had the right to take their property wherever they wished.

The North was aghast. In one fell swoop, Taney had invalidated every compromise made in the nineteenth century. The decision caused a sensation, debated endlessly in Northern and Southern papers, with people like Seward and Lincoln calling it nothing less than a conspiracy. The South was delighted.

In addition to this controversy, the United States was suffering a serious economic depression. Perhaps it would be more accurate to say that the North was doing most of the suffering. It was due to overproduction of goods and overexpansion of the railroads, while the South, being far less industrialized, was hardly affected by it. This added to their confidence that they could well do without the North and prosper as a separate country.

It was at this time that a senator from South Carolina, James Hammond, made his famous speech and proclaimed loudly and boldly that "COTTON IS KING." He wasn't just saying that the North couldn't live without it, but that the entire world was dependent on the Southern states for their source of essential cotton. Indeed, in the last years of Buchanan's presidency, the South became more and more convinced that it could, and should, do without being attached to the Northern states.

In the midst of this powder keg, John Brown once again inflamed the crisis. In October of 1859, he and his sons, together with some eighteen men, led the famous raid on the Federal Arsenal at Harper's Ferry. Having captured the arsenal, Brown meant to start a slave revolt which would spread throughout the entire South. The revolt did not happen, and the men could not hold the arsenal against a company of Federal troops led by U.S. Army Captain Robert E. Lee. After ten of his men were killed, Brown surrendered and was taken into custody. He was tried for treason in the state of Virginia and was hanged in December of 1859. The South was indignant and self-righteous, while the North was aghast at the execution. To many, this seemed to be another nail in the coffin of the Union.

The election of 1860 clinched matters; coming so soon after John Brown's raid on Harper's Ferry, the country seemed in a violent mood. The Democratic Party had, more or less, split into two, North and South, and some independent parties, offering various ineffectual panaceas to the grave problems of the Union.

The Northern Democrats nominated the "Great Debater", Stephen A. Douglas. The Illinois senator's platform was "Popular Sovereignty", in other words, let the people decide whether to have slavery in their territories. The Southern Democrats chose John Breckenridge, who promised to uphold the Dred Scott Decision, but was not a Secessionist. The Constitutional Union Party, comprised of old-line Whigs, called for enforcement of the Constitution and her laws, as well as an insoluble Union. They nominated John Bell, who promised to continue to compromise over the sectional differences. The Republicans met in Chicago, calling for no slavery in the territories and protective tariffs on imported goods. They nominated the less controversial of the front-runners, Abraham Lincoln.

In this national mood, it came as no surprise that North and South continued to move apart. One need go no further than Russell's fellow journalists, the editorial staff at the *Charleston Mercury*. In October, an editorial was written detailing the terrors that awaited an unsuspecting South if Abraham Lincoln was elected. The scenario was construed to be that the abolitionists would come south in such numbers as to divide her; that there would be a new protective tariff; that the Underground Railroad, spiriting slaves north to freedom, would become the Overground Railroad; and that slave property would be devalued by an estimated four hundred and thirty million dollars. They concluded that the so-called terrors of submission were vastly worse than secession. This was, in fact, the mood throughout most of the South.[43]

In November of 1860, after the second highest voter turnout in American history, the Southern fears of 1856 were confirmed. Abraham Lincoln was able to win the presidency without carrying a single Southern state, and only obtained 40 percent of the popular vote. After that, it was only a matter of time. By December 1860, South Carolina, Georgia and Florida seceded from the Union, and the battle lines were drawn.

Chapter Two

"...the sewer of the nations..."

NEW YORK CITY, MARCH, 1861

THE BATTLE LINES, Russell knew, were disproportionately drawn. The face-off between North and South could not have been more unbalanced. The North retained control of more than two-thirds of the states. Her population was roughly twenty-two million. The South, on the other hand, had nine million, one-third of whom were slaves. The North was a highly industrialized and diversified society, while, as Rhett Butler said, there were few factories south of the Mason-Dixon line. The North had more than twenty thousand miles of railroad, while the South had less than half that. In the final analysis, the North possessed more than three-quarters of the nation's financial resources, while the South, short of liquid capital, had great difficulty financing the war.

Nevertheless, the Southerners did have some advantages. They fought a defensive war with shorter lines of supplies and communication. The Southerners were accustomed to an outdoor life of riding and hunting, far more so than the Northern shopkeepers and factory workers. The South was endowed with outstanding military leaders, such as Thomas "Stonewall" Jackson and Robert E. Lee, while the North struggled much longer before finally finding its great leader, Ulysses S. Grant. Most importantly, the South had the will and spirit to fight for the "glorious cause." The Northerners were hardly happy fighting a war against slavery, nor was "States Rights" a clearly defined or inspiring opponent.

Before continuing with Russell on his journey through the United and Confederate States of America, there are a few additional pieces of the picture to examine. A look at the immense influence of *The Times* of London on the educated English public, indeed, the entire English-speaking world, is vital. The attitude of the educated English public towards America and her people must be evaluated. In addition, a look at the questions that urgently concerned England, as well as the Britons' odd conception of the typical American, would be beneficial.

The Times of London, stalwart bastion of Britain, was founded in 1788 by John Walter, a former underwriter of Lloyds of London. Initially, *The Times*, with an eye to appealing to a broad audience, wrote exciting stories about famous people. Amid the scandals and gossip, Walter wrote a story about the Prince of Wales that "rewarded" him with a two-year sentence in Newgate prison. Since he was also in the pay of the government, they naturally expected him to write favorable stories.

His son, John Walter II, did not agree with this particular arrangement. When he inherited control of the paper in 1803, he strove to create a publication that would be independent of government interference. To this end, he hired a group of journalists who would seek stories on their own, and who invested their jobs with a new concept, journalistic integrity. As one of *The Times* first great editors, Thomas Barnes, too, was responsible for this independence.

As time went on, the paper became critical of the government, and argued long and loud for parliamentary reform. In 1832, Sir Robert Peel told the House of Commons that *The Times* was the "principal and most powerful advocate of reform" in Britain.[1]

In 1841, John Walter II appointed twenty-three-year-old John Thaddeus Delane editor of the paper. Like Russell, Delane had started out as a parliamentary reporter, and strongly supported Walter in his quest for journalistic credibility. He believed that *The Times* should be independent of all political parties, and he worked side by side with the manager, Mowbray Morris, coordinating the paper's foreign correspondents. However, he also felt strongly that the paper should serve the nation's interests, and made sure that both of these principles would work in tandem. He shared this vision with John Walter III, who succeeded his father as chief proprietor. By now, *The Times* had earned a reputation as the "preeminent national journal and daily historical record."[2]

Though Russell's reputation as a war correspondent was unparalleled, the profound influence of *The Times* on the educated readers of the English-speaking world (including the United States and Canada) must also not be underestimated. Russell himself wrote that there was no power so potent in producing that effect on public opinion in England that would determine her course in a variety of affairs, foreign and domestic, as his ". . . own popular little periodical."[3] Further, the historian Goldwin Smith wrote in 1863:

> I think I never felt so much as in this matter the enormous power which *The Times* has. Not from the quality of its writing . . . but from its exclusive command of publicity and its exclusive access to a vast number of minds.[4]

Finally, John Bigelow, the nineteenth-century diplomat, diarist and Russell's friend, wrote that *The Times*, as a journal, had more power over the British government and public opinion than ". . . all the journals of the world combined."[5]

There were, nevertheless, those who found this all-encompassing power a dangerous tool in less than responsible hands. In 1865, an anonymous pamphlet discussing this very issue (the author of which was revealed later to have been British intellectual, Leslie Stephen) was published. This small work utilized the American Civil War as a subject for the analysis of *The Times* and its sway over its readers. Stephen explored the mystique of *The Times*, saying it "was . . . regarded by ordinary men and women as a mysterious entity, a concrete embodiment of the power known in the abstract as 'public opinion.'"[6] In describing how this force would extend across the water, Stephen lamented the ignorance of the British public regarding the average American, and the many reasons an American may have found himself involved in a civil war:

> In our ignorance of the cause of some great foreign convulsion, we judge of it partly by the way in which it affects our interest, and partly in accordance with certain traditional prejudices. There must be something radically wrong in a war which affects our supplies of cotton; and we cannot credit a race who chew tobacco and wear bowie knives with any heroic virtues.[7]

Curiously, Stephen himself was not free from these prejudices. He later stated, with regard to the insult of *The Times'* pro-Southern stand that ". . . no American—I will not say with the feelings of a gentleman, for of course there are no gentlemen in America. . . ." [8] More to the point, however, *The Times'* coverage of the Civil War was judged by Stephen, despite his opinion of Americans, and many others to have been a gigantic mistake. Furthermore, with regard to the newspaper's integrity and consistency, ". . . it has none."[9] He concluded on a reassuring note to the American public, saying that *The Times* did not represent the views of all intelligent and thoughtful Englishmen. Indeed, it ". . . only supplies the stimulating, but intrinsically insipid fare that most easily titillates an indolent appetite. . . ."[10] A scathing, but courageous, indictment of the most powerful and influential organ of the Victorian world.

All criticism aside, the fact remains that *The Times* was respected throughout the empire. It, therefore, becomes critical to understand just how it used its enormous power. *The Times* and, more importantly, its executive staff (whose views largely represented and reflected the bias of the upper-classes and the educated Englishman) were decidedly pro-Southern. John Walter III, an avowed "anti-Unionist", wrote: "Why should we be so very anxious to see the Union preserved? What has it done to command our sympathy?"[11] Despite a visit to the United States in 1856, John Delane was ignorant of American affairs and institutions. In addition, he was opposed to universal manhood suffrage.[12] Lastly, the foreign manager, Mowbray Morris, a conservative born in the West Indies, had decidedly Southern sympathies. About slavery and the South, Morris wrote to a friend:

> You will find much to interest you, but probably little ocular proof of the evils charged against their peculiar institution. As a rule the slave is well fed and housed, carefully attended in sickness & often cherished in old age: the exception is when the animal is not worth his hire.[13]

Though readers today find this attitude a little bone-chilling, this sort of pronouncement by *The Times'* executives raised Southern hopes that Britain would recognize the Confederacy. Parenthetically, *The Times* was the only major newspaper to give *Uncle Tom's Cabin* a poor review, finding it crude and bad propaganda. In all fairness, Morris tried to rid himself or, at least, the paper of its pro-Southern biases, advising another American correspondent to try to find something good about the Federals, but, inevitably, he greatly enjoyed hearing them abused.[14] Naturally, this all succeeded in driving a wedge between Britain and the North.[15]

Continuing this trend of English sympathy, James Spence, another zealous pamphleteer, wrote a most persuasive argument urging recognition of the South. He felt that the Confederacy should be ". . . another power added to the family of nations. . . ."[16] He further wrote that the *de facto* government of the South should be legitimatized, citing examples of other formerly ruled countries, such as Greece, Holland and Portugal, whose governments were recognized under hostile conditions. British animosity toward the North already existed, and the Union had already lost its prestige. Spence concluded that slavery would not be abolished unless the South willed it, that the war was hopeless and that, in the process, it was harming Europe. Therefore, the quicker Britain recognized the South, the better for all parties, including both of the belligerents.

In the face of all this self-righteous involvement, it was expected that the British would "gleefully" involve themselves in another international altercation. The average-educated Englishman felt compelled to express his opinions about whatever was happening, wherever it was happening. ". . . [I]t was inevitable for Englishmen—accustomed to meddling with abuses everywhere—to take sides in an American Dispute. . . ."[17] Most of the London and foreign press took sides. The majority of the London press supported the South, with the exceptions of the *Daily News*, the *Spectator* and the *Manchester Examiner*.[18] In January of 1861, the *Economist* wrote in highly anticipatory tones:

> . . . the tidings from what we can no longer call the United States bid fair . . . to surpass all others in interest and importance. . . . Nothing that passes beyond our shores can affect us so powerfully or concern us so much as . . . the great Federal Republic.[19]

Indeed, powerfully concerned as the pro-Southern Press were about the demise of the "Federal Republic", they regarded the internal institutions of the South, namely slavery, as her own business, thus leaving their consciences out of the matter entirely. Further, they compared the Confederacy with Brazil, saying that the Confederates, by establishing good faith externally, were excused from their conduct in internal affairs, thereby giving *The Times* and its readers a justification for ignoring the South's peculiar institution. Conversely, with the distance of an ocean, *The Times* and its journalistic colleagues felt no compunction about expressing extravagant opinions regarding matters which were not strictly their business.[20]

It is interesting to note that although *The Times* had initially adopted a neutral position, they, nevertheless, wanted to retain the freedom to pronounce mirthful condemnations of the antagonists. Soon, however, after some half-hearted wavering, the men behind *The Times* enthusiastically embraced, among others, the convincing reasoning of pamphleteer Spence. Taking a positive stand on the justice of the Southern cause, it seemed that ". . . a unified and implacable

South was a phenomenon which *The Times* found very difficult to resist. . . ."[21]

To be fair, however, John Delane, in his capacity as editor, did try to take a more equitable tone in dealing with the issues across the Atlantic. He fully published the letters of both his United States correspondents, although they were both pro-North. He tried to demonstrate ". . . the objective journalistic policy of *The Times*. . . . His correspondents . . . [told] . . . the truth as they saw it."[22]

In addition to the profound influence of the foremost daily journal, the thoughts and opinions of the group that Leslie Stephen skeptically called "Public Opinion" should also be considered. The British had definite opinions about the experiment in democracy in which its errant child was indulging. Furthermore, having abolished slavery many years before, the prevalent trends in Britain were decidedly against this "abhorrent" institution existing elsewhere. Clearly, a potential country who supported slavery could not count on British support. Neither could a country who was conducting a war for strictly venal economic motives.

Lastly, the Americans, themselves, were an enigma upon which the average Englishman could only speculate and stereotype. Regarding democracy, slavery and economics, full spectrums of opinion were eagerly expressed. The loutish stereotype of the rough frontiersman, however, the bumptious braggart who was convinced that he lived in the finest and freest country in the world, loomed large and without argument in the British psyche and, for that matter, the British press. Russell himself, as he traveled through the United States, was grateful for the slightest traces of civilization. Whether it was a good meal, decent accommodations, or finding the company of amiable and intelligent gentlemen, these were noted in his diary as being finds of immense delight, and seeming rarity. Equally, his diary was full of horrible food, terrible hotels without adequate spittoons, and the above-mentioned brutish clichés.

On May 14, 1861, Queen Victoria pronounced a Declaration of

Neutrality with regard to the American Civil War.[23] This declaration was seen in the North as a deliberately malicious act, and as a virtual and premature recognition of the South. To many Englishmen, however, the South had many of the attributes of an independent state: its own government, a culture and a way of life vastly different than that of the North, and the will to fight to be free of the Union. Britain, however, recognized the belligerent status of the South, not her independence.

This declaration did not alter the fact that upper-class Englishmen admired the gentility and elegance of Southern society. Moreover, the aristocratic Britons' fear of the alarming spread of republicanism was an important element of their support for the South. The revolutionary upheavals throughout the world made the privileged classes feel insecure.[24] Therefore, it was not difficult for this group to have publicly maintained its "neutral" position, while in private to have vigorously rubbed its hands with untoward glee at the thought of a failed Union.

Further, if the experiment was unsuccessful in America, clamors for more democracy at home could be easily squashed. Since the upper-class British felt the war was a direct result of democratic government, they fully expected to see it discredited as soon as possible. Democracy was a defective policy that would deteriorate into anarchy and despotism, dying a slow but natural death.[25]

John Walter III put it bluntly when he wrote: "The whole affair is looked upon in this country as a breakdown of democracy; that is one of the main causes of the absence of sympathy."[26] However, Russell saw another meaning, which he states in a letter to Charles Sumner:

I do not approve of the tone of many papers in Great Britain in reference to American matters . . . in reality it is . . . republicanism at home which most of those remarks are meant to smite—America is the shield under which the blow is dealt.[27]

Perhaps, had the thinking Englishman believed that the war was explicitly fought to end slavery, recognition of a moral purpose could more easily be given. In another letter to Charles Sumner, Russell wrote:

> There would perhaps be an overwhelming sentiment of popular sympathy with the North in this conflict if they were fighting for freedom; but the pretence that this was an anti-slavery war cannot be sustained for a moment. . . .[28]

President Lincoln himself quite clearly stated in his inaugural address that he had ". . . no purpose, directly or indirectly to interfere with the institution of slavery in the states where it exists." He believed that he had ". . . no lawful right to do so, and [had] no inclination to do so."[29] Americans, in the beginning, had no intention of stating clearly that this was a war against slavery; indeed, few would have thanked anyone who had made such a commitment.

For this same-thinking (and self-righteous) Englishman, pecuniary motives were insufficient to base any war upon, or the support of any war. Economic concerns, however, no matter how blatant, threw out moral considerations quickly enough, particularly when the flow of cotton became endangered.

During the winter of 1860–61, Europeans were willing to accept, with alacrity, the separation of the American republic. They could easily consider slavery an internal problem and none of their business, as long as this did not culminate in war, which could dangerously disturb the flow of business. However, culminate in war it did, and the economic sanction of blockade gave rise to fears that the wealthy textile county of Lancashire might easily revolt. It was estimated that one-fifth of the entire British population was dependent, directly and indirectly, on cotton prosperity and looked to the American South for 80 percent of their supplies.[30]

That the South ". . . received only the most illusory solace from the British aristocracy . . ."[31] did not prevent growing Northern animosity towards Great Britain. The Union felt that Britain took the South's part out of self-interest. However, to be scrupulously accurate, the moral reason (slavery) for support of the North was, initially, non-existent. The preservation of the Union itself provided scant interest to English newspaper readers, and certainly none to the English upper classes. Lastly, economic coercion, in the form of any kind of sanction, such as a blockade, was to be resisted at any cost.

Though the British found the contentious questions of the Civil War both puzzling and obscure, they delighted in news from America. In part, this was because, as stated, the United States was considered the country of the future, but even more so because the Britons found the Americans one step up from primitive exotics. It is interesting to note that, though American affairs were all that was talked of seriously in the British drawing-room, the bad manners and bad habits of the typical American (chewing tobacco and shaking hands), were endlessly ridiculed.

The English had come by many of these misconceptions honestly. In the 1830s, Frances Trollope, mother of the famous novelist, and Harriet Martineau had both published descriptions of Americans that ". . . contrived to offend Northerners and Southerners alike." To add insult to injury, after a visit to America in 1842, in which he was feasted and fêted, Charles Dickens managed to write ". . . in the American chapters of *Martin Chuzzlewit,* an account so ferociously contemptuous . . ." that he was unable to return to America for over twenty-five years.[32]

Through misunderstanding of the American and his love of country, the British attitude became one of contempt. It was obvious that

> . . . except for slavery, the issues of the war were incomprehensible to the British; they understood liberalism, in a constricted sort of way, but they never grasped nationalism. Perhaps their own nation had been around for so long that they could not recognize its analogue elsewhere.[33]

Not surprisingly, when the war did come, the British interpretation of events was guided by British traditions and interests. Their attachments, North and South, however sentimental, proved tenuous in the face of their own interests. Although understandable, this self-interest left relations with America mired in ignorance and misapprehension.

It was to this perverse climate of misunderstanding, coupled with the ambiguous nature of Anglo-American relations, that Russell would present his credentials and letters of introduction.

* * * *

Russell left Queenstown, Cork Harbor, in Southern Ireland, on March 2, 1861. The voyage was cold and miserable, with strong winds blowing, and, unfortunately, there were few good sailors among the passengers. As time went on, however, remnants of the passenger list began to trickle in for meals, and the gregarious Russell was saved from complete boredom. The food itself was very good. Russell wondered how such liberal meals, five times a day, could be managed; however, he was grateful for the abundance and said they were excellent for their kind.

Intrepid reporter that he was, Russell decided to begin his observations much before he set foot on American soil. Aboard the steamship, he began to study fellow passengers who came from both sections of America, and their broad spectrum of viewpoints. He talked to many who were pleased to discuss the situation. Among them was Mr. Julian Mitchell of South Carolina, a vehement "secesher", who expressed a particular dislike for the "rail-splitter", Mr. Lincoln, and had no love for William Seward and the Secretary of War, Simon Cameron. He was adamant about the States Rights issue, as well as Mr. Calhoun's Doctrine of Nullification.

Russell probed Mitchell closely—who would South Carolina look to if attacked from abroad? Herself? A host of sister states? Or, perhaps, the nation? Mitchell did not respond, but continued to criticize the new regime, saying: "No gentleman could tolerate such a government."[34]

There were two Louisiana sugar planters, whose main interests were not the legal principles involved, but whether their crops would continue to be picked by workers who would remain on their property. To them, secession was a measure that should be taken only in the most extreme cases, and, certainly, there should be no violence. Russell observed that Louisiana, whether she liked it or not, would have to go — or suffer isolation.

Representing the sentiments of the Union was a young merchant, Mr. Brown, from New York, a nephew of an English Member of Parliament. He was a well-educated man from a good Northern university. With typical insularity, the reporter pronounced him well-informed and intelligent because he had spent a great deal of time in England. The young man was resolute, but not violent, in his determination to keep the Union together. Another young man, a college friend of Mr. Brown and also a merchant, professed similar feelings. He expressed support for the Union, though it seemed not a tangible thing to him, but an abstraction, like truth or freedom.

Other passengers were Major Robert S. Garnett, from Virginia, a fervent States Rights man and blatantly antagonistic to the North; a family from Nashville, who was unenthusiastic about the possibility of war; a New Yorker with a decided prejudice against Irish immigrants; and, the most enthusiastic of all Northerners, the German immigrants.

In his conversations, Russell learned that President-Elect Abraham Lincoln had made a trip to New York, on his way to Washington, D.C. to attend his inauguration. Surprisingly, especially in view of the evident unpopularity of the President, he received a tremendous ovation from large crowds as he rode to his hotel. In New York, Lincoln was fêted for several days, going to the opera, teas, and even Barnum's Museum, a prime tourist attraction of the day. Indeed, the Prince of Wales himself, who had visited the previous October, had made a stop there. Mr. Lincoln learned that the city was extremely uneasy. Its leaders worried about what would happen if the country went to war against itself. Lincoln breakfasted with a hundred of the city's most wealthy merchants, and their main concern, like the men in Lancashire, was that the rhythm of business should not be disturbed. Lincoln knew that he would not let the South go lightly, and his feelings about keeping the Union from tearing itself asunder were too well-known. He could, therefore, give but few reassurances to the businessmen on that point.[35]

Russell further noted, from conversations with passengers, that the Northern army was made up primarily of Irishmen and Germans. As he had already heard from the New York merchant, he observed again that the Irish were disliked by Southerners. They complained that if it came to war, the best blood, meaning theirs, would be spilled by the lowest, meaning the immigrants. He noted too the utter contempt many on board had for Universal Male Suffrage in America. One American lady asserted that the Irish, now a familiar scapegoat, should not be allowed to vote as they were ignorant. She considered them useful, but only for building roads.[36] As for the Germans, they were swine, according to Major Garnett, ". . . who are swept out of German gutters as too foul for them. . ."[37]; he complained further that now they would be able to avail themselves of a country where they could do as they pleased. Russell himself chimed in with the general view of his fellow passengers, calling the Germans aboard, brutes and beasts.[38] The mentioning of the Irish and Germans wherever he found them was a common thread running through Russell's Letters and diary. The attitudes behind these references seemed quite in line with the sentiments expressed by Americans, even when they, themselves, had Irish or German in their family trees, as Russell himself did.

Regarding the American passengers, Russell noted that they were already two separate nations: they sat apart "with intense antipathies on the part of the South, which was active and aggressive in all its demonstrations."[39]

Though not distracted from his course by his private life, Russell, nevertheless, poured out his worry about his children and, in particular, his sickly wife, Mary, in his private diary too. He was constantly concerned about her various illnesses and conditions, and anxiously awaited letters from her.

In addition to his many conversations with the passengers, Russell did a voluminous amount of reading about the United States. He mentioned in his private diary having perused *The Cotton Kingdom* by Frederick Law Olmsted, the man who designed New York's Central Park. He wrote that a like picture of misery and ignorance could be seen in England, describing people who were "neither slave owners nor slaves."[40]

Russell came ashore at the Battery on March 16. He was anxious to begin his assignment, and did so immediately by assessing the harbor. He was satisfied that it could easily be defended. Indeed, it would be hazardous for the enemy to make a run for the batteries, unless possibly attacked by a large complement of ironclads.[41] He noted the numbers of Irish and Germans on the docks speaking Hibernianized or broken English. He was appalled by the lack of porters, though he eventually procured an Irishman to organize his trunks and secure a carriage.

Describing the people and places of America, Russell wrote as though he were talking about anthropological curiosities or, perhaps, an interesting kind of human zoo. One is given the impression of a tour director describing passing scenery and local novelties while his passengers sit wide-eyed and open-mouthed, their noses pressed against the coach windows. Nowhere is this more evident than in Russell's narration of his New York experiences. The city that Russell saw, as he rode up the New York streets to the Clarendon Hotel, was one noisily teeming with life and commerce. He called it the "sewer of nations,"[42] full of absolutely everything and everyone imaginable. During the drive, which he called long and tortuous, Russell saw more oyster-shops, saloons and people from all walks of life than he thought possible in one place. As the carriage continued uptown, however, things did change for the better. The streets were more attractive, with their churches, concert halls and private homes.

In the days ahead, Russell was to discover more about New York's ambivalence regarding the smoldering conflict to come. Many New Yorkers felt that a state that wanted to leave the Union had the right to do so, and no Federal government should prevent that state's secession. Russell mentioned that the President's inaugural address had exacerbated the forces at work to destroy the "cohesion of the Union."[43] New York herself had considered departing the Union, as the crisis mounted. Earlier in the year, her mayor, Fernando Wood, had proposed to his council that should the Union be no more, then New York should become a free-trade city.[44] The mayor reasoned that if New York became an independent entity, its citizens would no longer be subject to the crippling tariffs on imports imposed by the Federal government. A few months later, the issue became moot, since the seceded states announced large tariffs of their own.

The following day, March 17, St. Patrick's Day and falling on a Sunday, saw Russell amusing himself as he watched people going to Mass. He could see that the men were wearing insignia, indicating that they were Irishmen. As was his wont throughout the tour, Russell mentioned the meals, for good or ill, at the hotels. At breakfast this particular morning, the food was evidently not worth mentioning, and all Russell noticed were the white-jacketed waiters and accouterments for serving the meal. Afterwards, he took a walk up and down Fifth Avenue, observing the Sunday custom of parading along the avenue in various hats and costumes. People chatted with their friends, commending them on their apparel. He compared the broad promenade to the West End of London, with its handsome tree-lined streets and elegant homes. He examined the beauty of the American women and said that they need fear no negative comparisons from abroad. Amazingly, he found little fault with the females, outside of their lack of stature. Their beauty, he felt, might be surpassed only by the Hindu women he had seen in India.

That afternoon, Russell met with Mr. George Bancroft, a former minister to the Court of St. James. The journalist wrote that anyone with an "ex" carried no weight. "Ex-presidents are nobodies, though they had had the advantage, during their four years' tenure of office of being prayed for as long as they live."[45] The same went, he continued, for ex-ministers, such as Mr. Bancroft, for whom no one prayed at all. In their discussions, Bancroft praised the republican form of government, saying that it was the best in the world. He, too, however, felt that the South should not be coerced. As an historian, Mr. Bancroft would eventually produce a twelve-volume history of the United States. He would change his mind about secession during the strife, and counsel the President about historic precedent.[46]

Russell dined that evening with a New York banker, Mr. William Butler Duncan. Because Duncan was of British descent and educated in Europe, he was deemed by Russell to have given a dinner of great taste and distinction. Over cigars and brandy, the writer was surprised to see how sanguine the gentlemen were about the possible demise of the Union. Surely, he thought, they would have the most to lose in such a violent conflagration.

Russell also knew that bankers and merchants would feel the loss of business if there were an upheaval of the proportions that a civil war suggested. They feared that the Southerners, who were in great debt to them, could not make good on those debts should there be such a war. Therefore, it was strange to him that they sat and discussed such matters, as Mr. Brown's friend had done aboard the steamer during Russell's voyage to the United States, as nothing more than vague abstractions.

The day after, March 18, was actually celebrated as St. Patrick's Day. As a prominent Irishman, Russell was invited to dine at the Astor House with the Friendly Society for St. Patrick. There continued much parading on Fifth Avenue by the sons of Erin. Russell was amused: "The Americans appeared to regard the whole thing very much as an ancient Roman might have looked on a Saturnalia; but Paddy was in ascendant, and could not be openly trifled with."[47]

At the Astor House there was much feasting and toasting. Being the finest hotel in New York, and probably the biggest, it reminded Russell of a railroad terminal. He was, however, in his element, and happily went about the aforementioned feasting and toasting. He was, nevertheless, sorry to see so many natives of Britain express so much anti-English sentiment. When he was asked to address the conclave, he delivered a speech expressing a fervent desire that the Union stay together. He became emotional when he stated:

> I come among you at a period of great difficulty and excitement. . . .
> I cannot and will not believe that the people of the United States
> are about to whistle, a prey to fortune, the greatest legacy a nation
> ever yet received.[48]

He added that he'd never seen such a well-dressed group of Irishmen.

His speech was printed in the New York papers the next day. Barely remembering that he had delivered such an address, he wrote (with a bad hangover): "I am much affected by reading my speech in the papers. O, Lord, why did I do it?"[49] This rather indiscreet speech endeared him to the North, at least at the time. Whether Russell was pleased or not by a description of himself that appeared in the American press, one can only imagine:

> He has short iron locks parted down the middle, a grayish mous-
> tache and a strong tendency to double chin, a very broad and very
> full but not lofty forehead: eyes of a clear, keen blue, sharply obser-
> vant in their expression, rather prominently set and indicating
> abundant language.[50]

However, observations of the situation began immediately. Russell noted several New Yorkers' comments on the recent election. They were, it seems, ". . . disgusted at the election of such a fellow as Lincoln to be president and would back the Southern states if it came to a split."[51] He also remarked that New Yorkers thought Mr. Lincoln's administration was made up of completely undistinguished men.

That evening, Russell dined again with William Butler Duncan, the banker, and several other important gentlemen. Among them were the

Hon. Horatio Seymour, former Governor of New York, Samuel Tilden and George Bancroft. The evening's discussion centered upon the Constitution's ability to prevent secession. There was much argument for the document's being an agent of the people, as well as the states. They felt that the government was an agent for the states, particularly in dealing with foreign powers. This was similar to the stipulations in the Articles of Confederation, the predecessor to the Constitution. Russell had read the Constitution that very morning, but the lawyer in him did not feel any more enlightened by the conversation. He complained that the document seemed to refer itself to the Supreme Court. And, how would the Supreme Court act if armies were called up and battle lines drawn? Their joint conclusions seemed to be that the principle of secession could be injurious to capital and property.[52] Yet, the company seemed unmoved by the evacuation of Fort Sumter and the South arming itself. Though they all agreed, if the fort was threatened by a foreign power, the Federal government would quickly find a way to relieve it. New York, Russell concluded, ". . . would rather do anything than fight; her delight is to eat her bread and honey and count her dollars in peace."[53]

These very interesting gentlemen aside, Russell was surprised to find New York almost completely apathetic to the threats of secession. In his first Letter to *The Times*, he commented:

> If an intelligent foreigner . . . were to visit the United States at this juncture, he would fail to detect any marked indication of the extraordinary crisis which agitates the members of the Great Republic. No doubt there is great agitation and feeling, but it is not apparent. . . .[54]

Russell and all his opinions were much in demand. He was virtually inundated with invitations. John Bigelow commented: "His head is a little turned already by the attention he is receiving."[55]

During the day, Russell strolled the streets, taking in the sights. He wrote especially about the shops, such as A.T. Stewarts, and found them suitable to rival the best establishments of London and Paris. The bookstore, Appletons, boasted a million-and-a-half volumes, but had nothing available on the present difficulties. He did notice that there were a number of photography shops all over, and refered to them as a "plague."[56] And, because there was an absence of any sense of an old family-owned business, Russell felt that New York's commercial districts had the air of being nouveau riche: "There is about it an utter absence of any appearance of a grandfather."[57]

Several days later, the London correspondent had the opportunity to meet the editor of the *New York Tribune*, Horace Greeley. The *Tribune* was well-known for its lurid tales of the iniquities of slavery. There was a continual flow of articles observing first-hand the slave auctions, the strange and exotic "goings-on" on the plantations and the ugly mistreatment of the workers. The readers of the paper were alternately horrified and titillated.

Greeley, a staunch abolitionist, advised Russell to ". . . be sure you examine the slave pens. They will be afraid to refuse you, and you can tell the truth."[58] One imagines that Russell nodded his head in agreement with Greeley; however, his private thoughts were much different. In a letter to John Delane, Russell wrote that Horace Greeley was the "nastiest form of narrow minded sectarian philanthropy," who would be rid of all the whites in the South to satisfy his own conscience. In reality, however, according to Billy Russell, he was only ambitious, and a separation from the South would best feed that ambition.[59]

Whatever his ambitions, and they would later be presidential, Greeley rightly presumed that Russell would be offended by actually observing slavery in progress. Would it be as comfortable for this upper-class Englishman to criticize the practice after seeing it first-hand? Or, perhaps, since the class system existed in England, he might see it as the natural order of things in the United States.

Russell had been scheduled to visit many sites in New York, including the new state penitentiary, Sing-Sing, which claimed, he wrote, to be the first institution of its kind in the world. But the correspondent felt pressed to move on. He wanted to be in the thick of the action, and escape what he perceived to be the indifference of the New Yorkers.

Before leaving at the end of March, Russell read, experienced and formed a life-long impression of the American press. They delighted in ridiculing public figures, such as Lincoln and Greeley. Russell questioned a gentleman with whom he was conversing as to what he thought about the papers writing such contemptuous things about the President, and the man answered:

> Oh yes, that must strike you as a strange way of mentioning the Chief Magistrate of our great Republic, but the fact is, no one minds what the man writes of any one, his game is to abuse every respectable man in the country in order to take his revenge on them for his social exclusion, and at the same time to please the ignorant masses who delight in vituperation and scandal.[60]

Russell must have been glad that *The Times* was perceived to be above such chicanery.

The jocose, gossipy and personal manner in which, for example, the description of Russell himself was penned, however, was not nearly as offensive to him as the kind of language the newspapers used.

> "Slang" in its worst Americanized form is fully used in [sensational] heading and leaders and a class of advertisements which are not allowed to appear in respectable English papers, have possession of columns of the principal newspapers. . . .[61]

Russell also found it extremely strange that the newspapers purporting to represent the most civilized, enlightened and highly educated people on earth featured advertisements for sorcerers, wizards, fortune tellers and clairvoyants, as well as very unsavory personal columns. During his stay, Russell's impression of the press never improved. In his Letters and diary, complaints about its lack of ethics, quality of writing and sensationalism became chronic.

[41]

Just before Russell pushed on to Washington, he had a breakfast meeting with members of the New York Press Association. Among them were Henry Jarvis Raymond, editor of the *New York Times*, Frederick Olmsted, whom he described as "little, nice, lame Olmsted", and Charles Anderson Dana, managing editor of Greeley's *Tribune*. Naturally, there was talk of politics and, not unusually, a complete division of views. Secession and Sumter were the subjects on everyone's tongues . . . and everyone disagreed.

Having formed some interesting acquaintances, and having derived some impressions of New York, Russell was ready to proceed to Washington, D.C. In a letter to Delane, written on his first day in Washington, he discussed some of these impressions. They were days, he wrote, that were profitless and pleasureless, due to the cacophony and violence of opinions. He had, he said, never encountered such a "diversity of assertion & opinion extending even to the minute matters of fact . . . even in the House of Commons. . . ." Although he found New Yorkers charming, tremendously hospitable and willing to fill him up with meals that seemed big even to his healthy appetite, he was much more seriously concerned about the opinions he heard rejecting Universal Suffrage and Freedom of the Press. They would, however, be in favor of a foreign war that would remove this ". . . domestic cancer. Their bad leg of 50 years standing would they think be cured in an instant by gunpowder. . . ."[62] They would be motivated to relieve Sumter only if it were in danger from a foreign power, which Russell disdained.

As reprints of his Letters to *The Times* drifted back across the Atlantic, Russell's ideas would not only annoy New Yorkers (whose apathy evaporated, a fact duly chronicled by Russell), but would motivate the feelings that would lead to abusive attacks on the writer after more controversial Letters to London were reprinted.

→ *Chapter Three* ←

"... the insalubrious swamp ..."

WASHINGTON, D.C., MARCH—APRIL, 1861

ON THE EVENING OF March 25, Russell traveled by train to Washington, a trip that was extremely uncomfortable. On board, he was happy to find a Mr. Henry Sanford, the United States Ambassador to Belgium, who gladly took him under his wing. After stopping in Philadelphia, they thankfully acquired sleeping berths, which Russell considered an American institution of great merit. There was, however, one problem. A group of prize-fighters had decided to make the car their home for the night, enabling no one to get much sleep. Instead, the train rang with all manner of songs, and good-natured offers of drink. Several of these men, in highly gregarious moods, told Russell that they meant to go to Washington to get foreign missions. France was no good, they explained, because they didn't speak French and didn't care much for Frenchmen. They all thought England might be better, since it would be good to show John Bull a thing or two. Like children, they remained reluctant to go to sleep, but eventually the drinking took its toll. They were adamant that they would not "sleep unless they damned pleased," but, nevertheless, "slept and snored."[1]

The following morning, Russell arrived in a city that was unbearably hot and muggy. The Washington of 1861 little resembled the elegant city that it was to become. The population was small, about 63,000,[2] and there was little doubt in Russell's mind that this was surely due to the insalubrious climate and environment. The elevation was low, it was swampy and full of all manner of flying insects. In the summer, it was hot and humid, and in the winter, it was subject to floods. The sanitation left much to be desired, and diseases such as typhoid and tuberculosis were rampant. Socially, it was not at all what a sophisticated Englishman might want. Lord Lyons, British Ambassador, complained that Washington was not a good town for young men. For one thing, there were no decent clubs or restaurants, and for another, the city was full of saloons, brothels and gambling dens.[3] Though certainly a work in progress, the city on the Potomac was, nevertheless, a seething and exciting place to be.

Russell took his first walk along the wide boulevard of Pennsylvania Avenue. On a fine day, social, political and business leaders could be seen promenading up and down the broad thoroughfare. Men in top hats and ladies in wide hoop skirts wanted to be sure that they would see and be seen. Russell was only interested in seeing the unfinished capitol building. The dome was completely scaffolded, and the building itself would soon be used for a fort, a barracks and a hospital during the war. The dome, however, would not be completed until much later. Russell walked back up the avenue toward the White House and his destination—the splendid Willard's Hotel.

Willard's was an establishment well-beloved by the gentlemen of the press. It had been remodeled to six massive stories by two brothers from Vermont, and was, at that time, one of most popular hotels in Washington, D.C. Its popularity extended not just to the press, but it attracted an assortment of men and women from all over the country and the world. An interesting arrival was Georges Clemenceau, the French statesman, then employed as a young, fledgling scribbler for *Le Temps*.[4] In fact, nearly five hundred correspondents had poured into the city, and it seemed to Russell that they were all staying at Willard's.[5]

As were the other journalists who had arrived with him, Russell was given his key and shown to his room. Nevertheless, he quickly headed back to the public rooms to soak up the atmosphere. The rooms were enormous and crowded with people from all walks of life. Since there was some delay in receiving his luggage, the journalist decided to have breakfast. The dining room, again, was massive, easily able to accommodate twenty-five hundred hungry people. "Hungry" being the operative word, for when Russell saw what the others were eating, he was amazed. Being no shirker when it came to dining, Russell was, nevertheless, taken aback at the quantities of food his fellow diners consumed. A typical breakfast might comprise: fried oysters, steak and onions, scrambled eggs, all sorts of fish and game, as well as toast, blanc mange and pâté de foie gras. Russell did note, however, that there was a considerable waste of food. After this enormous repast, midday dinner was served at five in the afternoon, tea at seven-thirty and supper at nine. To add to all the other oddities, the dining hours were unusual for the Englishman.

After eating as much as he possibly could, Russell wandered back into the pandemonium of the main lobbies and drawing rooms. This quadrangular mass of rooms, he wrote, contained more scheming, plotting and planning than he had seen anywhere in the world. There were gentlemen everywhere with their pockets bulging with testimonials, letters of introduction, documents of great accomplishments and, sadly, simply not enough spittoons to accommodate them all.[6] Willard's, usually thought to be the most elegant hotel in Washington, was now not only filled to overflowing with Russell's fellow journalists, the "Bohemian Brigade", the nom de guerre of the Civil War correspondents, but also "choked" with a less than admirable group known as "office-seekers." Office-seekers were the natural result of the recent elections. There were appointments aplenty and hundreds of jobs to be had in the government, if only the office-seeker could get an appointment to see the right man. This was known as the "spoils system", as in the famous saying: "to the victor go the spoils."

Russell wrote that there was a "ferment" in Washington that could take place in no other part of the world. It was a singular "spectacle" that would make the observer wonder how any man could be persuaded to seek office or that governing could be ". . . conducted under such a system."[7] However, govern under this system the United States government certainly did; most notoriously so under the administration of Andrew Jackson. In a modified form, the practice still exists to the present day.

The other hotels of the city were also filled to capacity with these gentlemen. Indeed, ". . . the streets, railroad carriages, etc., bulge with them."[8] At the time of the newly inaugurated President, they came from every corner of the country, including the South. Willard's Hotel, as mentioned, was the center of this frenetic activity. However, anywhere else that these office-seekers could ". . . surprise a potential ally with letters, etc., they will do so!"[9] This particular point was brought forcefully home to Russell, when he presented a man with his letter of introduction. The gentleman said, "Sir, I know you must be a stranger because you did not stop me to present these letters in the street."[10]

Russell marveled that men may come thousands of miles to seek an office that may last for only four years, but "with true American facility have abandoned the callings and pursuits of a lifetime for this doubtful canvas."[11] He also marveled that President Lincoln was able to see all of these men, yet get any of his important work accomplished. He explained to his readers that the President was the head of this system, and must see office-seekers from morning until night. Russell was sure that this was certainly the moment when the President should be left to cope with more important and pressing matters. The opinions, speculations and rumors over these immediate issues settled over Washington like a miasma over a swamp, from which, at the time, the city was only one step away.

Because the issues of secession and the fortification of Southern forts had Washington wound up like a tight rubber band, the press was left with opinions, rumors and speculation. Everyone was waiting for something—anything—to happen. They were sure that it would be any minute but, as yet, waiting was all that they could do. With nothing to write, and as a consequence of constant conjecture, the press, it must be said, did very little to educate the public with the facts. To illustrate, Russell recounted a story of meeting a man from New York who had been sent by a daily to report on the Washington scene. He told Russell:

At first, I merely wrote news, and no one cared much; then I spiced it up, squibbed a bit, and let off stories of my own. Congressmen contradicted me . . . said they were not the facts. The public attention was attracted, and I was told to go on and so the Washington correspondence became a feature in all the New York papers.[12]

This did not enhance Russell's view of the American press, and, to his thinking, its authenticity became totally suspect.

As he became progressively more aware of all that was transpiring, Russell began to comprehend the snippets of conversation that traveled in Washington circles. The tense situation at the Federal forts in the South, Pickens and Sumter, was on everyone's lips, and Russell wrote, less than prophetically, ". . . any attempt to relieve Sumter would be attended with great loss of life."[13] The integrity of the Union, however, seemed of too little importance. He wrote that he met very few people who really showed any ". . . passionate attachment to the Union for its own sake. . . ."[14] Nevertheless, many looked to what Russell said and wrote. His veracity, at least, was not in question. He was thought to have great influence, not only with the British government, but as the primary arbiter of English public opinion.

Washington rumbled, and Russell had the experience to understand those rumblings. Three days following his arrival, he commenced writing home compelling and detailed Letters. This correspondence was the beginning of a long series that would eventually comprise the experiences of an incredibly tumultuous time. The Washington and Southern Letters were later published in a book entitled *The Civil War in America*. They recounted Russell's journey to the South and his return several months later. The remainder of the Letters,[15] unfortunately, were never published in book form.

Russell's diary entry of March 26, 1861 recorded that he dined at the home of his erstwhile train companion, Henry Sanford, the United States Ambassador to Belgium. There, he made the acquaintance of Secretary of State William Henry Seward, whom he had the opportunity to meet frequently in the following weeks. Russell described him as:

> . . . a slight middle-sized man of feeble build, with the stoop contracted from sedentary habits and applications to the desk. . . . [He had] a well-formed and large head . . ., keen eyes [which] were seeking . . . an adversary. . . . [T]he nose [was] prominent and aquiline. . . .[16]

Seward, earlier, had made an unfavorable impression on the English when he remarked to the Prince of Wales that ". . . when he became Secretary of State, it would be his duty to insult England."[17]

His hostility toward England evidently put aside, Seward made it a point to talk about secession and other issues of great immediacy. He, at least, showed great devotion to the Union. He told Russell that his brothers and sisters had "seceded" from the family home early in life, but had eventually come back. He was sure that the errant Southern states would also do so.[18] Though Russell doubted whether Seward had ever been in the South, he, nevertheless, began to talk authoritatively on the Southern states. He claimed that they were like New York at the turn of the century. He also discussed their dependence on black labor, and how they mistook idle extravagance for elegant luxury. They were nothing, he assured the company, compared to the Northern states. Seward also declared that Sumter would never be surrendered. The journalist duly recorded this statement in his diary, and not for the first time.

Consequent of this first meeting, Russell presented himself at the State Department the following day. Seward had promised to introduce him to President Lincoln. The State Department, Russell wrote, was a humble, even dingy two-story building, situated at the end of a "magnificent line of colonnade in white marble, called the Treasury. . . ."[19]

Anyone, he wrote, who was familiar with Downing Street could not be offended by the dinginess of the building.

Seward's son Frederick, the Assistant Secretary of State, met Russell and escorted him to the President who, coincidentally, also had an audience with the representative of the new kingdom of Italy. As an aside, Russell mentioned that Seward's young son did not have the appearance of a gentleman and had to suppress the urge to shake hands. He awaited his interview with the newly elected President with great anticipation.

> Soon . . . there entered, with a shambling, irregular, almost unsteady gait, a tall, lank, lean man, considerably over six feet in height, with stooping shoulders, long pendulous arms, terminating in hands of extraordinary dimensions, which, however, were far exceeded in proportion by his feet. He was dressed in an ill-fitting wrinkled suit of black, which put one in mind of an undertaker's. . . .
>
> [He has] the appearance of kindliness [and] sagacity . . . full of an expression which almost amounts to tenderness. . . . One would say that, although the mouth was made to enjoy a joke, it could also utter the severest sentence which the head could dictate. . . .[20]

Lincoln was then introduced to Russell, and this time extended his hand. Upon learning of his affiliation with *The Times*, Lincoln said:

> Mr. Russell, I am very glad to make your acquaintance. . . . The *London Times* is one of the greatest powers in the world. In fact, I don't know anything which has much more power—except perhaps the Mississippi.[21]

Russell was favorably impressed by Mr. Lincoln's sense of humor, his shrewdness, his wisdom and his noted use of anecdotes in illustrating a point. When dining with the President, he must have felt another kindred spirit, for Lincoln was also a noted raconteur. Throughout his stay, Russell's good opinion of Mr. Lincoln never wavered.

It is interesting to note that such a steadfast admiration was not extended to President Jefferson Davis of the Confederate States. During dinner that evening, however, Seward was full of praises for the personal qualities of the Confederate leader.[22] Russell's pen, nevertheless, was poised to reserve judgment until the eventual meeting. And, even after that meeting, Russell could not quite bring himself to admire Davis unreservedly.

During his stay in the capital, the journalist began receiving invitations to dine with all of the socially and politically brilliant figures of Washington. During meetings with various people, Russell made special note of the conversations and subject matter which were of immediate concern to Washingtonians. These topics were included in his Letters to *The Times*, in which Russell would instruct his reading public about the subtleties of the conflict.

One such theme, uppermost in American minds, was the concept of States Rights and its weighty bearing on the secession issue. In his Letter from Washington dated April 1, 1861, he wrote that it was ". . . scarcely possible for an Englishman, far less for the native of any state possessing a powerful Executive . . ." to understand the powers of a state, or how far a state may go to resist the authority of the Constitution. This, even though the state is a consenting party to that Constitution. His observations, however, told him that many in Washington sympathized completely with this doctrine. Again, his legal brain was trying to understand which powers the Constitution did and did not have.

Russell set about educating the British public on several subjects that were crucial to understanding the civil strife. As mentioned, his views about the Southern states returning to the Union were quite decided. Much space in his columns was devoted to clarifying the economic difference of the two sides; for example, free trade vs. protectionism. British readers were made aware that they were to play a part in the conflict: "The influence of England and of France on the destinies of the Republic is greater than any American would like to admit."[23]

Russell was struck by the passive way in which both sides seemed to treat events. Rather than act, they would just wait until something happened—there seemed no desire to influence the action. Finally, in regards to Lincoln's view of slavery, Russell noted, decidedly, that Lincoln would adhere to his inaugural policies.

Russell's time in Washington was spent dining, visiting, and being visited by most of the leading figures of the day. His March 28th entry noted that he had been visited by members of Congress. That evening, he was invited to Lincoln's first State Dinner at the White House.

The first official photograph of the White House was probably taken by famed photographer, Matthew Brady, during Lincoln's administration. It portrays a White House that is very familiar. Visitors could approach the house, which was designed principally by architect James Hoban, from either side of the driveway. This would lead into the north portico. The semi-circular drive of gravel in front of the portico no longer exists. On the lawns in front of the entrance stood a statue of Thomas Jefferson. This remained from 1841 until 1875. The facade itself is the one familiar to all: the large pediment supported by four Doric columns, and a balustrade around the roof.

Upon his arrival, Russell was amused that a servant seemed particularly "inquisitive as to my name and station in life."[24] When he discovered that Russell was neither a cabinet minister nor a foreign minister, he was more than a little disappointed, as well as suspicious, of his right to be there. The servant eventually relaxed his vigilance, but made sure that the reporter understood that what would happen next was completely extraordinary.

Russell was ushered into one of the larger reception rooms, the Blue Room, and was introduced to several people, while waiting for the presidential couple to make an appearance. Among the ministers, politicians and hangers-on, Russell met Salmon Chase, Secretary of the Treasury, and his vivacious and conniving daughter, Kate, who Russell described as ". . . attractive . . . and sprightly."[25] The ravishing Miss Chase was always a serious competitor to Mrs. Lincoln and, during receptions, virtually held her own receptions in the Blue Room.[26]

These two remarkable women notwithstanding, there was not, he felt, "a scrap of lace or piece of ribbon"[27] in the entire assembly. No one, he felt, was conspicuous or very elegant in their dress.

When she appeared, the hostess, Mary Lincoln, was ". . . of middle age and height, of a plumpness . . . natural to her years; her features are plain . . . her manners and appearance homely. . . . Mrs. Lincoln struck me as being desirous of making herself agreeable."[28]

Mr. Russell was, however, less compassionate with his comments concerning the dinner itself. The Marine Band played as the assemblage entered the State Dining Room. Guests that evening were seated according to a chart made up by President Lincoln's secretary, George Nicolay, and approved by Secretary of State Seward. The table was elaborately decorated with "flowers, ferns massed on great gilded plateau. Gas and candle light illuminated the textures of mirrors, gilt, silver, and crimson and white damask."[29] The room was impressive enough; however, the servants were too plainly dressed, and the dishes were all too obviously not the work of a culinary artist. The wines ". . . owed their parentage to France, and their weaning and education to the United States. . . ."[30] Mr. Russell was most certainly not making allowances.

Russell also alluded several times to the cold treatment Mary Lincoln received. At the dinner, he observed that the ". . . secessionist ladies at Washington have been amusing themselves by anecdotes . . . [about Mrs. Lincoln] . . . which could scarcely be founded on fact."[31] Visiting Mrs. Lincoln again, several days later, Russell found the same rather malicious behavior. The gathering, he noted, was very sparsely attended, for the ladies had not yet made up their minds whether Mrs. Lincoln was the fashion. It seemed that they missed their Southern friends.[32]

Whether Mrs. Lincoln was the fashion or not depended upon interpretation. Russell felt compassion for her, but there were others, then and later, who wondered whether what she deserved was compassion or contempt.

Mary Todd Lincoln, like her husband, was born in Kentucky but, unlike her husband, she had the advantages of wealth and education. She was the daughter of a successful planter and businessman. She went to live with a sister in Springfield, Illinois, and there was courted not only by young Mr. Lincoln but, as rumor had it, by Stephen Douglas. Whether true or not, Mary decided to marry Lincoln in 1842.

They had four sons, one of whom died before they reached the White House in March of 1861. Initially praised for her efforts to redecorate a very shabby White House, and for her lavish entertainments, the press compliments soon turned to derision after the first battles of the war were fought. She was maligned constantly. Curiously, she never seemed interested in correcting the impressions that the press gave about her extravagance, her manipulation of the moody President, or even that she was a Confederate spy. Members of her family were, in fact, fighting for the Confederacy. In the end, her only living son had her committed to an asylum, Bellevue. Though she was soon released, she spent the remaining years of her life in listless, unhappy wanderings, and using spiritualists to contact her three dead sons and her violently murdered husband.

* * * *

It was also during a dinner at the White House that Russell wrote down one of Mr. Lincoln's famous stories. The President evidently used these stories to get out of awkward situations. In this case, the Attorney General had questioned his appointment of a judge. Lincoln then began by telling the company that the judge was not as bad as he seemed. Many years before, Lincoln had been walking along a bad road making his way to court, which was a distance of some ten or so miles. This judge happened by in a carriage and had offered young Lincoln a ride. Once inside, Lincoln could not help but notice that the coachman was driving erratically and he said to the judge, "I think your coachman has been taking a little drop too much this morning." The judge agreed and shouted at the driver, who responded merrily,

"By gorra! that's the first rightful decision you have given in a twelve-month." While everyone was laughing, Lincoln was able to escape the Attorney General.[33]

After dinner, the rest of the evening was quite ordinary. The men retired to the Red Room for brandy and cigars, and the ladies to the small dining room to refresh their toilettes.

The following day, Good Friday, Russell had several conversations concerning the all-important issue of States Rights. From one young man from Virginia, a Mr. Banks, he heard the complaint that Mr. Seward would not see the three Southern Commissioners—representatives of the fledgling Southern government. Russell retorted that the Crown would never see anyone in the dominions who had seized forts or threatened war. The young man replied that this was different, being more like the Hungarians seeking redress from the Austro-Hungarian throne, or one of the German states, like Hesse, making claims at the German Diet. Russell shook his head. No one in Britain, he said, thought in terms of Texans or Virginians—they thought in terms of Americans. An older gentleman, Mr. Truman Smith, thought otherwise. He said that the compact under which the states lived obliged them to give up their sovereignty to the government. They couldn't take it back when it pleased them to do so.[34]

In the company of other gentleman, Russell made a visit to the Washington Navy Yard. Instead of describing it in minute detail, which was his wont with military installations, the journalist expressed his annoyance that the Americans were so outraged when the British destroyed this particular installation in the War of 1812. Wasn't it the privilege of belligerents to do this? Having said this, he expressed his deep abhorrence of war when he wrote: ". . . it is deplorable such scenes should ever have been enacted between members of the human family so closely allied by all that shall make them of the same household."[35]

In the beginning of April, Russell visited Mount Vernon. Being extremely patronizing, he called it the Shrine of St. Washington. He noted that he did not really understand the greatness of this General —since the French, in his opinion, had really won at Yorktown—or of the residence itself, which appeared extremely run-down. Continuing on to Fort Washington, he made the observation that twenty men with good revolvers could have taken the place.

That evening, Russell met with the three Southern Commissioners, Andre B. Roman, Martin B. Crawford and John Forsyth. They came to the capital to work out a peaceful separation of the conflicting "countries", maintaining the attitude of foreign diplomats in Washington. In terms of diplomacy, the South was directing its fledgling efforts primarily toward the United States.[36] These three ". . . unrecognized ministers plenipotentiary . . ."[37] reinforced Russell's belief that the South would never rejoin the Union. The Southerners were never received by the United States government, a fact that they obviously resented. They, in fact, stayed in Washington for several weeks hoping to be acknowledged, but, as Russell noted in his Letter of April 9, they failed to gain even a glimmer of recognition.

From his window, the journalist observed military units marching up and down the streets of Washington. He was scathing in his observations of their pasty faces, and the presence of Irish and German immigrants among them. In sum, a sorry-looking lot.[38]

During his stay in the capital, Russell had several visits with the "Little Giant", Senator Stephen A. Douglas. He was enormously impressed with Douglas's ability to have moved up to a position just short of the presidency. Senator Douglas expounded on many topics, all related to the current crisis. He spoke for a solid hour on the issues of Popular Sovereignty, the Kansas-Nebraska question; in short, topics that might normally have bored a foreigner. Nevertheless, Russell wrote that he spoke with great energy and thought, and was, therefore, most absorbing. In Douglas, Russell found one of the few men who was positive about keeping the Union whole. During another visit, Russell dined with Mr. Douglas and other gentlemen. His opinion of the Senator continued to be positive, while remaining realistic.

Few men speak better than Senator Douglas: his words are well chosen, the flow of his ideas even and constant, his intellect vigorous, and thoughts well cut, precise and vigorous—he seems a man of great ambition.[39]

Russell again dined with the three Southern Commissioners on the evening of April 5. At a French restaurant called Gautier's on Pennsylvania Avenue, he discovered the first idiosyncratic Southern custom that was little to his taste. The conversation turned to dueling, and its importance in upholding the honor of the white women of the South. Russell questioned the correctness of a standard which utilized the murderous use of a pistol or dagger. Could such virtue, perhaps, be open to some doubt? The three men were also of the view that the Southern white man was superior to the Northern one. This they explained by saying that the Northern men were liars and cowards. Look at Seward, they cried, he could never be relied upon to tell the truth. As for cowardice, look at the Sumner-Brooks confrontation. Russell protested at this juncture; hadn't Sumner been stuck behind his desk and unable to defend himself? No, they declared, that wasn't so. Brooks, the smaller man, had hit him slightly with his cane. He had only continued because Sumner irritated him with his cowardly demeanor.[40] Russell concluded: "I found there was very little sympathy with my views. . . ."[41]

The days following this dinner were rainy, muggy days. Russell complained fitfully about the weather. He perpetually worried about his wife and family. One received the impression, from the way Russell wrote, that his wife was the sort of woman who was more child than wife, and that in the good old-fashioned tradition, her husband had stepped in as a replacement for her father. Undoubtedly, the reporter felt some guilt at leaving his family for long drawn-out assignments, and possibly more so since he enjoyed these assignments so much.

On a particularly wet day, Russell continued expressing his annoyance with the New York press. He related how men in Washington would write articles to New York about Sumter and other pressing issues, who knew nothing about them. Nonetheless, newspapers would publish these reports as absolute truth. This lack of integrity greatly irritated Russell, who wrote and grumbled endlessly about it. On a more constructive note, the correspondent went with some gentlemen to see the Smithsonian Institute. He was shown around by American physicist, Professor Joseph Henry.[42] Together, they studied a map of North America, while the professor expounded on the extension of slavery and the ideas of slave empires. Russell pronounced the museum very interesting and the library a very good idea.

Russell's most important connection in Washington, however, was with Secretary of State Seward, with whom he attended numerous dinners, social events and engaged in many lively discussions. Seward was eager to discuss British opinion and reactions to current American problems. Moreover, he felt that in maintaining extended contact with the journalist, he could convey his views to the important British reading public. Russell, in his turn, interviewed Seward extensively, finding him to be a "quick subtle man, rejoicing in power, . . . [and] . . . bursting with the importance of state mysteries."[43] Interestingly enough, the man who was ready to insult England at every opportunity was, nevertheless, ". . . fond of talking of Lords, etc., and of his acquaintance with England", but he was "not at all communicative on subjects that really mattered."[44] Russell discovered that this taciturn attitude toward affairs of State did not always extend to a journalist who was the "gentleman from *The Times*." In an interview, the Secretary expressed fears ". . . even as the United States was at last preparing to suppress the rebellion, that the British might recognize the government in Montgomery."[45]* In addition, he was most adamant that if Great Britain recognized the Confederacy, he would be ready to threaten war against them.

---

* Montgomery was the capital of the Confederacy until the seat of government was moved to Richmond in May of 1861.

Seward used this threat as a rather peculiar solution for the problem of recognition. He told Russell that efforts were being made to preserve the integrity of the Union ". . . and hinted that it might be saved by a foreign war."[46] Being so anti-British, there was little doubt to which foreign country he referred. This "solution", which became widely publicized, was met with dismay by the Washington diplomatic corps. Lord Lyons, British Ambassador to the United States, warned, in typically British understatement, that Seward would be ". . . a dangerous foreign minister."[47]

Several days before the firing on Fort Sumter, Seward drew up a dispatch to Charles Francis Adams, United States Ambassador to the Court of St. James, saying:

> . . . if they [the Powers] determine to recognize, they may at the same time prepare to enter into alliance with the enemies of this republic. You alone will represent your country at London, and you will represent the whole of it there. When you are asked to divide that duty with others, diplomatic relations between the governments of Great Britain and this government will be suspended.[48]

Russell, who had been invited to Seward's home on April 8, ostensibly to play whist, was given a preview of this strong missive. While listening to the decisive statement, Russell concluded that even war with Britain ". . . may not be out of the list of those means which would be available for re-fusing the broken union. . . ."[49] Seward, however, felt it would not come to that. His hopes were that the South would see that the North meant no harm to their persons or property, and would react by rejoining the fold.

Seward's purpose in reading this inflammatory message to Russell was obvious. The reporter was not to keep this information to himself, but was to convey it to the British public through his correspondence. The theme of United States' threatened aggression against England was often mentioned in Russell's Letters. Since the early days of the war, the North expressed its insecurity by bragging that after subjugating the rebels, it would annex Canada, fight England, and so forth. Though Seward may have been quite serious about this "solution", the reality was that few would have agreed with such an enterprise.

It seems contradictory that, just a few days before, Seward would tell Russell, ". . . if the majority [of the Southern states] desire secession, [that he, Seward] would let them have it. . . ."[50] This seems doubly odd in the face of his dispatch to Adams. Subsequently, in a letter to William L. Dayton dated June 17, 1861, he, again, restated his position, saying that foreign powers were not to assume that there was a state of belligerency in the United States. He reaffirmed that ". . . there is here, as there has always been, one political power, namely the United States of America, competent to make war and peace, and conduct commerce and alliances with all foreign nations. . . ."[51]

* * * *

As the situation became increasingly strained, Russell realized that he must journey to the South while he could still do so. Seward, it seemed, had issued orders that secrecy from the press must be maintained. There continued to be more opinions, rumors and speculations, hence Russell's desire to see events first-hand. He wrote that ". . . matters look very threatening, I must go South and see with my own eyes how affairs stand there before the two sections come to open rupture."[52] He admitted that a week in Washington had already made him ". . . tired and weary of this perpetual jabber about Fort Sumter."[53]

In his Letter dated April 5, 1861, Russell assured his readers that the United States had no intention of giving up any possessions. The flags over Pickens and Sumter would remain Union, unless forcibly removed by the rebels. The Federal government could not recognize the rights of any state to take these forts. Any attempts to do so, he wrote, would provoke very strong feelings from the North. Inaction, however, could not last. He concluded that ". . . whatever may be the result of all these diverse sections, the Great Republic is gone!"[54]

Russell's woeful prediction echoed throughout Britain. It "provided the earliest confirmation of the Confederacy's determination not to re-enter the Federal Union. . . ."[55] Russell felt great sympathy for what he firmly believed was the Union's inevitable demise. He was enormously grieved that the ". . . great experiment of self-government had reached its end. . . ."[56] There was no false note in this sad pronouncement. Russell seemed genuinely moved by what he saw as a permanent rift in the democratic experiment. He deplored the glee that such a collapse would, no doubt, illicit among the enemies of the United States. In a letter to John Bigelow, about a month after his arrival, Russell lamented:

> I fear, my friend, you are going to an immortal smash. That little lump of revolutionary leaven has at last set to work in good earnest and the whole mass of social and political life is fermenting un-healthily. . . . [t]he world will . . . see . . . the failure of republican institutions in the time of pressure as demonstrated by all history— that history which America vainly thought she was going to set right and re-establish on new grounds and principles.[57]

In the end, even should the sections reunite, Russell said ". . . their co-hesion can never be perfect."[58]

The evening before his departure to the South, Russell dined at General Winfield Scott's quarters. Upon arriving at the general's home, Russell was surprised to find that it was heavily guarded. No doubt, the War Department was most concerned for their Chief of Staff. Parenthetically, John Bigelow included a letter in his memoirs that Seward had written to him. Seward said: "Assassination is not an American practice of habit, and one so vicious and so desperate can-not be engrafted into our political system."[59] Undoubtedly, it would have been preferable if Seward was correct.

The general, who was, at that time, in his mid-seventies, had al-ready gone through a war with Britain in 1812, and was well-known for his leadership in the Black Hawk Wars and the Mexican War. He had even run for president in 1852, though he lost to Democrat Franklin

Pierce. He was known as "Old-Fuss-and-Feathers" because of his attention to military detail and appearance. Now, however, he had grown so fat that he could not mount his horse. Nevertheless, he was honored and protected, though only months away from stepping down.

Russell noted that soldiers would often come by Scott's home and begin cheering, demanding that the General appear, which he often did. He would make a speech and then retreat. There was, Russell wrote, "no privacy for public men in America."[60]

Scott was the author of the strategy known as the Anaconda Plan, which would, in part, carry the Union to victory. It was so called since it was hoped that this plan would squeeze the life out of the South. Its elements were simple: blockade the Eastern seaboard and dominate the Mississippi in the West, thereby cutting the South in two. This was eventually accomplished.

The general, Russell wrote, was much admired by Americans. They did not spare him, however, some ". . . amiable weaknesses . . ."; but to Russell, his only fault was a ". . . little vanity. . . ."[61] This revelation aside, the dinner was an uneventful one, filled with discussions of the War of 1812, the Sepoy Rebellion and the Crimean War, including disputes on the issues closest to the minds of Scott, Seward (who was also in attendance), and Russell.

The following morning, April 12, the correspondent received an "intimation" that the Federal government was going to test the "sincerity of Secession."[62] The Commander at Charleston, it seemed, had warned Major Anderson at Fort Sumter that all communications between the city and the fort must stop. The Federal government, on the other hand, was now determined to resupply Sumter—peaceably if possible. The garrison at Sumter was ready, and the Confederates, who had positions around Charleston Harbor, were also ready.

While preparing for departure, Russell had occasion to speak to some ladies who told him that when he returned, there would be some much nicer people in Washington—the Davises. Others stated that

there was only one way such a battle could end between Southern gentlemen and Northern trash. Russell grasped the immediacy of the circumstances. After making a few last visits, and leaving cards for the
President and Mrs. Lincoln, General Scott and Senator Douglas, he
set off immediately to Baltimore—the first stop on his journey to the
South.

PART II

The South

APRIL–JUNE, 1861

→ *Chapter Four* ←

"Too small for a republic . . ."

WASHINGTON, D.C.—CHARLESTON, SOUTH CAROLINA
APRIL, 1861

RUSSELL'S INTENTION OF "ascertaining . . . the real state of affairs in that direction . . ."[1] was only a very small part of the discoveries made during his journey South. In the short span of two months, he traveled over land, rivers, swamps and open sea, visiting military sites, government chambers, small towns, plantations, major cities and, for the most part, uncomfortable hotels. As he delved into the palatable, and not so palatable, customs of the Southerners, there emerged a fascinating picture, illustrating how they lived and thought about a myriad of important issues.

On April 12, Russell traveled south to Baltimore. Rumors about Fort Sumter continued to be rampant. The reporter caught the six o'-clock train, accompanied by Mr. Frederick Warre of the British Legation. The train was filled with frustrated office-seekers. Disappointed by the current administration, no offices or favors granted, they were returning home. The talk was, of course, whether Sumter would be relieved, and whether or not that was the appropriate action. Russell, again, remarked upon the disrespectful way about which the President and his cabinet were spoken.

At eight that evening, they arrived and went straight to the Eutaw House. There, Russell learned, from his obliging landlord, that Sumter had been fired upon. The journalist went immediately to the public rooms, which were crowded to breaking point. People were

gleefully speculating about the Sumter rumors, and the possible results. Russell stood among them, listening to men whose faces were
flushed with excitement at the prospect of war. But there was no actual verification. It all continued to be conjecture and rumor.

The following day, it was confirmed that Sumter had been fired
upon, and command had been placed in the hands of General Beauregard. In speaking with some gentlemen of the city, Russell wrote
". . . the whole feeling of the landed and respectable classes is with the
South."[2] Their instant elation, however, eluded Russell. His comment
was ". . . the act seemed to be the prelude to certain war."[3] Obviously,
to the seasoned campaigner this was no cause for celebration.

* * * *

Russell commented often about the war mania that pervaded most of
the South. It seemed at its strongest in Maryland, though the state
never actually seceded from the Union. Like the other states in the upper South, Maryland was extremely divided in its feelings about the violent issues facing the country. With Kentucky, Delaware, Missouri,
and the new state of West Virginia, they were known as "border
states", since they were located literally on the boundaries between the
North and South. One of Lincoln's most compelling objectives during
the war was to keep the border states in the Union. The President often said that he hoped that he had God on his side, but he most certainly must have Kentucky there.[4] In actuality, when the Emancipation Proclamation took affect in January of 1863, one of its stipulations
freed only slaves in states then in rebellion. By this stipulation, the
President kept the border states in the Union and did not antagonize
the slave owners.

The firing on Fort Sumter was the culmination of months of posturing and uncertainty. Much of what Russell heard in Baltimore was
the same talk that he had heard day after day in Washington and New
York.

After the election of Lincoln, and the subsequent secession of the

Southern states, there were several Federal forts and other installations which had not been peaceably handed over to the Southern authorities. During the period between November and Lincoln's inauguration, President Buchanan, now a lame-duck, at last began to show some gumption and resolution. He was absolutely adamant that no state had a right to secede. He maintained this resolve, leaving it for the President-Elect to solve the conundrum of the forts—whether they should be supplied and reinforced, or whether they should be quietly abandoned.

In Russell's Letter of April 15, he explained to his readers that the Southern Commissioners actually thought that they had an unwritten understanding that the forts would go quietly to the South. Once Buchanan was out of office, they continued to insist that Washington had given its word not to reinforce any Southern forts without notifying the government in Montgomery. When Lincoln became President, this promise was possibly forgotten, but most certainly ignored.

Meanwhile, several months before, Major Robert Anderson of Kentucky had removed his men from Fort Moultrie and Castle Pickens in South Carolina. His purpose was to bring them all to what he deemed to be the most defensible fort of the three: Fort Sumter in Charleston Harbor. The Major, in order not to provoke the Confederates, evacuated the other installations in the dead of night.

In February of 1861, Brigadier General Pierre G.T. Beauregard became the Commander of Charleston. Beauregard, like so many of the men in command of the Northern and Southern armies, was a graduate of West Point. Being a great admirer of Napoleon, his classmates called him "Little Napoleon", or, because he was a native of Louisiana, "the Little Creole". One of his early assignments was with the Army Engineers. Later, he served on Winfield Scott's staff during the Mexican War. He resigned the United States Army in the beginning of 1861, and accepted the rank of Brigadier General with the Confederacy. Now, with Anderson's men garrisoned at Sumter, both Commanders waited for the next move of their respective governments.

Buchanan held firm in the new year of 1861. He insisted that he would defend Sumter "against hostile attacks from whatever quarter they may come."[5] This attitude was all very well when one would soon be leaving office. Lincoln, however, decided that it was important to relieve Sumter with men and supplies. In early April, Lincoln notified the Governor of South Carolina that a supply ship with an armed guard would resupply the fort. He also informed Beauregard, making sure that the General understood that no force whatever would be used.

In an exchange of letters between Anderson and himself, which began on April 11, Beauregard demanded that the fort be evacuated at once. Anderson politely declined. In speaking with his aides, who had delivered the first letter, Beauregard was told that Anderson spoke of being starved out if Confederate guns did not "batter" them to "pieces."[6] The Commander of Charleston demanded, once again, to know when Anderson would leave, and the Major replied that they would vacate the fort on April 15.

President Jefferson Davis felt that Anderson was dissembling and gave permission for Beauregard and his troops to commence firing. After extending an extremely civilized warning to the opposition, Beauregard did so at 4:30 on the morning of April 12. Later in the day, the elite of Charleston drove out to the shore to watch the firing. The bombardment continued for roughly thirty-six hours, with Anderson offering what little resistance he could. Beauregard wrote that the barracks of Fort Sumter itself were on fire, and the interior seemed completely untenable because of the flames, heat and endless bombardment. In fact, whenever there was a barrage from Fort Sumter, the Confederates on the opposing sides would cheer for Anderson and his men, although continuing to fire themselves.[7] In the end, only when the fort was virtually ruined, Beauregard accepted Anderson's surrender. As he and his men took the American flag down, Anderson could only speculate on what they might have achieved with adequate men, supplies and munitions. Probably, Beauregard was glad of what seemed like a benign engagement with his former West Point instructor.

Instructor or not, Anderson's only casualty came as the flag lowered, and a charge was set off. It killed one man and wounded five others. A Union steamer, the *Isabel*, which had been waiting in Charleston Harbor, quietly bore the men away, as the Confederates, lining the beach, silently removed their hats.

The fort had become a symbol of the impasse between North and South.[8] Now, after another set of shots heard "round the world", the two sides had come, again, to a place of deadlock, and another round of seemingly endless waiting.

Naturally, as a journalist, Russell was extremely eager to visit Sumter and observe the fortifications, the armaments and troop strengths for himself. In his April 15th Letter, he wrote:

> I hope to stand amid the ruins of a spot which will probably become historic and has already made more noise in the world than its guns, gallant as the defence may have been.[9]

* * * *

The following day, the landlord came to Russell's room, eager to confirm and discuss the bombardment. When he finally went down to breakfast, the room was buzzing with excitement. Talk of the tremendous events of the day before spilled over to the morning, as people theorized on what would come next and when. Many told Russell that Maryland would go with the South, and that Lincoln was not a gentleman and, therefore, completely unfit.

After breakfast, Russell, while being shaved, questioned his black barber. The man felt that nothing good could come from the firing on Sumter, and that slavery was surely coming to an end. "And what will take place then, do you think?" Russell queried. "Wall, sare, 'spose colored men will be good as white men."[10] The man, Russell lamented, seemed to have no understanding of the gulf between himself and the white man. How naive he was to think that emancipation would really mean equality!

That evening, Russell continued his journey south to Norfolk, Virginia. He felt a bit under the weather after eating crab salad, and complained about feeling "seedy." His night on the steamer *Georgiana* was an unpleasant one: noises of all descriptions disturbed his slumbers, and mosquitoes tormented him through the night, despite the curtains around his bed.

The morning saw the boat arrive at Fortress Monroe, and Russell's first soon-to-be Southern military installation. As he dressed, a black woman walked into his room and demanded his ticket. She identified herself as the ticket collector and a slave: "The latter intelligence was given without any reluctance or hesitation."[11]

In the light of the rising sun, Russell described all the color of nature and the bustling activity he saw . . . a low coast fringed with trees, anxious little wooden lighthouses and much oyster selling and eating. They set down along the Navy Yard in Norfolk with an excellent view of the ironclad ship, the *Merrimac*. On deck, all were already consuming mint juleps. Many wanted the reporter to join them, but he felt slightly constrained since it was before breakfast. All were surprised.

While waiting for a small steamer to take him ashore, Russell commented on a particularly disgusting American habit—chewing tobacco. "Although it was but 7:00 a.m., everyone had their quid in working order. . . ."[12] Humorous, good-natured references were made, throughout his diary, to this habit that Russell abhorred. Moreover, when he reached Norfolk, he was "doomed"[13] to make his quarters the Atlantic hotel; besides being dilapidated, malodorous and unclean, the unfortunate place had tobacco juice all over the floors.

The waiters, he wrote, were slaves. He noticed a tall, lean, badly dressed man leaning against the wall in the hotel. He asked one of the waiters who he was, and the waiter replied that it was "Professor Jackson." Russell did not speak to him, which he very much regretted later on. He never formally met the man who, after the Battle of Bull Run, would be known as Thomas "Stonewall" Jackson, Robert E. Lee's right-hand man.[14]

After yet another bad meal, Russell took a walk through the city. He was bedeviled by thoughts of his wife, complaining in his private diary that he had not heard from her. He, in fact, wrote a letter to his friend Bancroft Davis on that very day, instructing him to open all of his correspondence and give him word about Mary.[15]

Observing that men were discussing the news of Sumter with great joy and gladness, Russell refused to join in. He knew it was only the beginning of what certainly would be a long and tragic war. He continued to the black quarters of the city, and noticed that no one there discussed Sumter. They did not even seem to know that it had happened.

Russell returned to the hotel after his promenade, and had a dinner "to make one wish the desire for food had never been invented."[16] Looking forward to moving on to Charleston, he wrote that during the night the mosquitoes had been "aggressive and successful."[17] Thankfully, he was on his way to Charleston early the following morning.

The trip by rail was extremely interesting. Russell actually complimented the ride, waxing poetic as he described the countryside: the Spanish moss, the cypress and dogwood trees, as well as the tortoises, large frogs and alligators. He wondered at the appellation "Dismal Swamp", because he thought it so beautiful, but, he speculated, it was, no doubt, not so beautiful before railroads and canals easily traversed its length. He was equally thrilled with the feats of engineering that he saw. The bridges, he remarked, were "exciting in size & frailty, great skill engineering."[18] Eventually, they passed the swamps and came in sight of some wooden huts. "The right sort" of people, he was told by the engineer, lived here. They flew Confederate flags and shouted "huzzahs" for Jefferson Davis. The flag, Russell wrote, was not as gaudy as the "Stars and Stripes"; however, the two flags were very similar. The "right sort", he thought, were not particularly flourishing. They were pale and tawdry-looking and, for the first time since his arrival in the States, he saw barefooted people.[19]

In North Carolina, the reporter spent the night at an inn next to the railroad tracks. A long table was laid out for the passengers with various pickles, fish, meat and potatoes. Russell was revolted by the habit of eating with a knife, but he was even more disgusted by the fact that the proprietor of the inn expected him to share a room. He eventually talked his way out of that problem, but listened all night to three men snoring next door. There were, the proprietor explained, just too many people moving about.

The following day, Russell traveled through Wilmington, North Carolina. The topography was different, flat and uninteresting, nevertheless, with Confederate flags proudly waving. Everywhere they stopped, Russell saw evidence of preparations for war or, at least, some kind of militias. He saw men already dressed in military jackets and showing their swords, which had seen action perhaps in Mexico and, less possibly, against the British, though that would, no doubt, make the swords very old indeed.

In speaking with his fellow passengers, Russell decided to ask them whom they expected to fight. One young man said, "That's more than I can tell. The Yankees ain't such cussed fools as to think they can come here and whip us, let alone the British." The reporter wondered what the British had to do with it, and the young man assured him that the British would have to side with the South or "We'll just give them a hint about cotton."[20] That seemed to settle the matter completely and to the young man's satisfaction.

They went through customs in South Carolina. As they approached Charleston, Russell could see the shape of Fort Sumter with the Confederate flag flying. The scene excited many of the railroad passengers. It would have been difficult not to comment upon the euphoric celebrations subsequent to Sumter. Russell observed crowds of armed men, singing and marching through the streets. The ". . . battle-blood

... [was] ... running through their veins ... the 'flush of victory' ..."
was on their cheeks.[21] Indeed, as he crossed Cape Fear, Russell could
see no sign of ". . . affection to the Union. . . ."[22]

Russell busied himself getting to the recommended hotel, the Mills
House. He received his correspondence and was diverted by a letter
from Bancroft Davis. Apparently, much had happened in New York.
"You have missed the most extraordinary demonstration in history—
the rising of the Northern people en masse for their institutions. Fifty
thousand men are enlisted in the City of New York alone. . . . "[23] A
changed city without doubt. In addition to mail and news, Russell was
happy to meet his friend Samuel Ward, an acquaintance he had made
in the summer of 1860.[24] During a long talk, Ward gave him an account of the Sumter bombardment.

At the hotel, Russell was where he loved to be, in the very thick of
the action. Many notable South Carolinians had quarters there;
among them, Senator James Chestnut and ex-Governor John L. Manning. The journalist was introduced to General Beauregard, hero of
Sumter. However, it was not until several days after that he penned a
description of the General:

> He is a squarely built, lean man, of about forty years of age, with
> broad shoulders, and legs made to fit a horse, of middle height, and
> his head is covered with thick hair, cropped close, and showing the
> bumps, which are reflective and combative. . . .[25]

Anxious for the goodwill of *The Times*, Beauregard told Russell, "You
shall go everywhere and see everything, we rely on your discretion and
knowledge of what is fair in dealing with what you see."[26] Russell assured the General that he could, indeed, rely on his making no improper use of what he saw, but he cautioned, ". . . unless you tell me
to the contrary, I shall write an account of all I see to the other side of
the water, and if when it comes back, there are things you would rather
not have known, you must not blame me."[27]

After supper that evening, Russell repaired to the Charleston Club

with John Manning. After an ardent political discussion, and some irritating braggadocio, Russell asked his hosts if they felt that they could
defend against the Yankees, who had "such preponderance of men and
matériel, that they are three to your one, will you not be forced to submit?" There was a chorus of "no's" and "never's". "Then," the journalist continued, ". . . you alone, of all nations in the world, possess the
means of resisting physical laws which prevail in war. . . ."[28]

The gentlemen confidently reminded Russell of King Cotton
diplomacy, and he admitted in his diary that there certainly was a great
dependence on Southern cotton. In addition, the Charlestonians believed that they had the perfect society. It was one in which one race
of men worked, while another cultivated civilization. They further believed that this principle was upheld by God. In June of that year, in a
service of thanksgiving for the victory at Fort Sumter, Reverend
Thomas Smythe thanked God for the victory, and told his parish-
ioners that it was signal proof that God watched over them.[29]

A bell tolled at eight-thirty that evening. Upon asking what it
meant, Russell was told, "It's for all the colored people to clear out of
the streets and go home. The guards will arrest any who are found out
without passes in half an hour."[30] Russell noted this without comment.

After breakfast the following day, Russell strolled through Charleston, whose streets ". . . present some such aspect of those of Paris in
the last revolution. . . ."[31] He saw pamphlets lauding Sumter—never
had there been such brave men or such a battle. It was a bloodless
Waterloo, he thought, wryly.[32]

Russell went over to Fort Sumter with an entire party of senators,
soldiers and other gentlemen. They walked together down to the quay,
on a morning that the reporter described as swelteringly hot. Near the
wharf, there was a large white marble building in a near-finished state.
It was a customs building, he was told, but his hosts didn't think it
would be used much because "what we want is free trade."[33] Russell
saw groups of volunteers crowding around the pier. Major Whiting,
formerly of the U.S. Army Engineers, would guide them through the

fort. They embarked on the steamer, and Russell saw his "brethren" from the New York and local papers. One wrote a report of the day, saying that the entire party had been arranged for him. Major Whiting, despite being the appointed guide, expressed a great disdain for the press, wishing them all in the water. Russell discovered that the Southern distaste for freedom of the press was more ingrained than in the North. Though, he observed, it is not "accompanied by the signs of dread of its power which exist in New York."[34]

The fort was situated between James's and Sullivan's Islands. While imposing from afar, as they neared Russell could see that it wasn't as solid as he supposed, being made of brick and not of stone. As they landed at Morris Island, a crowd of men swarmed about them, wanting news and provisions. Russell was able to ascertain that the fort, under proper circumstances, could have withstood the attack, but that the works were not properly shored up, nor the fort properly armed. Nevertheless, all now were in a party mood.

As they walked about, every tent extended hospitality. There were cases of champagne, claret and pâté. Though Russell was, again, pressed to drink, he declined, prompting some rude remarks from the conquerors. "They assume that the British Crown rests on a cotton bale. . . ."[35] In a large tent, there was much toasting and camaraderie. Russell was told how much money some of the gentlemen there were worth, and he assured his readers that this "reference to a money standard of value was not unusual . . . it was made repeatedly."[36]

Russell and Whiting proceeded to Sumter, where they were met by an extremely inebriated Senator and self-styled Colonel, Louis T. Wigfall of Texas. Wigfall was a remarkable man, noted for his quick tongue, ever ready with an acerbic remark. He stood in the U.S. Senate, nearly to the last. Then, when, at last, the Confederacy was defeated, he went to England, never able to accept her fate.

Wigfall had played the interesting role of the emissary that finally encouraged Anderson to surrender the fort. The Senator/Colonel was determined that Russell should know all regarding his Sumter exploits. Major Whiting, on the other hand, wished only to show the journalist around, but had no opportunity to do so.

The wind was extreme, and fine dirt was flying into the men's faces as Wigfall continued to imbibe fearlessly from his flask. Russell dryly described the Senator, who was relating his Sumter moments, as expounding "'on some phase of his personal experience' with 'strong illustrations and strange expletives', all while his sword was dangling between his legs and 'involving his spurs in rubbish and soldier's blankets'."[37] While still in his cups, Wigfall was not above the boast that Russell heard constantly throughout the South, that they have only to shut off Britain's supply of cotton for a few weeks in order to create a revolution. Russell later communicated to his readers:

> Sumter, in fact, was a mouse in the jaws of the cat, and the moment an attempt was made to release the prey by external influence, the jaws were closed and the mouse was disposed of.[38]

In his beautifully descriptive Letter of April 21, the correspondent began the detailing of the military preparations and positioning of the South Carolinians. He singled out the organizational efficiency of Major Whiting and General Beauregard. In addition, he described Sumter in the minutest of detail: its cost, dimensions, how it was armed, and the numbers and classifications of guns used. Russell enumerated the damage to the fort, and concluded that Sumter was by no means destroyed. It was still useful for an efficient and sufficiently large force.[39] Interestingly enough, after discussing all these issues in exact detail, he noted that one thing about Americans was that they loved to know exactly how high something was, or exactly how much something weighed. They were far more precise in their measurements than were the British.

The walls were dented from all sides by shot marks, the entrance blocked by collapsed masonry. He saw men working to clean up the debris, while others were clearing the mines at the wharf. Russell decided that the heat and fire aside, there was no reason to surrender the place. The problem was that Anderson was not properly equipped, nor had a sufficient force, and that the Major had been unable to defend himself ". . . in the only way in which it could be done."[40] To round out the picture, Russell commented on the problems of the Union armaments. As the journalist completed his tour of the fort, he noted that shell splinters were being carried off as souvenirs and trophies by people in a holiday mood.

To his readers, Russell summarized by saying that, though not a single life was lost, a proper defense would have been very costly in casualties. It is interesting to note that these same readers were surprised that there were none killed or wounded at Sumter. This thought was also phrased throughout the South, though most expressed it as disappointment that more Yankees were not killed. Moreover, the English were surprised at the unexpected lull in hostilities. After hearing many overblown tales of American ferocity, they were sure that the delay of continuing battles was a farce.[41]

The party returned to Morris Island and had lunch. Senator Wigfall, still drunk, insulted Lord Lyons, the British Ambassador, but later apologized. By nightfall, they returned to Charleston, the city still ablaze with light, music and celebration. Russell proceeded to the Charleston Club with several gentlemen.

* * * *

In his next diary entry, Russell described the "goings on" at the hotel. It was crammed with people in uniform. The waiters were mostly Irish, not black. The meals were typical of American hotels, quantities of which an American will "consume in a few minutes in the morning."[42] The dining room was noisy, with chairs scraping, the rattle of newspapers and people walking in and out. Principally, there was talk of Sumter and the war, and of what "Old Abe and Seward would do."[43] Russell was continuously asked for his opinion.

The following day, after his visit to Sumter, Russell, Major Whiting and Sam Ward went to visit another fort important to the harbor, Fort

Moultrie. The journey by steamer was extremely unpleasant. At one point, they were in "actual danger." Major Whiting insisted on having a discussion with Russell about the writings of Thackeray, about which he was "lunatics."[44] After being tossed about and lurching in the drink of the harbor for more than two hours, they turned back to Charleston. They never saw the fort.

The newspapers were brimming with secession fever. Russell commented that Seward could not have understood the feelings of Southerners, or he would never have thought it would so easily blow over.[45] In a letter to Lord Lyons, he reiterated this sentiment, and said that the Confederates firmly intended to march to Washington, if only to move the war away from the Southern interior.[46]

The following day being extremely hot, Russell commented upon the strength of the sun and the unpleasant dust. He was afforded an opportunity to stroll through the Charleston streets and observe the architecture and gardens. He ambled into an open air market and perused the stalls. They were all attended by blacks, and he noticed that the "colored" people, whether buying or selling, were all dressed very well. He was most impressed by the quantities of fruits and vegetables, but noticed that there was no fish. He was informed that the fishing boats were not permitted to go out to sea, in case Yankee gunboats should come.

He walked over to General Beauregard's quarters for a brief conversation. The General spoke of the importance of the secession of the state of Virginia, which had not as yet happened. Afterward, Russell went to see the Governor of South Carolina, Francis W. Pickens. The Gubernatorial offices were very humble. The signs were not painted, but actually pasted on the doors. The Governor was not very impressive-looking, either. He was, however, the former Ambassador to the Imperial Court in St. Petersburg, and was not unaware of the importance of his former appointment. His ideas of slave economy versus Northern capitalism were quite typical, and Russell related his lecture in a somewhat comical fashion:

"In the North, then, you will perceive, Mr. Russell, they have max-imized the hostile condition of opposed interest in the accumula-tion of capital and in the employment of labor, whilst we in the South, by the peculiar excellence of our domestic institution, have minimized their opposition and maximized the identity of interest by the investment of capital in the laborer himself," and so on, or something like it. I could not help remarking it struck me there was "another difference betwixt the North and the South which he had overlooked,—the capital of the North is represented by gold, silver, notes, and other exponents, which are good all the world over and are recognized as such; your capital has power of locomotion, and ceases to exist the moment it crosses a geographical line."[47]

The Governor then wished to point out the various principles of Adam Smith that would reinforce his point. Russell, fearing that he might be forced to listen, looked at his watch, cleared his throat and much regretted that he would have to hear it another time, since he must leave urgently.

On his last day in Charleston, Russell visited the city newspapers, the *Mercury* and the *Courier*. Nothing about the offices was very re-markable other than the fact that the *Mercury* was the radical secession newspaper that had managed to scare its readers with the "terrors of submission" to the "abolitionist" regime of Lincoln and Hamlin.

The journalist wandered over to the cotton exchange and, thence, spoke to several of the city's merchants and bankers. They repeated the same litany that Russell had heard before, and would hear many times again. If the Yankees keep England from Southern cotton, Great Britain would be forced to act.

That evening, Russell dined with acquaintances he had made in Charleston, including John Julius Pringle, a rice planter,[48] and William Trescot, both of whom invited the reporter to visit their re-spective plantations. During dinner, Russell endured the same sort of talk that was becoming endemic in Southern conversation. However,

Mr. Trescot, who was Undersecretary of State under President Buchanan, had a wide British acquaintance. His ideas made more sense than Russell had previously heard. Trescot admitted to not liking the institution of slavery, but was unsure if and how it could be remedied.

Hearing reports that the officer commanding the arsenal at Harper's Ferry had quit the place after burning it down, Russell wrote, "How 'old John Brown' would have wondered and rejoiced, had he lived a few months longer."[49]

→ *Chapter Five* ←

"... two-legged cattle"

CHARLESTON—SAVANNAH, GEORGIA
APRIL—MAY, 1861

AFTER SUMTER, Russell began a round of visits to forts and plantations. He was taken "everywhere . . . and . . .," wrote Mary Chestnut, "poor Russell was awfully bored . . . He only wanted to see the forts, etc., and news that was suitable to make an interesting article."[1] Though they did not make the most exiting articles for his readers, nevertheless, the newspaperman did seem more than happy to visit places other than military installations, and began to garner several interesting impressions.

The first of these impressions was that the South would like to go back to a monarchical system. Russell contended that he had heard from many that they wanted one of the British royal family as their sovereign. He lamented that in the ironic shadow of George III, all who had contended against the great rebellion of the Thirteen Colonies could now ". . . clap . . . [their] . . . ghostly hands in triumph."[2] Henry William Ravenel, Southern diarist and famous botanist, wrote that Russell's Letters reported that the "general feeling" in the South was to return to British rule and the monarchy. Ravenel complained that an Englishman could not ". . .understand States Rights. . ." and, naturally, thought that the South was in a state of rebellion. In all fairness, Ravenel concluded that Russell ". . . seems, however, to do justice & gives his impression fairly."[3] Mary Chestnut joined in disputing the monarchical theory. She called Russell to account ". . . for saying we wanted an English prince to the fore. Not we, indeed! Every man wants to be at the head of affairs himself. . . ."[4]

Yet Russell wrote later that the South became increasingly aware that it would have to fight for its independence. He wrote further that they would give anything, money, labor and even life itself, to carry out their theories, ". . . [and barring all that] . . ., said an ex-governor of this state [Alabama] 'Sir, sooner than submit to the North, we will all become subject to Great Britain again.'"[5]

It was inevitable that in such a climate, Russell continually heard abuse of the North. The Southerners called their Northern counterparts bigoted blackguards and torquemadas. Furthermore, they reviled the North as a corrupt and evil place. New England came in for special abuse as the birthplace of impurity in women, abolitionism, free love, rotten philosophy and persecution.[6] The animosity illustrated the feelings of the gentry of the South towards what was, in their minds, the low rabble of the North.[7] Further, "the New Englander must have something to persecute and so he has hunted down all his Indians and burnt all his witches and persecuted all his opponents to death."[8] Therefore, he must persecute the South and had invented abolitionism for that purpose. Finally, they expressed the heartfelt wish that the Pilgrim Fathers' ship ought to have sunk.

Russell commented also about the puzzling doctrine of States Rights. It seems that the slave states maintained that each state was as independent as England or France. The Federal government was empowered to act only as an agent of the state when dealing with foreign governments. These powers were very similar to the powers given the Federal government by the Articles of Confederation—the governing document of the United States before the Constitution was promulgated in 1787. Russell, however, was more convinced that ". . . the invocation of States Rights was for 'protection to slavery, extension of slave territory, and free trade in slave produce.'"[9] Of all, the Europeans seemed to find this doctrine the most difficult to comprehend, and the most difficult with which to sympathize.

Russell spent most of the last week of April stopping as a guest at several agricultural establishments. His first visit was to the small farm of Mr. William Crafts, just outside of Charleston. Traveling with his friend Porcher Miles, a former member of Congress and something of a hero during a Yellow Fever epidemic some years previously, they wandered in the oppressive heat and humidity, through "thick Indian-like jungle, filled with disagreeable insects."[10] Since they had arrived unexpectedly, Mrs. Crafts could only promise them potted meats and a good bottle of wine. One can imagine Russell's anticipation of any good bottle. The family lived in what Russell termed a cottage-like residence surrounded by slave huts. The slave children were trotted out and commanded to sing for the visitors. Slowly and shyly, they emerged from behind trees and the little huts. They were shoeless, dirty and ragged-looking, and seemed almost wild. They began to dance listlessly and sing a spiritual about the River Jordan. Afterwards, they were all invited to a fête champêtre, a sort of country fair, on a broad lawn with large trees. Russell speculated on the great American love for large trees. He wrote that it was because large trees were not indigenous to America and that Americans admired objects of great "dimension and antiquity"[11] because they lacked tradition in the usual forms. Their flora would have to make up for this deficiency.

The party continued on to the Pringle plantation, near the Peedee River above Georgetown—up the coast from Charleston. In the company were Pringle, Sam Ward and Nelson Mitchell, a lawyer noteworthy for later defending the rights of black Union soldiers captured at Fort Wagner and making sure that they were treated like prisoners-of-war.[12] Russell thought him a nice man.

At seven in the morning, aboard the steamer, Russell and his friends were invited to the bar. The reporter demurred, but stood with the gentlemen as they imbibed mint juleps since it was a good place to share the news. The discussion was about Lincoln's blockade of the Southern ports. The President had given orders to treat Confederate ships as "pirates", which caused general outrage. Little incidents were also related—the attacks on some Northern military companies in Baltimore were cheered, and all anxiously peered at the horizon, trying to locate blockading ships.

As they progressed upriver, they were boarded by men in uniform hungry for news. Russell described their "gray tunics, slashed and faced with yellow, stiff belts, slouched felt hats, ornamented with drooping cock's plumes, and long jack boots,"[13] which only emphasized what seemed as a Cavalier versus Roundhead association. The activity at the shoreline had a party feeling about it, with people calling back and forth. Women in carriages suggested a large holiday picnic. They, at least, seemed little concerned with blockades.

They arrived in Georgetown, which had what Russell called an air of quaint simplicity and old-fashioned quiet. From their steamer, they proceeded through the quiet, pristine woods, and then ferried across the Black River. Upon arriving at the Pringles' home, called the White House, they could see broad expanses of fields planted with crops. The plantation house reminded Russell of country houses that were found in Ireland or Scotland a hundred years ago. The reporter, in fact, seemed to feel that much of the South was about one hundred years behind the times.

They were shown graciously through the house, and Russell saw evidence of foreign travel in the furniture, the books and the paintings. Upon being shown to his room, he pronounced it delightful. Certainly, the Pringles' home was a welcome change from the awful hotels he had thus far experienced. After a short rest, the entire party gathered for dinner. For the first time, he was happy with the meal which had been "cooked by negroes and served by negroes."[14] The wines were excellent and the conversation was naturally of great interest as the Southerners expressed the wish that a king or at least a prince would come to rule over them. The discussion turned to duels, and as an afterthought, how happy and relieved they were to be free of the Union at last.

During the meal, Russell had an opportunity to converse with his host on the daily existence of the slave population. While enjoying his food, served by the aforementioned majestically attired black servants, Russell made the observation to his host that there were no locks on the doors, and but one gun on the entire premises. The planter explained that he had nothing to fear from his slaves.

Julius Pringle was not concerned with the fidelity of his servants; he knew them to be completely loyal to his family. Russell found this a curious statement in view of the tales of murder and violence previously heard.[15] However, Pringle's confidence in them was such that, as Russell had noted, the doors were unlatched. Russell noticed that the slave owners reiterated constantly that they were not afraid of their slaves. This was a sentiment expressed so many times that it troubled the reporter. He heard so much about the assaults, slave toward master, and he began to think the owners protested overmuch. However, he saw Pringle as a kind man and a good master, keeping his slaves as one did children: feeding, clothing and caring for them when they were ill.

The next morning, the journalist, relaxing on the veranda, enjoyed the peace of a hot spring day. Later, when it was cooler, the company walked about the grounds inspecting the flat fields and the idle slaves. As Russell noted, this was a time of year when there was not much for them to do. The children were fishing and their parents, shunning Russell and his party, kept to the background. Pringle, it seemed, knew the slaves that worked the fields very little, professing to know only his house servants intimately.

At dinner that day, the conversation took its familiar turn and Russell duly noted their reluctance to return to the Union. The company preferred to return to Great Britain. The reporter, however, had more immediate problems. He determined that, despite many invitations from other plantation owners, he would leave the White House that very evening. The steamer that had brought them to the plantation was returning to Charleston and, because of the blockade, Russell felt that he should hurry back. He bid his host goodbye at midnight.

The *Nina*, as the steamer was called, reached Charleston the following afternoon. Russell was relieved not to have seen any blockading ships, and he resolved to go to his room at once and write letters. That evening, he met with General Beauregard once again, and noted that the General was very proud that, despite his small stature, he had great strength.

On April 25, Russell sent out the second of his Southern Letters (the first had, naturally, been of Sumter). He felt it prudent to pass it through a messenger to Lord Lyons at the British Legation in Washington. He feared that the Letters were being tampered with and did not want to use the post office. That evening, he dined with James Petigru, an old gentleman who was a decided Unionist. Mr. Petigru was credited with the quote: "South Carolina is too small for a republic and too large for an insane asylum."[16] However apocryphal this quote may seem, Mr. Petigru was very much concerned. "They have this day set a blazing torch to the temple of constitutional liberty," and he very much feared that there would be no peace, forever.[17] The Charlestonians humored him because they wanted to show how open-minded they were. After all, Petigru was most definitely a rarity. General Beauregard again joined Russell's party. He expressed his concern lest the North attack before the South was prepared. He was also worried that the Federals might stoop to cutting the levees on the Mississippi River above New Orleans. That would flood and, therefore, ruin many of the larger plantations in that area.

Russell looked forward to his next visit, which would be to the home of William H. Trescot. The journalist and Fred Warre left Charleston at the end of April in order to visit Sea Island. This time, they boarded a train heading southwest towards Georgia. Russell remarked upon the flatness of the countryside, which he did continually. During the train ride, he had overheard snippets of conversation from Southern ladies on the train, noting that the gentler sex was the most fiercely loyal of all, and that ". . . the least good-looking were the most bitterly patriotic, as if they hoped to talk themselves into husbands by the most infeminine expressions toward the Yankees."[18] Needless to say, he did not find them to be the fabled flowers of womanhood. Perhaps he did not consider that, no matter how things went, the women usually had the most to lose.

Finally, they reached Pocotaglio, where they were met by Trescot and taken to his island which lay in the Port Royal Sound. They were obliged to drive several hours through flat country, stopping at a neighbor of Trescot's for a meal. Indulging in his interest in ornithology, Russell noted some of the more unusual specimens which, to his horror, his host thoughtfully shot for him. At sunset, they came to a river and, after an hour's journey, arrived at Trescot's estate on Barnwell Island. Russell noticed that the rowers sang spirituals throughout the crossing, which was to him a "strange scene."[19]

Once disembarked, the party followed Trescot closely to a house that was barely visible in the velvet darkness. They were welcomed by Mrs. Trescot and served tea before going off to bed. Not, however, before the comment by the lady that she could easily feed a Confederate Army since she had "experience in feeding her negroes."[20]

Russell observed first-hand Eliza Trescot's responsibilities. As the chatelaine of the plantation, she carried the keys to all the storerooms and outbuildings, she supervised the house slaves, gave orders to the cook, the pastry chef, the maids and the seamstresses. This particular night, she sat up with a slave mother having a baby. Russell hastened to write that unfair motives should not be attributed to these acts of kindness by the master and mistress towards their chattel. "When people talk of my having so many slaves, I always tell them it is the slaves who own me . . .," Mrs. Trescot explained.[21] Property, Russell observed, has its duties as well as its rights.

The house itself was large, constructed of wood, with a lovely garden at the back. Large cotton fields were visible from the garden, as well as views of the river. After breakfast, a drum fishing expedition was organized. The men went down and sat by the river, lazing and conversing while waiting for neighboring friends, the Elliots, to arrive with their fishing boat. At last, the boat arrived, powered by six slaves, with extra servants and provisions for the alfresco meals along the way. Once aboard, the rowers were ordered to sing, which they obliging did. However, down river, as the party approached the more ideal spots for the drum fish, they were told by several other groups that there were no fish to be had. Eventually, after some attempts to catch the strange fish, Russell and his friends headed back to the plantation. It ended up a very long day, and they arrived home in time for supper and bed.

The next morning, a Sunday, Russell was awakened by a slave child. When he asked her if she went to church, she replied that she heard prayers from "Uncle." The reporter wondered at the constant title of "Uncle" and "Aunt" that was commonly used among the slaves. Where were the children's parents? What Russell did not know, or chose to ignore, was the fact that children were often sold away from their parents, so that adults in their new situations would take over parenting tasks. Also, slave marriages were not recognized so a child might or might not know its father, even if it were lucky enough to be raised by its mother.

Russell's day was spent walking around the place, looking at the cotton fields that were not in bloom, as well as the cotton mill which was not in use. Sea Island Plantation was typical of those on the coast of South Carolina. It raised a particular type of cotton, a long, staple, silky variety with smooth black seeds, very much like the kind grown in India. This crop was so profitable that many planters bought land in other states, such as Arkansas, in order to increase their crops.

Life here was also very typical. The house was not as impressive as the ones of legend. It was, as Russell wrote, made of wood, possibly on four stilts, and of clapboard. It was the dominant unit, and the out-buildings and slave quarters surrounded it, all usually inside some kind of enclosure.

Sea Island had over one hundred slaves, but this was not typical. Usually slave owners had two or three slaves; it was only the very richest of Southerners who had over twenty or more slaves. There was definitely a slave hierarchy, the house servants being closer to the white family and therefore more privileged than those who worked outside.

The plantation was usually self-sufficient. The slaves would produce their own food, have their own "mills and shops of various kinds, its milliners and mantua makers, tailors and barbers" as well as dairies and weavers. In fact, they purchased very little. [22] Russell and his companions strolled by the quarters of the older slaves, and Russell described them as dirty and shabbily-dressed. Neither did they express much pleasure at seeing their master. Russell saw padlocks on the doors of some of the outer huts, belying what Julius Pringle had said some nights earlier. Trescot told him frankly that things would be stolen if the doors were not locked. Mrs. Trescot, however, vouched constantly for the honesty of her house slaves. They might take sweets or sugar, but they would never take money or jewels. The answer was simple enough to Russell; there was little a slave *could* do with jewelry or money.

When they returned to the house, Mr. Edmund Rhett, a prominent South Carolinian, was waiting for them. Rhett was the son of Robert Barnwell Rhett, the so-called Father of Secession. His son was very much in line with his father's ideas. He repeated the notion of wanting a prince from Great Britain as his sovereign rather than the hated Yankees. He intimated that the ladies and gentlemen of the South were more like those of England. The gentlemen were people of leisure, who had the education and opportunity to serve the public, which made them the most ideal people to do so. They were certainly superior to the low class of people who were elected to Congress in the North, or as diplomatic representatives. Russell ventured to interject that there were many able people holding public office in the North. His views, however, were not met with great sympathy. Rhett ended by telling Russell that Great Britain "must recognize us, Sir, before the end of October."[23] And the reporter wryly commented that Rhett must think that the Lord Chancellor sat on a bale of cotton.

After several days of observing plantation life, Russell headed toward Savannah, Georgia. He occupied his time reading and once again noting how flat the area was in that section of the country. His first impression was that the Georgians were not quite as vehement in their hatred of the North as were the South Carolinians.[24] On his first day in Savannah, he stayed in and wrote a good deal. This resulted in his Letter of May 16. This descriptive Letter captured much of the slow, tranquil beauty and indolent grace of the planter's life. Because of his visits to slave-holding establishments, Russell's sentiments became markedly abolitionist, despite the fact that many of the masters took very good care of their slaves. Nevertheless, he declared that treating men like chattel was one of the Southern institutions he found most abhorrent.

After Russell had described an incident where the wife of an ex-cabinet minister stood on her back piazza and hollered at a servant three fields away, Mary Chestnut, the avid diarist, took great exception, writing that ". . . I daresay there are bawling, squalling, vulgar people everywhere."[25]

Russell and Fred Warre reached Savannah in the late afternoon, and were met by Mr. Charles Green, a British-born Savannah merchant[26] whose home was to be Russell's home in that city. Observing the white population, the reporter wrote that they looked sallow and listless, while the blacks were gaily dressed and perpetually busy. The city was a network of squares, fenced and adorned by greenery and many large trees.

The house reminded the reporter of the mansions he had seen on New York's Fifth Avenue. He was full of praise for the Italianate style and the luxury of the bathrooms with quantities of cold water. After settling in, the men drove to see Brigadier General Alexander Lawton, who was in charge of the defense of Savannah. He conducted the party on a tour of his house, and showed them the cartridges that Mrs. Lawton and a group of ladies were making for the war effort.

Russell also received the news of the day, which had not been accessible when he was at Sea Island. Seward had rejected the Governor of Maryland's plan to have Lord Lyons arbitrate between North and South. The Southerners seemed to find this terribly amusing. Seward and Lincoln, it seemed, were drowning their unhappy plight in alcohol, as was most of Washington. On a more sober note, Robert E. Lee, late of the United States Army, was named Commander of the Forces of Virginia—which had finally seceded. In addition, the Governor of Georgia announced that no more payments on debts to Northerners would be made until the war's conclusion. In all the Southern states, calls for volunteers were being answered.

During his stay in Savannah, Russell was taken to visit the Bonaventure Cemetery. It was a strangely beautiful sight. The drive there was particularly satisfying, and the journalist, in his naturalist mode, described the trees in great detail. He reiterated his theory of the reason for American reverence for trees—because they were older than anything else in the country.

At dinner that evening, where the guests were, among others, Brigadier Lawton and Commodore Josiah Tatnall, Russell noted that though the Georgians might not hate the Yankees as much as their South Carolinian brothers, they were just as determined to fight. Contrary to previously heard remarks, they also expressed no interest in becoming part of England or borrowing a prince from that country. Most importantly, the Georgians were determined to be independent.

The following day was as beautiful a day in May as one could wish, the weather not unlike England's best effort. Russell was pleased to enjoy his favorite American pastime—examining military installations. He visited Fort Pulaski, a fortification named for a Polish patriot who helped defend Savannah from the British during the Revolutionary War. The fort was located at the mouth of the Savannah River, making it invaluable to the defenses of the city. His guides were old Commodore Tatnall, a gentleman who had spent nearly all his life in service to the Union and was now ". . . quietly preparing to meet his old comrades and friends, if needs be, in the battlefield . . . his long service flung away, his old ties and connexion severed . . ."[27], and Brigadier Lawton.

Russell scanned the harbor for ships and saw few anchored there, probably as a result of the blockade. He decided that "Uncle Sam" had better hurry and bottle up the harbors before the Confederate States of America raised its privateer flags and began its trade all over the world. He wasn't convinced that England would take this opportunity to trade with the rebels. There would be few in England to take "letters of marque and reprisal" (which was, in effect, a government grant to engage in privateering).[28]

While viewing the banks of the river, Russell observed that the huts and slave dwellings looked much like a camp in the Crimea. As they steamed down river to the fort on board the *Camilla*, Russell was able to see a Confederate flag flying atop Pulaski. When the party landed, Russell noted the outdated weapons carried by the guards, and the uniforms which were a rag-tag mixture of different colors and allegiances. The complement of the fort was made up of planters, clerks, West Pointers, as well as some who had seen action in Mexico and probably even the Crimea. Included among the wooden huts was one that served as a hospital since many of the men were suffering from a mild bout of measles.

As the Commodore entered, the guns fired a salute, and the band played an enthusiastic welcome. As the reporter walked through the fort, as was his metier, the armaments and troop-size were noted in precise detail. Russell pointed out the weaknesses as he saw them. Pulaski was on low land, and very accessible to boats and approaches from the city side. Brigadier Lawton was confident that he could take care of the Yankees on land, and the Commodore would stop them on the sea. He added, "We beat off the British fleet at Charleston by the militia—ergo, we'll sink the Yankees now."[29] A mistaken notion at best, Russell thought, since past glories were scant assurances against modern weapons and tactics. Tatnall summed it up in a much more pragmatic manner when he said, "I have no fleet. Long before the

Southern Confederacy has a fleet that can cope with the Stars and Stripes, my bones will be white in the grave."[30] In the end, Russell wrote that ". . . what I saw did not satisfy me that Pulaski was strong or Savannah very safe."[31] Nevertheless, he was pleased that they served a good lunch.

As they steamed back to the harbor, there was a small alarm. A ship hoisting the Stars and Stripes turned out to be a cotton merchant's ship from Liverpool. However, Russell thought to himself how vulnerable Savannah Harbor, one of the South's few harbors, was.

They were home that evening, quite late but, nevertheless, had a party at dinner. Russell spent the time with a strong, well-informed Southerner, regretting that "there are some who are neither—or either . . . ."[32]

Preparing to move on to the Confederate capital of Montgomery, Russell wrote in a letter to his friend Bancroft Davis that the Southern swagger and exaltation had cooled down markedly in the near month since Fort Sumter. The idea of marching to Washington never occurred to them. They were still hoping for British intervention to clear the Yankee blockade; "they swear they'll keep every bale of cotton for a year to try how Lowell & Manchester can stand."[33] Russell later wrote to his editor, John Delane, "If we must have it [cotton] I think the old island is doomed for our weakness is so apparent. . . ."[34]

On that beautiful May Day, Jefferson Davis made his Declaration of War to the Southern people. Russell commented that it was ". . . steeped in moderation."[35] His further comments were that the Southerners did not expect England and France to ". . . allow this thing to go on."[36] The following day, he wrote another letter to Bancroft Davis, complaining about the state of the post. He had only just received letters from home, a constant worry to him, and he wondered if his Letters to *The Times* might arrive without obstruction if he put them in bottles and flung them into the ocean.[37]

That morning, he breakfasted with the Hodgsons. William Hodgson had been a U.S. representative to such exotic places as China, and his servants served the meal in liveries that smacked, Russell thought, of the Orient. They discussed the concept of whether blacks were human or "two-legged cattle."[38] The idea that this discussion took place with the servants in attendance made Russell decidedly uncomfortable. The usual point was made that slavery elevated the slave and civilized his mind. They were sure that if emancipation came, the slaves would revert to their barbarian state. Russell felt that the slaves were, in reality, no safer in America than they had been in Africa, when capture was a danger every minute. Here in the States, they could be sold or separated in some other way from their families—indeed, legally their families did not exist. In his private diary, Russell noted: "Breakfast service very fine. Good house baddish pictures."[39]

After the breakfast, Russell walked around town again, as though to give himself a final impression of what he was seeing—the squares, the trees, the churches, the institutions and the fascinating mix of people everywhere on the streets. He noticed among the Southerners a great deal of Irish and German immigrants. He knew that as they had been so steadfast and loyal in the North, so they would be in the South and would fight to the death for the Confederacy.

He began to worry, what with the bad post and the martial situation ready to break at any moment, how long his own lines of communications would be open before he might have to beat a hasty retreat. And so, he said goodbye to his host, Mr. Green, and, sorry that he would not be able to see more of Savannah, he left with real regret.

→ *Chapter Six* ←

"... 'possums', raccoons, frogs and other delicacies ..."

MACON, GEORGIA—MOBILE, ALABAMA
MAY, 1861

INTREPID JOURNALIST that he was, Russell remained un-daunted and pushed on. His subsequent destination was Macon, Georgia. During the train trip, he was introduced to the Rev. Mr. El-liot, Bishop of Georgia. Mr. Elliot, Russell thought, was of fine stature and handsome countenance. Nevertheless, the journalist was dis-gusted at his pro-slavery arguments, particularly those which he based on Scripture. Russell opined that a nation that could "approve of such interpretations of the Scriptures and, at the same time, read the *New York Herald,* seemed ripe for destruction as a corporate existence."[1] He continued:

> The miserable sophists who expose themselves to the contempt of the world by their paltry thesicles on the divine origin and uses of slavery are infinitely more contemptible than the wretched bigots who published themes long ago on the propriety of burning witches or on the necessity for the offices of the Inquisition.[2]

Russell concluded that if the Confederacy ever won its independence, it would most certainly have to grapple with the rest of the civilized world on the question of this "peculiar institution."

During the trip, Russell stopped at an outdoor restaurant. The meal

[95]

was adequate, served by slaves, but when Russell went to pay the landlord, that gentleman protested. He did not want gold or anything that had eagles or stars on it, he wanted his "own paper,"[3] Confederate currency. Russell assured his readers that the man was serious, and he had to borrow a couple of Confederate Greenbacks from his traveling companions.

The party reached Macon at dark and went on to what was termed the best hotel in town. On his room door, Russell noted that there were the usual warnings about pickpockets, and a list of all the rules and regulations of the establishment. America's railways and hotels were plagued, the journalist assured his readers, with gamblers and thieves, or so it seemed from all the dire warnings.

In the morning, Russell had the opportunity to take a quick drive around town. He thought the country very pretty and the houses, detached, painted white and standing in their own grounds, charming. He also saw signs such as "Smith Co., advanced money on slaves, and had constant supplies of Virginian negroes on sale or hire."[4] These particular buildings had enclosures, or slave pens, as Horace Greeley called them. However, Russell had no chance to inspect them, as Greeley had asked, since he departed for Montgomery that very morning. This journey, Russell wrote, had little to recommend it, being similar to most of the journeys he had made thus far in the American South. The people seemed "rawer, ruder, bigger,"[5] and a great deal of swearing went on. There were, he said, no rustics in America. Everyone affected to dress the same, so that distinctions were not necessarily observed. Obviously, however, distinctions could be made in terms of the quality of the cut and material of a suit that a man would wear.

Again, to a man, his fellow passengers were loudly pro-secession. There was flag-waving and cheering at every stop and junction. News, as always, was exchanged and opinions given. The fact that Federal troops had come in to protect Washington made it less likely that the South would try to secure Baltimore. Nevertheless, martial spirits were still at a high pitch.

Coincidentally, General Beauregard and James Manning alighted the train at one of the junctions and were immediately pounced upon for speeches. Beauregard told Russell that they had tried to board unobserved, since demands that they speak seemed to happen at every station and stop. Manning, being a former Governor, apparently couldn't resist an opportunity to make a speech, and made one on the topics currently dearest to the Southern heart: secession, abolitionism and States Rights. He was then carried off on the cheering crowd's shoulders.

Upon arrival in Montgomery, Russell's first diary entries were complaints about the wretched sanitation at the hotel and the awful meals. The unhappy journalist was crammed into a room with five other men. It was filthy, and there were only three beds, obliging them to "double up." Had it not been for the flies, he wrote, the fleas would have been intolerable, but one nuisance neutralized the other.[6] The meals he found lamentable. He was served odd courses of ". . . unknown fishes, oyster-plants, 'possums', raccoons, frogs and other delicacies, and, eschewing toads and the like really make a good meal . . ."[7] on dirty dishes. Adding to his displeasure, the hotel was similar to Willard's, with office-seekers nested there waiting . . . and waiting. That evening, Russell was glad to be able to put his mattress on the floor in order to dodge projectiles of tobacco juice. One of the other men, he marveled, had the entire process down to a fine art. His only worry was that the man's attention might come his way at a crucial moment. He was much relieved when he heard the other's loud snoring. It was, he said sorrowfully, the worst hotel he had stayed in thus far, though he charitably forewent naming the offending institution.

One of Russell's party complained about the crush at the hotel. The office-seekers filled the halls much in the same way they did in Washington, D.C. However, these people were much more difficult to pass, since they seemed to be bonier, with sharp elbows. The clerk, however, pointed out to that gentleman that he was wrong. What he was feeling, the clerk explained, were simply implements of offense and defense. "I suppose you and your friends are the only people in the house who hadn't a bowie-knife, or a six-shooter, or Derringer about them."[8] Russell and his friends doubtless were unhappy at being thus exposed to danger and completely unarmed.

Russell was not impressed with this seat of the Confederacy. He described it as a small Russian town with place-names and shops that indicated their owners were of German and French origin. Montgomery, he wrote, ". . . has little claims to be called a capital. . . . I have rarely seen a more dull, lifeless place."[9]

He observed slaves lounging around the doors of the shops and buildings of the town, and not overly fearful of reprimand, nor were their owners seemingly worried about escape. "It is not in its external aspects generally that slavery is so painful."[10] They are, the reporter observed, well-fed, protected, their aged ones looked after, children provided for . . . something, like pigs in a sty. Then, "the hour comes when the butcher steals to the sty, and the knife leaps from the sheath."[11] Further, he wrote that the United States was represented to the world as a free society. In that respect, it was only the West and North that could be represented; the slave states were not part of the larger society. Russell was beginning to feel uneasy, but the worst was yet to come.

That evening, Russell dined with a number of Confederate officers and congressmen. Afterward, he walked over to staff headquarters. The talk was, as usual, about politics, and Russell was not spared the various speeches aimed at Great Britain and comments regarding her mortal fear of France, which he dutifully noted, without further comment.

On May 6, he toured the city with his friend, Senator Wigfall, now sober and not nearly as amusing, nor, thankfully, as insulting. The environs of Montgomery were far more pleasant than the downtown of the city. The homes were those same detached wooden villas set on grounds that Russell had noticed throughout the South. There were public gardens, and it was not unusual to see women riding on horseback.

The two men walked to the capitol building, which Russell called

a "true Athenian Yankeeized structure. . . ."[12] Though many would disagree, he apparently disliked the Federal style in which so many public buildings in America were designed. Before entering the building,
the reporter came upon an auctioneer disposing of some "living ebony
carvings"[13]—in other less euphemistic words, slaves—to a small crowd
who had more curiosity than cash. This was, he thought as he passed
the group, a bad introduction to the Southern legislative body. Seated
in that body at the beginning of the session, Russell heard an invocation, tremendously inspirational to the listeners, and deeply fanatic in
its extremism extolling the divinity that is slavery. After this invocation, the legislature proceeded with its business. The speaker, however,
immediately declared a "secret session." As Russell made a move to
leave, Mr. Rhett, the gentleman whom he had met at Sea Island Plantation, said to him, half-jokingly, "I think you ought to retain your
seat. If the 'Times' will support the South, we'll accept you as a delegate." The reporter demurred, quietly. He could not act as a delegate
to a Congress of slave states.[14] This was a decision resulting from the
lingering, and now constant, revulsion to what he had just witnessed
on the way to the session.

On leaving the capitol building, the pair went over to listen to the
auctioneer whom they had seen earlier. He was presently auctioning
off one of the so-called "living ebony carvings." The auctioneer was an
ill-favored, dissipated-looking man, and next to him was the "mer-
chandise" he was about to sell. The slave was a stout young man,
poorly dressed with dilapidated shoes. In his hand was a bundle of his
earthly goods. He regarded the crowd listlessly. More men gathered,
soldiers and laborers, and the auctioneer began his spiel—"A prime
field hand! Just look at him—good-natured, well-tempered; no marks
. . .,"[15] and he began the price at nine hundred and fifty dollars. Russell's reaction was vehement:

I am neither a sentimentalist, nor a black Republican, nor negro-
worshiper, but I confess the sight caused a strange thrill through my

heart. I tried, in vain, to make myself familiar with the fact that I could, for the sum of $975, become as absolutely the owner of that mass of blood, bones and sinew, flesh and brains, as of the horse which stood by my side. . . . He was by no means my brother, but he was a fellow creature.[16]

The man was sold for a thousand dollars, and there were comments all round that he had gone cheap, that, indeed, most slaves seemed to go cheap nowadays. For a split second, Russell reflected upon what it would be like to own a man in much the same way that he might own a horse or an ox; a man who would be subject to his whims at any time, and whose very life was his to command. That thought, however, left him with strong feelings of disgust. Lest we find the journalist too enlightened, these feelings also stemmed from the fact that Christian men were conducting these proceedings in English. Slave markets in the East were evidently more palatable to Russell; as he said, they were an entirely different matter.

As Russell left the capitol building that day, he reflected on the misery and cruelty engendered in the building of the city and the tilling of the soil. He thought of the degradation of a society that had wanted-posters for runaways, describing the marks, scars and whip marks.

Interestingly enough, reactions to the journalist's descriptions were mixed. Orville James Victor, a staunch abolitionist, felt that Russell had not spoken strongly enough against the evils of slavery. He wrote:

Every letter yet written by Mr. Russell shows that he studiously avoids the great social, moral and interstate bearing of controversy, viewing it only in its commercial and material relations.[17]

Mary Chestnut felt decidedly distressed:

. . . Russell . . . tries to tell the truth unpalatable as it is to us. Why should we expect a man who recorded so unflinchingly the wrongdoing in India to soften matters for our benefit. . . . God knows, I am not inclined to condone it . . .[18]

Russell, who may have been unhappy about slavery in the past, now became a staunch opponent. His journey south had ". . . enhanced and crystallized his hatred of slavery and made him positively unable to act as a defender of the Confederacy."[19]

The abolitionist pamphleteer Orville Victor zealously condemned Russell, since he was convinced that *The Times*, influenced by Mr. Russell, would lead England into war with the United States, as long as they kept their ". . . Special Correspondent at the Confederate Court, to write up the greatness and glory of King Cotton. . . ."[20] It seems that Victor, again, missed the point of Russell's Southern Letters.

A major theme that ran continually through Southern conversation was the conviction that England would have to back their efforts for independence because of her reliance on supplies of raw cotton. "Whilst Russell was first to acknowledge that an interruption in the cotton supply would produce serious economic distress across the Atlantic . . .,"[21] he became increasingly weary of the repetition of the slogan "King Cotton" as the primary material consideration of England and Europe. He wrote: "They believe in the irresistible power of cotton."[22] He later observed how astonishing it was that all these people felt that England was absolutely dependent on cotton for her very existence.[23] With all this braggadocio and self-satisfaction, it must have come as quite a shock to the South that the

> . . . Union Naval blockade of the Southern coastline compounded the difficulty of communications. In the last analysis, Southerners depended too much on the political power of cotton, the failure of "King Cotton" was one of the greatest blows to . . . [the Confederacy]. . . .[24]

Later that day (May 6), W.M. Browne, the Assistant Secretary of State of the Confederacy, visited Russell. They spoke of many things including, interestingly enough, the Confederate issuance of letters of marque and reprisal not only for England, but also for merchants in Boston. It was not so astonishing, however, when one remembered that many northeastern merchants continued to trade with England during the War of 1812. Browne further told Russell that Jefferson Davis intended to take full charge of the army and make all the appointments. Russell, once again, urgently wrote to his friend Bancroft Davis. Since there was little hope of getting anything through, either to or from the South, Russell was worried about his family and hungry for news of them.

On May 7, President Davis issued an official Declaration of War between the Confederacy and the United States, along with the issuance of letters of marque and reprisal. In the declaration, Davis invited any willing vessel to fight the wicked Northern aggression and break the blockade. Senator Wigfall, ubiquitous as ever, brought Russell to the State Department to meet the President. Seward had told Russell that had it not been for Davis, the South would never have seceded, for he was the only one with the brains and courage to bring the thing about. The center of the Confederacy was a large brick building with a flag waving atop the edifice. Russell and Seward proceeded to the first floor and a door marked "the President." After seeing some men out, Davis invited Russell to sit with the words, "Mr. Russell, I am glad to welcome you here, though I fear your appearance is a symptom that our affairs are not quite prosperous."[25]

Jefferson Davis was born in Kentucky and was a graduate of West Point. His first wife, who died shortly after the wedding, was the daughter of his Commander, Zachary Taylor. Davis later married Varina Howell. He was a member of the United States House of Representatives, and served gallantly during the Mexican War. He was later elected to the Senate, became Secretary of War during the administration of Franklin Pierce, and was re-elected to his seat after Buchanan took office. An avid supporter of States Rights and secession, he made an impassioned speech on those subjects on the floor of the Senate in January of 1861. Afterward, he left Washington for good, and was elected President of the Confederate States of America in February.

Russell and Davis spoke of general matters. Russell described President Davis as a man of slight, sinewy figure, rather over middle height, soldier-like in bearing and with regular, well-defined features. The face, however, he found thin, wrinkled and haggard. He was a calm, resolute man, the journalist noted in his private diary, slight, spare, a lean Cassius with an eye tic. However, he was thrilled to relate that the President did not chew tobacco and was neat and clean. This first visual assessment was more flattering than the following impression that was noted in his diary: "I had the opportunity of observing the President very closely; he did not impress me favorably as I had expected. . . ."[26] It was disappointing that Russell did not elaborate on his reasons for this negative impression.

The two talked of Russell's experiences in the Crimea and in India. The reporter remarked to the President about the eagerness with which the Southerners responded to a call to arms. Davis was pleased with his comment and told Russell that they were a military people. Russell requested some sort of protective document for his travels. President Davis, most anxious to please an important representative of the British press, issued Russell a safe conduct pass, signed by the Secretary of War, which stated:

The officers in the service of the Confederate States will recognize my signature, and facilitate your observations within those limits, I feel satisfied your own tastes will prescribe.

Your well-known worth in private, as well as public life, will always command the social attention of gentlemen where ever, within our bounds, you may think proper to proceed and sojourn.[27]

During his conversations with President Davis, recognition of the South by Great Britain was discussed. Davis was well aware of the ad-

vantages for both sides, whether for or against such an acknowledg-
ment. He felt, nevertheless, that if the South was not given the nod by
England, it would be a sign of ". . . hostility and alliance to the enemy."[28] However, he also realized that the North would consider such
a recognition as a virtual declaration of war. Russell reported, as an
aside to his readers, that the question of recognition was no immediate problem for Great Britain, because the cotton-loading season
started in October—therefore, the trial of the rights of neutrality
might conceivably not become an issue until then.

Davis wanted to know if the English people thought there would
be an all-out war between the states. Russell answered that it was his
impression that the English public did not think there would be actual hostilities. Davis replied that the South would be driven to it to
protect their "rights and liberties." As Russell left, Jeff Davis assured
him of his government's cooperation, and that he would always be
glad to see him.

After the meeting, Russell proceeded to the office of Judah Benjamin, Attorney General of the Confederate States. His impression of
Benjamin was quite positive. The Attorney General was judged to be
". . . the most open, frank and cordial of the Confederates whom I
have yet met."[29] In his private diary, Russell was less circumspect and
flattering. He described Benjamin as "Israel of diverse orbed bright-
ness. Clever, keen well yes! What keen & clever men sometimes are."[30]

Judah Benjamin was born in the Virgin Islands, and came to the
United States at the age of fourteen to study at Yale University. From
Yale, he went to New Orleans, where he met and married a Roman
Catholic Creole lady named Natalie St. Martin. Benjamin prospered
and, in 1854, was elected to the United States Senate. When the difficulties between the states began, he left his post in Washington. President Davis chose him to serve as Attorney General, Secretary of War
and, eventually, Secretary of State for the Confederacy. When the
South was crushed, Benjamin could not stay in his defeated home and
went to England, where he eventually became a Queen's Counsel.

The two men spoke of the issue of privateers. Benjamin assured Russell that if the United States executed any Southern privateers, the South would respond by executing two Northerners. He added that if England did not recognize the Southern privateers, it would be tantamount to a declaration of war. Great Britain, Russell thought wryly, was in the midst of a great dilemma. Seward had declared that if she recognized the South, it would be a declaration of war, and if she did not recognize the Southern flag, it would be the same. A classic conundrum.

That afternoon, Russell was invited by Mrs. Davis to a reception at the presidential home, along with Benjamin and Benjamin's brother-in-law, a Creole from New Orleans. The house in which the Davis family lived was painted white, "another White House,"[31] and had a small garden. Russell was introduced to Varina Davis, whom he called "a comely sprightly woman, verging on matronhood, of good figure and manners, well-dressed, ladylike, and clever, and she seemed a great favorite. . . ."[32] Mrs. Davis was a native of Mississippi. She met and married the Confederate President seventeen years before. An extremely capable woman, she ran the plantation during her husband's political service to the United States. However, like her counterpart Mary Todd Lincoln, she aroused rumor and anger in the press for the supposedly royal manner in which she conducted herself and the affairs of the presidential household. The reception, Russell thought, was without ceremony or affectation. He noted that the ladies seemed slightly jealous of "Queen Varina." After receiving an invitation from her to dine the following evening, he left.

Later, at dinner, Senator Wigfall joined the trio, and a heated discussion of rights of neutrals and the legality of the blockade ensued. Benjamin felt strongly that President Lincoln must understand that there was no legal way that England could recognize the blockade as long as they conceded that the ports still belonged to the United States.

The following day, Russell attempted to write his articles, but was constantly interrupted by the comings and goings of the people in the communal room. The ubiquitous Senator Wigfall came to persuade Russell of the truth of his ideas. However, these ideas, such as they were, were presented with "a wonderful lucidity and odd affectation of logic all his own."[33] What he told Russell seemed absurd by any standard. Southerners, he began, were a primitive but civilized people. They had no cities and did not want them, had no press or literature, no merchant marine or navy and did not want them, either. As long as they had cotton, rice, tobacco and sugar, he concluded, they could get what they needed from the rest of the world. Russell, no doubt, mentally rolled his eyes heavenward; nevertheless, he nodded politely and solemnly wrote Wigfall's words in his diary.

Russell received an official invitation to dine at the Davises. Having decided to move on quickly to Mobile, he had to send his regrets. It was most important to complete the Southern tour "speedily as all mail communication will soon be suspended from the South. . . ."[34] Indeed, Russell was worried that time was running out for free passage of his Letters from Southern ports. Further, he worried about the destruction of avenues of communication and possible escape routes for himself. The ". . . bridges . . . [were] . . . broken, rails . . . [were] . . . torn up; [and] telegraphs pulled down."[35]

His diary entries for those few days in Montgomery reiterate much of what Russell had seen and heard, along with the impressions he received throughout the South. In addition, he was not convinced that his strong feeling that the South would not be coerced back to the Union was wrong. He felt that the South would only be forced back by a strong siege that would lay it prostrate—words that General Sherman, no doubt, later took to heart. Such a conquest, however, would change the North and the Federal government, as well. It would have to become a much stronger force. Prophetic words, indeed. Neither side, he stated bluntly, was ready for the aggression or power of the other.

Russell's last night in Montgomery was spent making farewells.

There was a further reunion in his crowded bedroom, when Wigfall, Benjamin, Browne and others came to say goodbye. On the morning of his departure to Mobile, his "faithful" Wigfall returned again. He wanted to show Russell comments about his Letters, which were making their about-face from Great Britain and showing up in the *New York Times*. The newspaper was, it seemed, angry about Russell's comments describing New York apathy. Further, the editors were extremely upset at Russell's pronouncements, and pointed to their outburst of Union fervor after the fall of Sumter as proof of their strong feelings.

This enthusiasm would have been much more useful had they evinced it before Sumter. The *New York Herald*, he recalled, compared the Confederate cabinet to the cabinet of the Union, and found the Union wanting. The Confederates "were gentlemen—(a matter of which it is quite incompetent to judge)—and would, and ought to succeed."[36] Russell, evidently, smarted under criticism, but could comfort himself with the idea that he had seen it all first-hand. If one remembered what New York had been like in March, it would be difficult to disagree with the correspondent's assessments or his judgments of the fantasies in which the New York press was now indulging just two months later.

Before Russell boarded his steamer that afternoon, his Montgomery friends came to bid him adieu. Naturally, he had one more gripe about the food at the hotel, then was off on the steamer *The Southern Republic* to Mobile. He left Montgomery with no regret, except that he had to desert the new friends he had made. It was his opinion, after leaving the Confederate capital, that though neither side was ready for any kind of fighting, the South presented a solid, united front, and the North did not.[37]

The trip down the Alabama River was monotonous. The captain was an Irishman and regaled Russell with amazing tales. The reporter just hoped that the captain wasn't foolish enough to think that he believed anything he said. The land on both sides was cotton-growing land and, therefore, extremely valuable. That night they reached Selma, which was built on a high bluff and reminded Russell of Edinburgh. After an uneasy night, full of creaks and whistle sounds, the journey continued on much the same. During their discussions, the captain became most anxious that Russell believe how happy the slaves were, and how good slavery was for them. To that end, he trotted out a young boy of twelve, half-naked, and began to confirm his hypothesis.

"Are you happy, Bully?"
"Yas, sar."
"Show how you're happy."
Here the boy rubbed his stomach, and grinning with delight said, "Yummy! Yummy! plenty belly full."[38]

The captain remarked to the reporter that there were many in his country, meaning Russell's, who could not say as much.

An incident occurred that evening which further supported the journalist's personal revulsion to slavery, as though, at this point, any further incidents were needed. Again, in order to show how happy the slaves were, a dance was arranged by the captain. This need to show others the felicity of the slaves was "a favorite theme of Southerners."[39] There would be more attempts, in later visits to plantations on the Mississippi, to show Russell how blissful was the slave's life. "Yes Sir, they're the happiest people on the face of the airth!", the captain assured Russell cheerfully.[40]

On May 11, they arrived at Mobile. Entering the harbor, Russell could already see the initial effects of the blockade on the Southern economy. There were, he wrote, only five ships in the harbor, and all were British.[41] During his stay, Russell was told that the harbor at Pensacola was not actually blockaded. There were, however, squadrons of Union ships there, as well as at the harbor in New Orleans, which prompted Russell to lament that ". . . the mails are stopped; so are the telegraphs; and it is doubtful whether I can get to New Orleans by water." Luckily, he was wrong.[42]

As he walked along to his hotel, the Battle House, Russell observed the large warehouses on the quay. The hotel was a fine building, though, as usual, it was crowded with tobacco-chewing men. It was a far more commodious experience than its predecessors. Better, he wrote, than Willard's or Mills House in Charleston. The room was private and well-furnished, with gas lighting. The meals were far superior to the "oyster-plants, 'possums' and toads" he had been forced to consume in Montgomery.

After registering, the journalist went for a drive around Mobile. Though the weather was hot, Russell enjoyed the charms of the city, seeing, again, detached villas, fragrant orange trees and magnolia groves. The beautifully wide streets and roads were made of shell and sand.

Among Russell's first callers were Mr. James Magee, acting British consul in Mobile, and John Forsyth, one of the Commissioners whom he had met previously in Washington. After pleasantries were exchanged, Forsyth extended an invitation to Russell to visit the forts.

The first evening was spent with Mr. Magee and a Dr. Josiah D. Nott, who was noted for his studies of cranial size and the coordinate deduction that blacks were inferior due to reduced cranial capacity. According to the good doctor, who professed to detest slavery, ". . . questions of morals and ethics, pertaining to its [slavery] considerations, ought to be referred to the cubic capacity of the human cranium—the head that can take the largest charge of snipe shot will eventually dominate in some form or other over the head of inferior capacity."[43]

Both men, however, strived to convince the correspondent that Mobile was as fully secessionist as the rest of the South. This reinforced Russell's own conclusions that, after visiting four Southern states, he saw no loyalty to the Union. Even had they not been enthusiastic about secession before, which most were, they were now ardently supporting the inevitable. If an officer of Southern birth elected to remain in the Federal Army, he was reviled and his property was confiscated. There was no room in the new Southern republic for ambivalence or, it seemed, freedom of conscience.

After dinner, the men strolled about Mobile. Russell saw oyster saloons, lager-beer and wine shops, and dancing and gambling establishments. He noted that the place reminded him of St. John's in Liverpool on a Saturday night. Mobile and its environs, about which Russell was unusually complimentary, was the most "foreign-looking" city he had seen in the States so far. Nevertheless, nice as the city might be, Russell was far more interested in visiting the surrounding military installations, which he looked forward to on the morrow.

Chapter Seven

"... all the unanimity of a conspiracy ..."

MOBILE—UP THE MISSISSIPPI
MAY—JUNE, 1861

DURING THE NEXT FEW DAYS, Russell enthusiastically visited several military installations. On May 12, Russell's first stops were Forts Gaines and Morgan, which he described in minute detail. Munitions, matériels and especially the vulnerability of Fort Morgan were clearly and exhaustively delineated. The party visiting the forts was made up of officers, journalists, merchants and politicians, anxious to visit the scene where history was being made. The day was warm though breezy, and the Bay of Mobile, Russell wrote, was shallow. Finally, after four hours, they reached Fort Gaines. The garrison itself was filled with a company of bored young men who were waiting, like so much of the South, for something to happen. Russell sympathized with one soldier, who said he'd prefer a day against the Federals as opposed to an entire week against the mosquitoes.

Fort Morgan was a far more substantial stronghold. However, since its broad wall faced the sea, Russell realized that it was more vulnerable to attack. It held a larger complement of men, about seven or eight hundred, commanded by a like number of officers, some of whom had returned prematurely from their grand tours of Europe to take arms with their respective states. Though Russell was delighted to indulge in an excellent lunch, he could see that the way in which the fort, as it was presently garrisoned, "would suffer exceedingly from heavy bombardment. . . . All the barracks and wooden buildings should be destroyed if they wish to avoid the fate of Sumter."[1]

The following day, Russell was busy preparing for his visit to Fort Pickens at Pensacola. Though Pickens was a Federal fort, Russell was sure that his neutral credentials would stand him in good enough stead to get through the blockade. Forsyth, the Southern Commissioner, had asked him to take several gentlemen of Mobile with him, passing them off as friends. Russell consented to the men joining him, though he made it quite clear that he would not lie for any of them if they were questioned, or even say that they were friends.

> "Surely you will not have Mr. R____ hanged, Sir?" said the Mayor of Mobile to me when I told him I could not consent to pass off the gentleman in question as a private friend. "No, I shall do nothing to get Mr. R ____ hanged. It will be his own act which causes it. . . ."[2]

On May 14, at about nine in the evening, Russell boarded the steamer *Diana* with his party. Their destinations were Fort Pickens and the Warrington Naval Yard. Included in their stores were a British flag, lent to Russell by the consul, Mr. Magee, and a white tablecloth to be used, if necessary, as a flag of truce. They were seen off by a crowd, who were convinced that they were going to the scene of an impending battle. They, themselves, knew better, and Russell, more than ever, was quite convinced that there would be no battle. As they steamed along, keeping close to the coastline, Russell particularly enjoyed the way the moonlight reflected on the waves. The little boat traveled through areas that were unpleasant, swampy, and full of mosquitoes and alligators.

After a listless night, Russell was awakened by the captain announcing that he could see small specks on shore as he peered through his spyglass. It was, doubtless, some of those "damned Yankees 'conoitering' for a road to Mobile."[3] All on board were ready and willing to commence fire, but Russell strongly objected on grounds that he was a neutral, and that a battle at this point would be entirely arbitrary. So, the heroics were deferred.

Arriving at Pensacola, they could see two forts, Pickens and McRae, with rival flags atop their poles. A small blockade schooner, the *Oriental*, came alongside the *Diana*, and an officer jumped onto her deck. He identified himself as Mr. Brown, Master in the United States Navy, commanding the *Oriental*. After questioning everyone, Brown had no doubt that it would be all right to let them pass and gave such instructions. They were to moor alongside the schooner *Powhattan*. The Master was exceedingly courteous, Russell thought, while the Southerners were as black as thunder.

The *Powhattan* was commanded by the famous naval officer David Dixon Porter. Porter, the third generation of a prominent naval family, was a young midshipman in the Mexican Navy before joining the United States Navy at the same rank, at the age of sixteen. He had been involved in blockading the entire gulf coast since the beginning of hostilities. He would later be instrumental in the capture of New Orleans for the Union.

Porter also questioned Russell and his fellow passengers. Theirs was not the only schooner tied alongside the *Powhattan*, and Porter confided to Russell about a little clandestine operation that was taking place. Confederate merchants would set out of Mobile with cargoes of fruits and vegetables, with the stated intention of running the blockade. They would be captured, given a fair price for their goods, then go home and moan about how they were plundered by the Yankees. After this confidential talk with Porter, Russell was invited aboard the Union flagship *Sabine*, which was commanded by Captain Henry A. Adams. He received a pass to go through the blockade, but was advised by Adams to show the white flag of a neutral. Adams also felt that the Mobile gentlemen ought not to go on the excursion to Pickens. Russell quickly agreed. Adams greatly feared that he was exposing himself to general attacks by what he termed the unscrupulous misrepresentation of the press. He relied on Mr.

Russell's character to be truthful and make no improper use of the permission.

Of great interest to the correspondent, Adams began to tell Russell about himself. A Pennsylvanian by birth, he had married a girl from Louisiana and settled on a plantation there. One of his sons joined the Confederate Army, and two others had joined the army of Virginia. He shook his head sadly, saying, "God knows, when I open my broadside but that I may be killing one of my children."[4] His daughter, a supplier to the troops in New Orleans, wished him to starve if he persisted in his wicked blockade. Nonetheless, the old gentleman was gallantly determined to do his duty.

Russell returned to the *Oriental* to inform Lieutenant Porter that he had obtained the necessary permissions. One of the officers expressed astonishment that Russell was able to go freely to Pickens with the editors of Southern papers. Russell angrily assured him that there were no journalists, himself excepted, in the company.

The captain informed him that General Bragg, who commanded ". . . over there . . .", had sent word that he considered the Northern blockade a declaration of war, and that he had every intention of firing on any vessel which approached the Naval Yard.[5] Prudently, then, the somewhat dirty white tablecloth, which showed them as neutrals, proved very useful for Mr. Russell's peaceful purpose.

Upon reaching Pensacola, Russell was able to see Fort Pickens, which he described as ". . . a solid, substantial looking work . . . [reminding] . . . one something of Fort Paul at Sebastopol . . ."[6] in the Crimea, and the Confederate Naval Yard. Going over first to the Naval Yard, Russell detailed all the facets of its batteries, troop strengths and physical structure. The Yard was surrounded by high walls, and, within, was a focus of tremendous activity. There were tents and houses, which Russell called the model of neatness. There were gardens adorned with the most lush and beautiful tropical flowers. The walks were shady and put Russell in mind of the "dog days of Calcutta."[7] The officers were mostly Zouaves from New Orleans, so named after the original French company and known distinctively for the dashing jackets they wore, and the older gentlemen, who were Europeans and had seen action in various corners of the earth. He learned that Jefferson Davis, Mrs. Davis and his "faithful" Wigfall had been visiting the works that very day.

After a very satisfactory dinner, with champagne, Russell went to the officers' quarters, where he met General Braxton Bragg.

> [Bragg is] . . . about forty-two years of age, of a spare and powerful frame; his face is dark and marked with deep lines . . . his eyes sagacious, penetrating and not by any means unkindly. . . . His manner is quick and frank and his smile is very pleasing and agreeable.[8]

Bragg had graduated from West Point in 1837, and served with great distinction during the Seminole Indian Wars and the Mexican Wars. He left the United States Army in 1856 in order to take care of his plantation in Louisiana. He had now rejoined to serve his new country, and was one of only eight men who achieved the rank of full general in the Confederate Army.[9]

It was at this point in his writing that Russell decided to comment on several curious American habits. The first was that of hand-shaking. He considered it a ". . . remnant of barbarous times, when men with the same colored skin were glad to see each other."[10] He also observed that Americans seemed to have an almost universal curiosity about everyone they met. They were warm at first acquaintance, unlike Englishmen who were reserved, but later, if they liked you, they would shake hands. After Americans had had a drink with you and your party, they no longer found you interesting. Russell thought this in bad taste and extremely ill-bred.

Bragg, meanwhile, offered another argument for slavery that Russell had already heard from many in the South. He claimed that, in the Southern climate, a white man could not do the work that a black man was capable of doing since his body could not tolerate the heat as well as the black man's body did. As an illustration, he said,

[115]

On the other day, Colonel Harvey Brown, at [Federal Fort] Pickens over the way, carried off a number of negros from Tortugas, and put them to work at Santa Rosa. Why? Because his white soldiers were not able for it.[11]

Then, Bragg pulled out a map and told Russell everything he knew about Pickens, having been stationed there after he graduated from West Point. After supper, Bragg told him, "as a mark of complete confidence,"[12] that he was hardly ready to open fire on Pickens.

Russell was escorted back to the *Diana* by one of Bragg's orderlies who, in his former life, had been a planter. He'd turned his land to corn only and had left his plantation in the care of his twenty-five slaves. Russell asked whether he was worried that the slaves might rise. The planter replied that no, they were ignorant creatures, but faithful. Here was an intelligent man "who had come to do battle with as much sincerity—ay, and religious confidence—as ever actuated old John Brown, or any New England puritan to make war against slavery."[13]

The following morning, Russell was wakened by a reveille that was identical to those he had heard in the Crimea. Arriving on deck, the captain was anxious to know whether he wished to partake in some bitters. The recipe was brandy, tonic roots and sugar. Russell decided to go against his own rule and partake, though it was early in the morning. Afterwards, another of Bragg's orderlies came to fetch Russell and take him to tour the Yard. In the works, they encountered a man who had been at the Battle of Balaclava, and had been close to Lord Cardigan when his horse had been shot from under him. He had spent eleven months in a Russian prison camp until he was exchanged. The man had come to America to better himself, and was now in the Confederate Army. He told Russell that he did not know what his old commanders would think of his new company. As Russell wandered through the establishment, he could see that the ferocious descriptions of the works that had been written by the Union press were completely inaccurate. Instead of hundreds of guns, the actuality was nearer to

tens. But, great work was being done, though it was done in the typical way Russell had observed in the Southern army—much discussion
between men and their superiors before any work was undertaken.
Russell concluded that Bragg was completely correct in his view that
to open any attacks on Pickens, or anywhere else for that matter,
would be disastrous.

When Russell returned to staff headquarters at the Naval Yard, he
found General Bragg not only writing out letters of permission, but
also letters of introduction. So, having obtained the needed permission for a "look around", Russell hoisted his tablecloth and crossed
over the harbor to inspect Federal Fort Pickens. He left his party of
Mobile gentlemen behind, and the captain of the *Diana* was most put
out to have to moor next to that "darned Yankee Fort."[14]

As they approached the beach, the sentries were demanding explanations. Russell, meanwhile, pondered the loyalties to flags; just different combinations of colors and shapes, and yet many had and would
lay down their lives for them. The correspondent went ashore, where
he was given a guided tour. He observed that the United States regulars were not "comparable in physique" to the Confederate volunteers,
but were "infinitely superior in cleanliness and soldierly smartness."[15]

The fort, unlike some of the others Russell had seen, was strong on
the sea face, but weak on the land side. The Confederates would have
been happy to know that, as the summer was approaching, the climate
at Pickens was unbearable. In addition to the heat and mosquitoes, the
men had to deal with diseases such as Yellow Fever and dysentery.
However, despite all, Russell opined that he would rather be on the inside of Pickens in case of a bombardment. A Federal officer tried to ex-
tract "rebel" information from the reporter. Russell, however, who
kept his Northern and Southern facts in separate pockets, felt duty
bound to honor the trust both sides had accorded him:

> Probably no living man was ever permitted to visit the camps of two
> enemies within sight of each other before this, under similar cir-

cumstances, for I was neither spy or herald, and I owe my best thanks to those who trust me on both sides so freely and honorably.[16]

After seeing everything possible at the fort, Russell and his friends returned to the *Diana*, and sailed from Pickens to the Naval Yard to retrieve the Southern gentlemen. Then, tablecloth aflutter, they headed back between Pickens and McRae. The reporter had to admit that there were several anxious moments when they all wondered if one of the forts or the Yard might open fire on this little boat. Curiously, they were chased for several hours by an unidentified ship. Russell was sure that it was the Union schooner, the *Oriental*, although the captain was equally sure it was not. On those early hours of May 17, the little schooner quietly distinguished itself by entering open sea and actually breaking the blockade.

At five that evening, the *Diana* and her exhausted passengers arrived in Mobile. A very tired Russell made his way back to the Battle House. He watched several companies marching through the streets and executing various drills: "The air was filled with sounds of bugling and drumming."[17] That evening, Russell had many visitors who were interested in hearing about his impressions of the forts.

The following day continued as hot and uncomfortable as its predecessors. Russell commented, again, on the nuisance of the mosquitoes. He asked a waiter at his hotel if they were always numerous. The waiter answered by wishing for a hundred times the number "'. . . because we would get rid of those darned black Republicans out of Fort Pickens all the sooner.' The man seemed to infer they would not bite the Confederate soldiers."[18]

That evening, Russell dined with the anthropologist, Dr. Nott, and Judge John Campbell, late of the American Supreme Court. Judge Campbell gave Russell a long lecture about the Dred Scott case, explaining both sides and expressing his own satisfaction with the decision of Justice Taney.

Sir William Howard Russell (1820–1907), about 1880, called the First Professional War Correspondent. When any event of importance happened, the public asked, "What does Russell say?" (*Hulton Archive*)

John Thaddeus Delane (1817–1879), about 1865, Editor of *The Times* of London and Russell's close friend. (*Hulton Archive*)

William Henry Seward (1801–72), Secretary of State, about 1860. He was a "slight middle-sized man of feeble build, with a droop contracted from sedentary habits and applications to the desk. . . ." (*Hulton Archive*)

Abraham Lincoln (1809–65), 16th President of the United States. His face, Russell wrote, was "full of an expression which almost amounts to tenderness." (*The Stapleton Collection/Bridgeman Art Library, London*)

The interior of Fort Sumter, Charleston Harbour, South Carolina, after shelling by the South, April 14 1861. "Sumter, in fact, was a mouse in the jaws of a cat. . . ." (*Hulton Archive*)

City of Montgomery, Alabama, from *Harper's Weekly*, 1861. Montgomery "has little claims to be called a capital. . . ." (*Library of Congress, Washington DC, USA/Bridgeman Art Library, London*)

Left: Confederate General Pierre Gustave Toutant Beauregard (1818–93), about 1860. He told Russell, "You shall go everywhere and see everything, we rely on your discretion and knowledge of what is fair in dealing with what you see." (*Hulton Archive*)

Below, left: Attorney General Judah P. Benjamin (1811–84), Secretary of War and Secretary of State in the Confederacy, about 1860. He was "the most open, frank and cordial of the Confederates whom I have yet met." (*Hulton Archive*)

Below, right: Jefferson Davis (1808–89), the first and last President of the Confederate States of America, about 1865. "I had the opportunity of observing the President very closely; he did not impress me favorably as I had expected. . . ." (*Hulton Archive*)

Above: Confederate volunteers at Warrington Navy Yard, Pensacola, Florida, wearing an assortment of "uniforms", 1861. The tents, houses, gardens and shady walks reminded Russell of "the dog days of Calcutta". (*Hulton Archive*)

Right: Colonel Ephraim Elmer Ellsworth (1837–61), about 1861. He and his troops occupied Alexandria, Virginia, May 1861. He was shot while removing a Confederate flag. Russell decided that no matter how injudicious his actions were, he was in the performance of his duty. (*Hulton Archive*)

Union soldiers at Arlington house, the former home of General Robert E. Lee, June 28 1861, now General McDowell's Headquarters. Russell was surprised about the inactivity of the men. They were loitering about and there was no order whatsoever (*Hulton Archive*). *Inset:* General Irwin McDowell (1818–85), about 1865. Russell never lost his admiration for McDowell's "philosophical temperament" and great sense of duty. He felt he was sorely wronged for his part in the Battle of Bull Run. (*Hulton Archive*)

Union Army sentries standing guard at the ferry which connects Georgetown in the district of Columbia with Virginia across the Potomac River, 1861. Russell found the sentries a "loafing" group of men who handled their firearms like pitchforks. (*Hulton Archive*)

Above: Confederate troops making camp at the Manassas Junction railroad station, Virginia, about 1862. Things were done in the Confederate Army, Russell noted, in a typical Southern way – much discussion between men and their superiors before any work was undertaken. (*Hulton Archive*)

Left: A group of small boys watching Union cavalrymen watering their horses in the stream at Bull Run, Manassas, Virginia. The US soldiers were not "comparable in physique to the Confederates, but they were infinitely superior in cleanliness and soldierly smartness." (*Hulton Archive*)

US President Abraham Lincoln standing with General George McClellan, about 1862. "McClellan does not appear to me a man of action, or, at least, a man who intends to act speedily as the crises demands." (Diary, September 2 1861) (*Illustrated London News*)

Captain Charles Wilkes (1798–1877), about 1865. During the Civil War he intercepted a British ship and forcibly removed three Confederate Commissioners. His actions almost brought Great Britain into the war against the Union, averted in the eleventh hour by Prince Albert. Wilkes was, Russell sneered, ". . . the hero of the hour. . . ." (*Hulton Archive*)

The dedication of the monument to the men who died at the Battle of Bull Run, Virginia, June 1865. Of his infamous Letter, Russell wrote: "Let the American journalists tell the story their own way. I have told mine as I know it." (*Hulton Archive*)

Russell put forward to his readers another argument that the Southerners used as an excuse for slavery. In this one, he could not be sure that they were wrong. There might have been a good basis for the assertion that Britain might not have emancipated her slaves if they had actually lived within her borders—say in Manchester or Liverpool. Russell thought there was little inconvenience for mainland England when the slaves were emancipated, although it wreaked havoc, at least temporarily, with some of her possessions such as Jamaica.

On his last day in Mobile, so hot that he had little desire to venture out, Russell visited the country home of a merchant, Mr. Stein. This was no fort, no naval work, just a tranquil country residence, Springhill, growing a brand of grape, the Scuppernung, that Russell had never seen or tasted before. Cherokee plum and rose trees were also in abundance. It was a quiet and beautiful day, just before he set out to New Orleans.

The steamer *Florida* left Mobile Bay early in the morning on the 20th. The decks were crowded with the inevitable men in uniform. Russell noted that among the rules and regulations posted on his cabin door was the following caveat: "All slave servants must be cleared at the Custom House. Passengers having slaves will please report as soon as they come on board."[19] Russell described the beauty of the trip, the countless bayous, flocks of pelicans and schools of fish visible from the deck. There was some anxiety with regard to U.S. cruisers looking for blockade runners; however, there were none to disturb their journey.

As they left the Mississippi Sound and approached Lake Pontchartrain, they saw a large schooner flying the Stars and Stripes. Happily, they were allowed to proceed without incident. As they sailed inland on the approach to the city, Russell was charmed by the little towns, villages and elegant villas he passed. They were the summer homes of the gentry of New Orleans. The structures were of all architectures, painted in the brightest colors with flowers—magnolias and rhododendrons—adorning the gardens. Each home had a little pier jutting out into the water, with bathing machines and small boats at the moorings. Russell enjoyed this scenery, but complained that the passengers discussed politics all the "livelong day."[20] These discussions ceased only when they were eating or drinking, which was done with great frequency and in vast quantities. Spitting, sadly, was not an activity that ceased during vigorous exchanges. After dinner, the reporter witnessed another typical Southern predicament. Two gentlemen had argued vigorously, and guns emerged in preparation to give satisfaction to at least one of the two. In the end, Russell was spared the spectacle of a duel as the combatants agreed to postpone the argument and meet at a hotel in New Orleans instead.

The following morning, Russell awoke to find the vessel alongside the wharf in New Orleans. That day, the journalist was to be the invited guest of the British Consul, Mr. William Mure. In his Letter of May 22, Russell gave his readers a description of his arrival at the city, and its wonderful French flavor. He took a hackney cab to Mure's home and decided, on the way, that New Orleans had more claims to being called a great city than did New York. The Frenchness, which he liked, was in evidence from the people in the restaurants and the cafes. Even the black servants spoke French, and were particularly well-dressed.

The heat, however, was unbearable—the temperature topping out at 95°, making it prudent to stay indoors. Writing to Lord Lyons, Russell described his visit to Forts Morgan, McRae and Pickens, and his meeting with General Bragg. He emphasized that nothing in the letter should be made public since this knowledge came from a particular courtesy from both sides and could not be known except for that courtesy. He told Lyons of his firm conviction that General Bragg could not take Pickens, despite his familiarity with the fort. Moreover, the correspondent was convinced that the Southerners had an exaggerated idea of their own strength and readiness for battle. But, the soldiers are "wild splendid dare devil ill-armed men. . . ."[21]

By now, Russell's Letters and dispatches were getting more and more difficult to post through the usual channels. Regular mail between the sections had been suspended, and express companies were forbidden to carry letters. However, he was able to send a large packet through, by way of a British firm who had offices in the North.

On the evening of May 23, Russell dined with a large group of merchants and politicians. They were served by a "yellow" boy, whom his host, Major Henry Ranney, told him was a son of Andrew Jackson. These gentleman had no fear of slave revolts should hostilities begin. They expressed the sentiments that there was no desire on the part of the slaves for any such thing. Russell reported hearing, once again, the irritating refrain that ". . . our negroes, Sir, are the happiest, the most contented, and the best off of any people in the world."[22] The house servants, Russell commented, dressed well and were healthy and happy looking, but not so the ones he had observed on the streets of the city. They were "morose, ill-clad, and discontented."[23]

The following day, there was real war news to report. U.S. ships had attacked Fortress Monroe. Both sides happily claimed victory. Also, some Confederate vessels were captured by the blockade. The biggest news was that Federal Marshals had seized all telegraphic dispatches in all the large Union cities for the last twelve months—a definite suspension of Constitutional liberties that, unfortunately, marked a real state of war. Russell continued writing Letters, getting packets ready for his editor, Delane, as well as missives to Mary, who, as usual, was unwell. All of Mary's letters were "sad & low in tone,"[24] and Russell quietly asked God to comfort her and make him worthy. However, he was obviously unwilling to do what was necessary to ameliorate her condition—comfort her, himself.

On the 25th, Alexandria, Virginia, was seized by Federal troops. When a Union colonel, Colonel Ellsworth, tried to cut down the Confederate flag from an inn, he was shot to death by the innkeeper. Depending on which side you were on, and which newspapers you read, each of the men was either a murderer or a traitor, or both. However, Russell decided that no matter how injudicious the colonel's action was, he was in performance of his duties in attempting to remove the flag. In reviewing the state of the military in New Orleans, Russell remarked that ". . . the military enthusiasm is in proportion to property interest of the various classes of the people. . . ."[25] He mentioned the draft and how difficult it was to get all to serve. In addition, the journalist discussed the inexperience of the men, aggravated by a lack of munitions.

That evening, Russell was invited to the home of John Slidell, one of the gentlemen who would later be involved in the "Trent Affair." He noted that Slidell's wife and his sister-in-law, Madame General Beauregard, were quite charming. Senator Slidell was one of the Southern Commissioners whom Russell had met in Washington, D.C. The entire atmosphere of the house was delightful. As the ladies carded lint, they carried on their conversations in French. Though Slidell was born in the North, he was as ardent a Secessionist as the most vehement South Carolinian. Convinced that recognition of the South must come soon, he was, nevertheless, completely satisfied that the South was an established and independent country. Russell enjoyed the company, and remarked that the regret expressed by Washington society concerning their absence was much justified.

The following days in New Orleans continued to be too excruciatingly hot and humid for much outdoor activity. Russell postponed visits to forts and plantations, preferring to stay in, trying to sleep and write. The climate had put him in mind of the heat and misery that he had suffered in India in 1859, when he had come down with dysentery. New Orleans at the end of spring was a painful reminder.

The current news was that Confederate troops were on the march to Virginia, and the Congress had decided to move the capital up to Richmond. Russell felt that the propinquity to Washington was certainly a provocation and a possible cause for conflagration. General Scott was taking precautions to hold Baltimore, while the Northern papers were calling for an immediate advance to Richmond. When the reporter did venture outdoors, it was to watch the different and colorful companies drilling. Most of the men were either heading to Richmond or to the camp at Tangipao. All were furiously engaged in preparations.

An interesting side note appeared in Russell's Letter of May 28. It seemed that the chiefs of the five civilized tribes—the Creeks, Choctaws, Seminoles, Cherokees and Chickasaws—were passing through New Orleans. They were on their way to Montgomery, where they were interested in throwing their lot in with the Confederacy and in negotiating terms with the government. According to Russell, "The chiefs and principal men are all slaveholders."[26]

During this time, most of Russell's correspondence was about his dining partners in the evening, what they spoke about, and, particularly, what they ate; he simply did not have the energy to do much else. The 29th, for example, he dined with the Governor of Louisiana, Thomas O. Moore. The correspondent commented on what he termed a peculiarity: this was "the preponderance and influence of South Carolinian Jews, and Jews generally . . ."[27] in the South. The Governor, he averred, was somewhat under the influence of the "Hebrews", although, in the end, it seemed that he was able to think for himself. Russell's observations are, again, curious considering that he held Judah Benjamin in high esteem.

Russell also made a tour of the camp at Tangipao, about fifty miles from New Orleans, under the command of Major General Tracy. It gave, he wrote, "an occasion for obtaining a clearer view of the internal military condition of those forces of which one reads so much and sees so little. . . ."[28] Numbers of men and divisions were discussed, and Russell described the camp in precise detail. The correspondent informed his readers that Colonel Tracy had never served in anything but a militia, and that there was not one West Pointer among them. It would take a war to shape these men up, and, in fact, it would require ". . . months of discipline to enable them to pass for soldiers, even at the North. . . ."[29]

The South, he continued, was beginning to feel the effects of the blockade. He noted with interest that the railroad car in which he made the trip to and from Tangipao ". . . was built in Massachusetts, the engine in Philadelphia, and the magnifier of its lamp in Cincinnati. What will the South do for such articles in the future?"[30] So, Russell explained, with the stoppage of all commerce on the Mississippi, the South would be deprived of all but home goods.

Before leaving New Orleans, Russell was determined to see everything he possibly could. To that end, he and Mr. Mure even visited the New Orleans jailhouse. The sheriff complained about the high crime in the city and how it would, no doubt, continue until it became unlawful to bear arms. But, by law, "every American citizen may walk with an armory round his waist, if he likes."[31] Russell wrote a long description of the place, filled with the foulest murderers and lunatics, but also children accused of thievery. He left the prison in no charitable mood towards a city that sanctioned such treatment, but, where would he find better?

A much more edifying visit was to the levee that protected the city of New Orleans from the waters of the mighty Mississippi. The levee needed constant attention for, should it give way, millions could be lost in damaged crops and buildings, not to mention there being an unspeakable loss of life. Paradoxically, if the river were too low, the levee would not have the benefit of the water pressure and would cave in upon itself.

As he strolled through the city, Russell could not help but be impressed by its beauty, despite its crime and its far from comfortable tropical climate. The squares were magnificent, surrounded by lemon and magnolia trees. There were peach trees everywhere, as well as enormous cypresses hung with Spanish moss. Russell was feeling positively American in his admiration of trees. The journalist observed that the layout of the city was in a rectangular style. He wrote that this American style was reminiscent of the forms he had seen in Russia and in British India. He noted that in some of the squares, there were markets teeming with goods and patrons of all descriptions and colors. However, the stoppage of commerce with the North was already having a negative affect on the city and its services. The municipal authorities were forced to disband the police and close the public schools due to lack of funds.

Arriving at the British Consulate, Russell found it filled with English, Irish and Scottish nationals who wanted to be sent either up North or back home, since there was no work. Unfortunately, Mr. Mure did not have the means with which to help them. In addition, there was disturbing news. Something similar to impressment was happening—this time, however, not to Americans but to British subjects. Englishmen were being seized and forced to serve in the "volunteer" ranks and work gangs. Fortunately, this was quickly remedied when Mr. Mure forcefully intervened.

It was to be expected that grumblings about Russell's Letters, on the American side of the Atlantic, would continue after reprints of the New Orleans Letters seeped into the American press. Mary Chestnut complained that Russell was abusing the South in his Letters from New Orleans. She continued that people cared a great deal about what the journalist said since ". . . he represents *The Times*, and the London *Times* reflects the sentiment of the English people."[32]

Just before Russell's departure from New Orleans, he related an incident that greatly distressed him. A free black man, who was a member of the Royal Navy, applied to Mr. Mure for protection. If the Consul could not, or would not, do so, the man would be liable to imprisonment since, as a free black man, he could not walk the streets of the city. Mr. Mure was able to help him, but the reporter was greatly disturbed since he felt that London's position toward its citizens of color abroad was shameful. He said that it enabled the Americans to treat those citizens shamefully and, indirectly, to treat Britain with disrespect. Free blacks, he wrote, were subject to seizure, imprisonment and even sale. "It is too bad. This state of things ought not to be tolerated at all."[33]

Most importantly, worries about the dwindling access to mail made Russell decide to leave New Orleans on June 2 and to make his way back North. As the steamer sailed out of the city, Russell had a multi-faceted, sweeping view of New Orleans. The Mississippi levee put them roughly nine feet above the city, and the view was breathtaking. There were also the not so beautiful sights of shanties—poor, ugly shacks—but the rest was panoramic: the churches, the houses and the wide tree-lined avenues.

Describing his travels up the Mississippi, Russell gave his readers a picture of the river, its embankments, levees and the beautiful dwellings on the shores that brought to mind the glorious French chateaux.[34] During the frequent stops, he had further opportunities to visit plantations. His vessel landed first at "Cahabanooze", or "The Duck's Sleeping-Place", as it was in an Indian dialect. This plantation belonged to yet another of the Southern Commissioners, Andre Roman, ex-Governor of the state of Louisiana. The Governor received Russell and led him up to a two-story wooden mansion. Russell's quarters were a small cottage with a library and sitting room of its own. Monsieur Roman asked the reporter if he would like to look at the slave quarters, which were situated at the back of the house. Russell saw some young black women walking by in white crinolines, pink sashes and head scarves. He queried Roman and was told that they were going to a dance. The Governor permitted them to dance every Sunday. Visiting the huts of the slaves, however, Russell noticed that they had no windows and were extremely primitive. A partition divided the room in half, and pegs on the walls served as wardrobes. Some plain chairs and a table furnished one part of the room, while a mattress or two served as sleeping quarters in the other. Even here, there was hierarchy. The huts of the house servants were separated from the huts of the field slaves. Russell felt a certain repugnance in looking around the homes of these "poor creatures."[35] He felt that he had no right to intrude. The children seemed generally contented, though ill-clad. They were very well-fed and healthy-looking. That Sunday, they were listening to the music of some fiddlers, while the very old slaves were dozing. He found every evidence that they were being treated well by their master. Yet he saw, in their faces, a look of almost universal frustration. He was struck more and more by ". . . that deep defection . . . [that] . . . is the prevailing, if not universal, characteristic of the race."[36] It was fascinating to Russell. Here there was clear evidence that the people were well-cared for, and yet they had a pervasive look of sadness on their faces. The conclusion was obvious.

Roman's was a sugar plantation, and they walked over to the sugarhouse to examine the process. Roman explained that the juice was extracted from the cane, boiled, then granulated, preparing it for the refinery, which was another large brick building on the premises. Since this was not the time of the year for refining, the refinery was presently being used as a dance hall for the slaves.

That evening, several Creole gentlemen from other plantations came to visit "Cahabanooze." The talk, naturally, was of politics and the hoped-for recognition by Britain and France. The planters were resolved that Northern ships should never carry their goods again. Yet they reckoned that the combined forces of the French and British Merchant Marine would not be sufficient to carry Southern goods to Europe. At dinner, the talk was all of Jefferson Davis. The question that Russell was invariably asked all over the South was echoed, once again:

> "Have you seen our president, Sir? Don't you think him a very able man?" This unanimity in the estimate of his character, and universal confidence in the Head of State, will prove of incalculable value in a civil war.[37]

The South, commented Russell, had all the unanimity of a conspiracy.[38]

Russell rose very early the following morning, and found people up and around and the plantation bustling with activity. He rode over the fields with Governor Roman, watching the slaves eating their breakfasts, working in the cornfields, hoeing and weeding. They returned to the house for their own breakfast, in an atmosphere that Russell felt reminiscent of seventeenth-century France. He remarked on the quiet of the plantation after the very noisy city. There were barely any vessels sailing up or down the rivers, neighbors were fairly far away, the slaves worked quietly, and even the mockingbirds gave up singing during the hottest parts of the day.

After the very French hospitality of Governor Roman, Russell continued his journey on June 4. After being awakened with an offer of absinthe, he packed up and was off to Mr. John Burnside's sugar plantation. Again, Russell observed the slaves closely and was ". . . in no degree satisfied that even with [Mr. Burnside's] care and kindness even the 'domestic institution' can be rendered tolerable or defensible, if it be once conceded that the negro is a human being with a soul—or with the feelings of a man."[39] Russell further pursued this facet of Southern life when he questioned one of the slaves on Burnside's plantation. He asked the slave if he knew how to read or write. Further, had the slave gone to church or chapel and, lastly, had he ever heard of ". . . our savior?"[40] To all of these questions, the slave replied "no." Russell was greatly disturbed by what he felt was an irretrievable lack in the life of a slave. What was more important, he had no hope of salvation. The overseer, however, told him, "We don't think it right to put these things into their heads so young, it only disturbs their minds, and leads them astray."[41] He shook his head in disbelief, writing, ". . . no education—no God. . . ."[42]

Russell finished his ride with the overseer, deciding that the more well-organized the slaves were in their work, the better cared for when they were sick, "the more orderly, methodical, and perfect the arrangements for economizing slave labor—regulating slaves—are, the more hateful and odious does slavery become."[43]

But—breakfast was good.

Mr. Burnside's typical breakfast consisted of at least several mint juleps before coming to the table—the better to fight the ill-effects of the climate. Then a huge variety of dishes at the side-board: grilled fowl, prawns, eggs, ham, fish, potted salmon from England, preserved meats from France, as well as claret, water, coffee, tea, hominy mush and African vegetables. After such a repast, the newspapers were distributed and consequently rattled, read and forcefully commented upon. Then, more rides to other plantations, so that Russell began to feel that ". . . one plantation is like another as two peas."[44]

As he continued up the river, he mused: ". . . a planter is a denomadised Arab;—he has fixed himself with horses and slaves in a fertile spot, where he guards his women with Oriental care, exercises patriarchal sway . . ."[45] and was like his counterparts in the Middle East— enormously hospitable. His musings were interrupted by scenes of slaves in irons. They were, he thought, doubtless runaways, being returned to their masters. Russell feared that somehow ". . . the fatted calf-skin would not be applied to their backs."[46]

On June 7, Russell had news. The papers in New York were calling for a march on Richmond, while the papers in Richmond were calling for a march on Washington, D.C. There were rumors abounding that there were hordes of Indians at Harper's Ferry, ready to scalp the first Federal that came along. Major General George McClellan marched a force into Western Virginia, while General Irwin McDowell was put in charge of Federal forces in Virginia. The Confederates were amassing a large force at Manassas Junction near Bull Run.

When, at last, Russell had seen as many plantations, cornfields, sugar-houses and slave quarters as would satisfy him, he commenced his journey northward once again.

Chapter Eight

"Along the 'Mrs. Sippy'"

THE MISSISSIPPI—CAIRO, ILLINOIS, JUNE, 1861

WITH A GREAT SENSE OF URGENCY, Russell speedily traveled North. On June 12, he continued his journey up the "Mrs. Sippy" River, as he jokingly called it. He boarded the little steamer, the *Mary T.*, at Baton Rouge and traveled on to Natchez, which he reached the following morning. He found that his sense of urgency reached to his stomach. The first order of business was to find breakfast. All the little bars, normally open until the early hours of dawn, had already closed their doors. Even with money in his pocket, Russell feared he might starve. Thankfully, he was rescued by Mr. Levin Marshall, a prominent sugar planter, who invited the reporter to his home for breakfast.[1]

The journalist was enchanted by Mr. Marshall's plantation, with its broad expanse of lawn and trees, reminiscent of an English country house. Russell spent the following days looking at the fine homes and plantations for which Natchez was justly famous. Since time was of the essence, however, he continued upriver on the two-storied steamer the *General Quitman*. Arriving at Vicksburg, Russell proceeded to the Washington Hotel. Being hungry, as always, he went straight to the dining saloon. Upon entering, he was impressed by the sight of a long table at the end of the room, where black servants were carving and serving up joints, roasts and a variety of other dishes. The proprietor, proud of the establishment and its fare, proclaimed to the room, "Now then, here is a splendid goose! Ladies and gentlemen, don't neglect the goose and apple-sauce. Here's a piece of beef that I can recommend! Upon my honor, you will never regret taking a slice of the beef . . ."[2] etc., and so he continued, extoling the virtues of the oyster-pie and the turkey as well. It was a semi-barbarous scene, Russell decided, but not unlike old London, where a taverner might call out when meals were ready. Certainly, the food looked both good and plentiful.

After dinner, Russell adjourned to the train station with several men who wanted to discuss the events of the day. Among the other news and tidbits they exchanged, Russell was interested in the Supreme Court case of *Ex Parte Merryman.* The facts were this: a gentleman named John Merryman of Baltimore, a Secessionist, was arrested. President Lincoln had suspended the *Writ of Habeas Corpus,* or the right to a speedy trial, almost immediately after sectional hostilities had begun. Judge Roger Taney, of Dred Scott notoriety, protested this on the part of Mr. Merryman, who was currently languishing in jail. Taney, of course, thought it was illegal. He felt that Congress was the only body that could suspend the Writ, not the President. Having no means to enforce any decision, he remained with a frustrated sense of justice.

After many cigars and whiskeys, Russell boarded the train for Jackson, Mississippi, where he had been invited to meet with Governor John J. Pettus. That evening, the reporter, walking over to the state house, was able to observe the capital city of Mississippi. The houses, he noted, were very much like those he had seen throughout the South: detached, white, wooden and in the usual rows. The architecture of the churches and public buildings were, Russell thought, vulgar. However, when he reached the state house, the reporter was immediately impressed by its simplicity. After he was shown to the office of the Governor, he was even more impressed by how accessible that man was. Men were going in and out "as though they were in a public house. . . ."[3] Governor Pettus was tall, silent and grim; however, he became positively talkative when discussing his state. He was tremendously proud of Mississippi, and was content with the knowledge that here was the most civilized place on earth, even if they did have one murder a month.

He conversed with Russell on a variety of issues, but the central point he was concerned with making was that

> England is no doubt a great country, and has got fleets and the like of that, and may have a good deal to do in Eu-*Rope*; but the sovereign state of Mississippi can do a great deal better without England than England can do without her.[4]

The continual expression of this sentiment was beginning, understandably, to irritate Russell, who began to resent the smug and insular way in which such comments were presented. Little else was noted about the meeting.

That evening, after writing his letters and articles for home, Russell went out to enjoy the cooler, waning hours of the day. He chanced to meet a gentleman who obligingly explained the "ins and outs" of dueling. The man recounted incident after bloody incident in which he, himself, had been involved. The very air around them was purple, the reporter thought, with the passion for violence. There may be security of property, but, Russell concluded, no one was safe from a stray bullet on a Southern street.

On June 16, after only several day's stay, the correspondent continued his journey to his next destination, Memphis, Tennessee. Again, he traveled by train, which was crowded with soldiers traveling up to Virginia. They seemed to be thoroughly enjoying their time away from home, as though they were on the way to a picnic or visiting with friends. As an after-effect of hearing so many tales of dueling and other violent acts, Russell was feeling uneasy. He felt sure that he was in some sort of barbarous frontier town, where laws were barely enforced and only the strong survived.

Russell reached Memphis on June 17. After taking care of his baggage, he walked over to the Gayoso House, which boasted a panoramic view of the Mississippi. Memphis, which he called a "resuscitated Egyptian city", was far handsomer than he had expected, with its broad avenues and impressive public buildings. The hotel, which was quite large, was able to accommodate over six hundred guests, all of whom, he lamented, seemed to be in the halls at the same time. Gayoso also served as the headquarters for General Gideon Pillow, who had been ". . . charged with the defences of the Tennessee side of the river. . . ."[5]

Immediately upon Russell's arrival, General Pillow sent his aide-de-camp with his calling card. The aide invited him along to inspect the batteries and the camp at Randolph, sixty miles upriver. Russell agreed with alacrity to the expedition, which was to take place the next day. Then the aide took Russell to see his commander, his revealing comments about the General being of particular interest:

> General Pillow . . . is, in fact, an attorney . . . and was the partner of Mr. Polk, who probably, from some of the reasons which determine the actions of partners to each other, sent Mr. Pillow to the Mexican war. . . .[6]

Of the General's fortifications, Russell wrote:

> The General has made his entrenchments as if he were framing an indictment. There is not a flaw for an enemy to get through, but he has bound up his men in inexorable lines also.[7]

Pillow had been working on his plantation before the latest hostilities began. One of the officers told Russell about an incident during the Mexican War when the General, a political appointment, had thrown up a battery which, unfortunately, faced the wrong side.

The trip to the batteries and Randolph would be overnight. Russell and General Pillow went by carriage immediately to the bluffs above the Mississippi, where the reporter could see that the river had been completely blockaded. This was done to prevent any Federals from penetrating from Cairo, Illinois, just two states north on the Mississippi River. After viewing the batteries and blockades, they boarded the steamer *Ingomar* to go to the camp. During that evening, Russell was introduced to seventeen colonels and one captain.

After breakfast the following morning, the party went ashore. They witnessed some cannons firing for their benefit, of which the skill and the mettle of the guns themselves were highly suspect. Russell, however, was much more interested in the camp. He paid particular attention to the minute details of the base, the troops, entrenchments and armaments. The men made their way through the lines, walking along rows of tents. Most of the volunteers were drilling on the field; however, Russell ascertained that their officers were sadly lacking in the rudiments of military science. The General, nevertheless, gave a rousing, patriotic speech to the hot and listless troops. He assured them that, among other things, black slaves would relieve them in the next day or two. This was the only announcement that elicited a cheer, albeit an apathetic one. He closed with the remark that, in their hour of danger, "I will be with you."[8] This sentiment seemed ineffectual, and rightly so when one considers that, the following year, Pillow fled the scene of his first battle at Fort Donelson. Russell wrote prophetically, in view of later events, that a ". . . flotilla might get past the guns without any serious loss in the present state of their service and equipment."[9]

Boarding the steamer for the return trip to Memphis, the band struck up "Dixie" and "The Marseillaise". Russell saw young men, already sick with dysentery and other maladies, being carried on board on stretchers. Apparently, there was no one to treat the sick men. Russell felt obliged to bring his quinine, calomel and opium on deck in order to tend them. When he asked one of the officers where the doctors were, the officer replied that most of the men wanted to fight, not doctor.

Upon his return to the hotel, Russell dined with the General and his staff. They engaged in heated discussions concerning the sovereignty of states. Pillow explained that while he was in charge of the defenses of Tennessee, he would not dare cross into Kentucky. Kentucky was, herself, a sovereign state and Pillow could not violate her rights. The fact that, as a border state, they were neutral and, therefore, a host of cowards, was another matter.

At this point, the safe passage of his Letters was becoming a serious problem, and Russell realized the necessity for swiftly completing his journey to the North for,

> unless I could write, there was no use in my being on the spot at all. By this time, the Federal fleets have succeeded in closing the ports, if not effectually, so far as to render the carriage of letters precarious. . . .[10]

Russell had been invited by Jefferson Davis to visit Richmond, but felt there was no use in going if his Letters could not pass through the blockade and properly communicate with his paper. Being based in Richmond would effectively cut him off from the rest of the world.

During his journey up the river, Russell began to set down his impressions of all that he had seen during his two months in the Southern states. Throughout his visit, Russell demonstrated a keen awareness of the obligations expected of him as a Special Correspondent. There was, in his Letters, and even in much of his diary, the conviction that he maintain stringent objectivity throughout.

When he left the North, Russell believed it was suffering from a political paralysis or, perhaps more accurately, an amputation following which the patient continued to feel his absent limb. The only signs of life, movement or even optimism were a few sluggish militias drilling in the streets of Washington, and Secretary Seward, who was absolutely sure that the rebellion would be short-lived. Russell saw nothing tangible during these months to support this supposition, except possibly some letters from Bancroft Davis about the mobs in New York joining the regiments. Naturally, Russell would have to confirm these happenings for himself. What had apparently changed was the attitude of the press. The newspapers, who had once been so scornful of Lincoln and his cabinet, were now calling out for all to support them in their noble efforts.

[135]

Nevertheless, it became obvious to his readers that whatever positive opinion Russell held of the South disappeared between April and June. He saw nothing of States Rights that convinced him that it was anything other than a philosophy meant to protect and extend slavery. The perverse idea that slavery was civilizing and good for the slave and even, some said, ordained by God was spurious to the reporter, and he grew to detest hearing it. He was shocked by the ". . . barefoot, shoeless, stockingless children . . ."[11] and the villages that were ". . . miserable places compared with the trim snug settlements one saw in New Jersey."[12] In addition, he was revolted by the violence he had witnessed in Southern life. He found it unsound and untenable, not to say distressingly dangerous. Overall, his impression of the slave states and the institution itself was completely unfavorable ". . . both in regards its effects on the slave and its influence on the master."[13] He firmly believed that the more deeply slavery was probed, the more thoroughly its evils would be understood. Even though he realized that his own investigation had been hasty, and somewhat cursory, he believed that a deeper investigation would most certainly support this conclusion. The constant cry that the blacks were happy and comfortable was ineffective if one considered human standards to be anywhere above those of the beasts in the field. In addition, were the Southerners to win the victory, there would be, Russell wrote, of necessity, some kind of revival of the slave trade, which England could never countenance. "A slave state cannot long exist without a slave trade. The poor whites who will have won the fight will demand their share of the spoils."[14]

As to the new Confederate military establishment, from all that he had seen he had little faith in its success. The love of display and resolve could not make up for the lack of training and preparedness. In spite of the few West Pointers he met, there was still a dearth of officers with fighting experience. As a concluding thought, Russell felt that the immigrants who made up a large part of the fighting ranks, both North and South, were mostly inexperienced and, therefore, in his mind a useless liability. They were mercenary, he wrote, in their objectives and had no fixed principle for fighting on either side. What Russell failed to include in his reasoning was the fact that a land that would give a man such unheard of opportunities for material and social advancement inspired not only gratitude but fierce allegiance and love.

He concluded:

Never did a people enter on a war so utterly destitute of any reason for waging it, or of the means of bringing it to a successful termination against internal enemies.[15]

PART III

The North

JUNE, 1861–APRIL, 1862

Chapter Nine

"... fast churning up—a great fight ..."

ILLINOIS—WASHINGTON, D.C.
JUNE—JULY, 1861

AS RUSSELL COULD MOVE no further upriver by steamer it became necessary for him to proceed by rail to Columbus, Kentucky. From there, he would pick up a steamer, once again, to take him to a Federal position. With this rough itinerary in mind, he arose unusually early on June 19 to make an early train. He was seated with officers who were making the most of their morning inactivity to commence drinking their daily quota of whiskey.

A panorama of people got on and off the train. When they arrived at Union City, Tennessee, a large group of well-dressed people boarded. They were on an outing to visit a camp of Tennessee and Mississippi regiments. The ladies boldly advanced into the carriages and gave the impression that they would sit on the occupants unless they swiftly surrendered their seats.

The men made an exodus to the platform, where they stood in the hot sun. Russell, once again, regaled his readers with a full account of what he called the usual process of American Introductions. A stranger would come up to you and introduce himself and "if he finds a hand wandering about, he shakes it cordially."[1] Then this man, who was your new intimate, would introduce you to the entire company before you had made up your mind whether you wished to know the first gentleman. This process continued until your "acquaintance becomes prodigiously extended," and your "hand considerably tortured."[2] In the end, Russell was even introduced to the engineer and the stoker. These were the most felicitous contacts because he was proffered a seat on the engine, evidently far more comfortable than standing with the crowd on the platform.

When they reached the camp at Union City, Russell watched as the train disgorged its occupants. The mothers, sweethearts and wives of the men embraced them earnestly, and with the fierce pride of the whole Southern people. His trained eye looked in vain for the appearance of any sort of military order or discipline. The train also carried a large amount of stores, which for the next two hours were unloaded.

Russell continued to receive invitations to stay in the South, especially from the officers at the camp. "Why not stay with us, Sir; what can a gentleman want to go among black Republicans and Yankees for?"[3] He explained to them that he needed to be somewhere where his correspondence could go unimpeded in and out of the country. Being "Southern gentlemen," they took the explanation with good humor.

The train continued to Columbus, on the banks of the Mississippi. From there, Russell boarded a steamer to Cairo, Illinois. Evidently, this steamer was among the last that would use this route on the river, since both Confederate General Pillow and Federal General Benjamin Prentiss were determined to bottle up the Mississippi. After several hours, the captain pointed to the shore and said that was the camp of the Unionists. After two months of seeing the Stars and Bars everywhere, it was almost a novelty to see, finally, fluttering in the breeze, the Stars and Stripes.

Cairo itself was full of small, wooden buildings, completely unimpressive. There was a large hotel, owing to the fact that this was the southern terminus of the Central Illinois Railroad. The rest of the town, however, seemed dull and dreary. Russell made straight for the hotel, which was, naturally, full of soldiers and people coming to visit their friends and relatives who were living at the camp. In the dining room, Russell was introduced to the Commander, General Benjamin

Prentiss. He was an agreeable person, Russell thought, who had nothing of a soldier about him.

During his sojourn in Cairo, as would happen during many conversations in the North, Russell was forced to defend England's recognition of the South's rights of belligerency. He told people that England's neutrality was not a slap in the Union's face, nor any sort of aggression. Conversely, Russell wrote that the North did not feel it needed to take a defensive or groveling stance to any nations of the world. In her diplomacy, since its inception, the United States had managed to offend nearly every country with whom it had relations: "If the United States have astonished France by their ingratitude, they have certainly accustomed England to their petulance."[4]

More to his distress, the reporter was closely caught up in the insect situation that evening. In his room, he was completely absorbed in the ineffectual fight with the mosquitoes. The following afternoon, Russell toured the Union camps with General Prentiss. Russell could see that this position was better supplied than the Southern camps. As in the South, he was constantly invited to have a drink. The national anthems of England and the United States were played, and speeches were given. To his horror, Russell was eventually called upon to say a few words to the troops. He muttered some platitudes about

"mighty struggle", "Europe gazing", "the world anxious", "the virtues of discipline", "the admirable lessons of a soldier's life", and the "aspiration that in a quarrel wherein a British subject was ordered, by an authority he was bound to respect, to remain neutral", God might preserve the right.[5]

The men cheered and threw up their caps.

Russell spent several days with the men in Cairo, and noted a lack of respect for officers, a lack of efficient supplying and no evident facilities for the sick and wounded. The men were volunteers from their states, and somehow did not consider themselves part of the Federal Army or feel any particular respect for their commanders. Certainly, they felt no need at all to renew their conscription when the three months were up. The sentries, however, did an excellent job of keeping unauthorized personnel out, although the password signs and countersigns were often mixed. It was, after all, an army that had not engaged in conflict, and was not battle-toughened.

The news from the North was that battle was inevitable. The antagonists were massing in large numbers in Virginia and Washington, and there was little doubt as to what would happen next. Russell wrote that ". . . it can no longer be doubted that a battle between the two armies assembled in the neighborhood of the capital is imminent."[6]

Russell wrote to his friend Bancroft Davis, "I have at last got out of the land of Dixie & whiskey, & am speeding on towards Washington. . . ."[7] In this same letter, Russell was beginning to sense that he was not very popular in New York or the North in general. He couldn't help it; he wrote, "I must write as I feel & see & I believe I may have the consolation accorded to the impartial of finding myself still more unpopular in the South. . . ."[8]

On June 23, Russell boarded a train for Chicago. In his usual friendly way, he made conversation with a man about property and capital. The gentleman thought it would be a great service to the entire world if the journalist would write about how cheap land was in Illinois. Russell felt that it was all very well for an American pioneer, but a man who came from Europe might not be prepared to clear the land of forests, till the land and build a house, never mind possible incursions from Indians, bandits or other uncertainties of the virgin prairie. From this conversation, Russell observed that a man's worth was measured quite differently in the United States as opposed to England. Here, it was determined by a man's entire capital; in England it was determined by how much he had a year.

Russell spent the night on the train, and remarked how much cooler the nights were the farther north they traveled. This part of the world had a decidedly un-martial feel about it. From his window, Russell saw small prairie towns and hamlets, large fields and church steeples. He learned about what he described as a large species of partridge or grouse called a "prairie chicken" and another species called the skylark. As they approached Chicago, Russell caught glimpses of enormous Lake Michigan.

Arriving at the city in the morning, the reporter quickly took shelter at the Richmond House. There were welcome letters and news waiting. Virginia was invaded by various armies, two camping above Washington, and one below. However, as yet no clash had occurred. Southern privateers were stopped in their tracks by the British declaration that they would receive cruisers from neither side. The North was annoyed, just as they were about Britain granting belligerency rights to the South. Russell, however, was concerned with reports about his observations regarding New York in that city's press. He had written about the calmness with which many of the leaders in New York and Washington had received the news of the secession. Now, however, the papers said that this was not the case at all, and that Russell was bearing "false witness."[9] The reporter was resolute. He had seen so many strange interpretations of his writings that he decided it was best not necessarily to be indifferent, but not to bother to correct the wrong impressions.

For Chicago, Russell had unaccustomed praise. He believed it to be a city of which its occupants could be proud. The boulevards, the streets, the luxurious hotels, the handsome shops and stores were all to his great liking. As long as Europe wanted her grain and corn, he wrote, Chicago would continue to grow and prosper. It was, in fact, the perfect place to relax and recover from his Southern trip. Nevertheless, he continued his mission and spent his time determining the allegiance that Chicagoans had toward the Union and Mr. Lincoln.

He made a visit to the grave of Stephen A. Douglas. His untimely death, earlier in June, had made an impression on Russell, who had so recently met and liked the Senator. There were busts all over the city commemorating the man, though, the reporter observed, his widow was living in near poverty.

"Senator Douglas", observed one of his friends to me, "died of bad whiskey. He killed himself with it while he was stumping for the Union all over the country." "Well", I said, "I suppose, sir, the abstraction called the Union, for which by your own account he killed himself, will give a pension to his widow."[10]

This appeared not to be the case; the United States, Russell opined, was not grateful for the contributions of its great men.

Among the friends Russell met in Chicago was Augustus Dickens, the brother of writer Charles. The younger man had come to America after deserting his wife. He and Russell dined together several times, but of those meetings, nothing further is recorded.[11]

Russell left Chicago on the 27th to travel to Niagara. He thought it would be a shame to come to the United States and not see the great falls. He entered Canada at Windsor. The customs inspectors said that it was amazing that the Yankees let him leave unscathed, since he had not constantly praised them. When his train finally reached Niagara, Russell walked to the Clifton Hotel, along the St. Lawrence River bank. It was three in the morning. After the train left the station, he could hear the sounds of the falls and, as the sun rose, he saw the white steam rising from the crashing waters. Russell felt overcome with admiration. Words could not describe the thoughts and feelings he had as he gazed upon Niagara Falls.

He reached the hotel, which was a favorite with Americans, both from the North and South. Russell complained that the falls was too "touristy." Writing another letter to Bancroft Davis, he lamented the state of affairs between the United States and England. He surmised that the "hostile spirit" was caused by troops sent to Canada from England. Nevertheless, Russell felt that, in view of the troops amassing south of the border, it was a good idea to be prepared. In addition, it seemed to him that the elements of discontent in Canada might seize the opportunity to create problems while the entire world was focused on events in America.

Russell was planning an excursion to an Indian village when he received the news that General Scott had ordered troops, which were positioned in front of Washington, to move down toward Virginia. Abandoning his sightseeing plans, he quickly found a place on an overnight train to New York City. The next morning, looking out the window of his sleeper cabin, he could see the village of West Point.

He regretted that he could not stop and visit the celebrated military academy there. He would have to content himself with "the handiwork of some of the ex-pupils."[12] West Point, from what he could gather, was the closest thing America had to an English public school; the camaraderie between the men was similar and the product of the school, a sort of military aristocracy, was comparable. North or South, men would define their relationships with others by when they had attended the prestigious academy.

By nine in the morning, the train had reached New York City. This time, however, Russell was a guest of the young banker William Butler Duncan, with whom he had dined on several occasions the previous March. He decided to stroll around the city and see what had happened since his trip south. What he saw was a confirmation of all that his friend Davis had written in the letters he had received down south. He noted with surprise that many changes had occurred since his last visit. All apathy, it seemed, had fled. Now, everyone was in uniform or in some form of martial garb. It was, indeed, a frenzy of recruiting posters, military tailors and shops devoted to militia equipment.

As he walked through a city that was now a profusion of flags, Russell encountered men who, four months earlier, had argued ". . . coolly and philosophically . . ." but were now furious at the thought of secession.[13] The streets were filled with patriotic songs, such as "Hail Columbia" or "The Star-Spangled Banner" (which was not yet the national anthem), and should one not know these songs, the words and music were plastered all over the windows of music shops and book sellers. Russell continued strolling down Wall and Pine Streets, which were hung with patriotic bunting. He noticed crowds gathered around a window, which displayed, on a small exhibit, a gray cap. This cap had been a "Cap of Secession officer killed in action."[14] At another building, he saw women and children huddled together—Russell was informed that these were some of the families of the volunteers who had gone off to war, leaving them destitute.

Russell returned to write his Letters and correspondence. He felt that his conclusion was obvious: "At present dismiss entirely the idea, no matter how it may originate, that there will be, or can be, peace, compromise, union or secession, till war has determined the issue."[15] Everything he had seen for the last months had convinced him of these facts. As long as there was a possibility that the struggle would not take place, the New York businessmen were quiet and hoped for the best. The South, indeed, expected this. However, when violence seemed the only end result, the New Yorkers, who had once, for a moment, considered leaving the Union, were now Union men to the core. Russell concluded that the change was remarkable. He further wondered what Seward would say now. He had been so sure that the seceded states would come back at the rate of one a month. Russell, however, was very sure of one thing. Had the people of New York talked, acted and felt the preceding March as they did now, the attack at Sumter would most certainly have been avoided.

As Russell acclimated himself to the Northern atmosphere, he resumed his avid perusal of the New York newspapers. His contempt for the dailies grew only in proportion to his astonishment at the credulity of the American people in reading, and accepting, the boasting and advice that came from these popular organs. His opinion of American war correspondents was hardly more flattering. Russell viewed his American colleagues with condescension and amusement, while sneering at their accounts of battles. Of the Battle of Bull Run, for example, he said that the reports were written while ". . . they stood their ground as well as any, in spite of the shot, shell and rifle balls that whizzed past them for hours. Discriminating projectiles, truly."[16] He

[148]

wrote further that ". . . if you desire to understand how far faith can see and trust among people . . . [who] . . . consider themselves . . . civilized and intelligent . . . you will study the American Journals."[17]

Some of the more lurid writing actually shocked Russell. When shown a clipping in which a Union General was described as ". . . a miserable hound, a dirty dog . . . a treacherous villain, a notorious thief, a lying blackguard . . . [who kept] . . . his hide continually full of Cincinnati whiskey . . .,"[18] Russell was genuinely astounded. The British journalist observed that there was, indeed, much sensational journalism, more errors and much inaccuracy. Since the reporting could only be as good as the sources, it became apparent that, at the very least, those sources were misused, if, indeed, they ever existed. And, if there was some veracity in the source, it was most often inaccurate, if not grossly exaggerated.[19] In addition, Russell saw that many scribblers felt little compunction in making up the news as needed. Besides the creative Washington correspondent Russell had previously encountered, there was the case of Junius Henri Browne of the *Tribune*, who manufactured a complete account of the Battle of Pea Ridge.[20]

> The Indian press is really respectable journalism compared to the section of the New York papers which are generally quoted in England, & I find that no one of any weight in society attaches the least importance to the opinions or leaders of such a paper as the N.Y. Herald for example tho' they read it for the news.[21]

Russell realized that having no standards to fall back on, and no precedent to follow, the members of the "Bohemian Brigade" were on their own, "[They were] . . . unhampered by any legal or traditional restrictions on military news. . . ."[22] Because of this lack of any kind of guidance, Robert E. Lee said that he always looked for a particular column in the *Philadelphia Enquirer* because the reporter ". . . knew what he reported and reported what he knew."[23] General Winfield Scott had complained the previous summer that the government would achieve much more after they had hanged several spies and, at least, one newspaper reporter.[24]

Russell continued to denigrate the press at every opportunity. As late as November, he was railing about ". . . contorted falsehoods, contending statements. . . ." The sensationalism, he complained, had to be produced night and day to satisfy the craving of the readers. If these journals were credible, ". . . we would have believed in a victory at Bull Run and a number of pitiful skirmishes as so many . . . Waterloos."[25] Even considering the bitterness Russell must have felt after the reception of his Bull Run Letter, these were still harsh criticisms, indeed.

Russell stayed a day in New York, and was on the train to Washington early on July 3. As he traveled, he again marveled at the changes four months had wrought. He observed the men in the railroad car, and saw the complete differences in their attitudes, as opposed to their Southern counterparts. Southerners swaggered and boasted, while the Northern men were quiet and contemplative. He saw less vehemence and bitterness in these men, but felt it would be a mistake to think that they were less determined.

The train passed through Baltimore, a city under martial law. The press, Russell was told, was not allowed to print its secessionist sympathies, and the ladies dressed their children in Confederate colors. As they left Baltimore and headed toward Washington, there were military camps on both sides of the tracks, and tents as far as the eye could see.

Russell disembarked and continued up Pennsylvania Avenue to his lodgings. Wanting quieter digs than Willard's could offer, he took a small lodging next to a wine shop. Given the propensities of soldiers, whether North or South, quite why Russell thought that this place would be quieter is anyone's guess. Again, he noted the patriotic fervor that gripped the city. It was no longer the "scene of beneficent legislation and of peaceful government."[26] Washington was at war, and its street scenes provided confirmation.

Russell's first move was a visit to Lord Lyons at the British Legation to discuss his Southern journey. Those difficult months, from the recognition of belligerent rights of the South to the build-up of British troops in Canada, had taken their toll on Lyons, whom Russell thought looked careworn and pale. Dealing with Mr. Seward, while the Confederacy was gaining steam, turned out to be a burdensome and exacting task.

The following day was the Fourth of July, American Independence Day. Though there were celebrations everywhere, the reporter found it interesting that Congress had chosen that day to meet. They would decide, according to reports, whether to save the Union and invade the South. When they met, however, typically it was to organize and get committees chosen, and nothing was decided. The news was that General McDowell would attack the Confederate forces in Northern Virginia. Congress would have to start making decisions about how to proceed with a war. Russell was honored to be introduced on the floor of the Senate by Senators Charles Sumner and Henry Wilson. Thence, he spent time at Sumner's desk, writing to England until the Senate adjourned.

From the Senate, Russell walked over to the State Department to see Mr. Seward, who congratulated him on his safe return from the South. He, too, looked more tired and drawn than he had the previous April. Seward informed him that he would need a passport signed by Lyons himself, and additionally by General Scott, before he could travel freely about and with the army. Russell thought that in the land of the free this was despotism, though he did not relay his thoughts to Seward. Further, the Secretary of State told him that President Lincoln was dealing with an insurrection, and that England's granting the South the rights of belligerents had not made things easier. Indeed, if friendship between the United States and Britain were not so important, the United States would not hesitate, should some conflict arise. Inevitably, he concluded, it would not be the United States which would have to "lament the results of the conflict."[27]

Russell could not help but admire Seward's fearlessness. As he walked back to his lodgings, he watched a group of soldiers celebrating the day, some by the "internal use of fire-water, others by an external display of fire-works."[28]

The following day, Russell's good friend John Bigelow arrived, much to the reporter's pleasure. Together, they set out to look for a horse for Russell. Unfortunately, there was no decent horseflesh available. Later, the two men went over to the capitol building, which Russell described in great detail for his readers. But for all the talking, debating, newspaper rattling and spitting that went on, there was, as yet, no movement forward.

Early the next morning, Russell and Bigelow rode over to the military headquarters at Arlington, the former home of Robert E. Lee, which was now a Federal encampment. It was here that the ill-fated Commander of the Union forces at Bull Run, General Irwin McDowell, was quartered. In his diary entry for July 6, Russell wrote of the General:

> He is a man about forty years of age, square and powerfully built, but with rather a stout and clumsy figure. . . . His manner is frank, simple and agreeable, and he did not hesitate to speak with great openness of the difficulties he had to contend with, and the imperfection of the arrangements of the army.[29]

During their talks, McDowell expressed his opinion decidedly on political generals, men who had secured their appointments out of political influence—he despised them. Nor was he particularly keen on the volunteers, having served in Mexico. His experiences with them were most always unfavorable. He asked Russell for news about one of his old school friends from West Point, General Beauregard. McDowell walked the journalist back to his lodgings. Russell noted that ". . . not one of the many soldiers he passed in the streets saluted him, though his rank was indicated by his velvet collar and cuffs and a gold star on the shoulder strap."[30] Finding a "kindred spirit" in Russell, McDowell encouraged the correspondent to accompany him around the military camps and headquarters. He joked that war correspondents "should wear a white uniform to indicate the purity of their character."[31]

Russell accepted the invitation, and afterwards proceeded to the White House lawn to listen to the United States Marine Band. He was joined by Captain Cecil Johnson, an old friend attached to the British Legation, and several other friends. Russell called the sight "pretty, foliage green, the hills covered with tents, artillery practicing at Potomac,"[32] while citizens and soldiers lounged on the lawn, listening to the rousing music.

On his way over to listen to the band, Russell had run into General Scott, who was so enfeebled that he had to be supported by two men when he walked. The General promised to make sure that Russell had a signed passport, as well as some time for an interview. The reporter wrote to Seward's son Frederick, the Secretary's assistant, in order to get the proper documents for the needed signatures.

The next morning, Russell breakfasted with Mr. Frederick Olmsted. Olmsted was now a member of the New York Sanitary Commission, an organization made up mostly of women. This commission was organized and ready to do anything necessary to prepare New York for the sick and wounded that would surely result from the conflict.

After breakfast, Russell, who had finally been able to procure a horse, rode over to Arlington. Together with General McDowell, Russell rode through the encampments. The journalist was able to observe the condition of the Northern defenses. Lincoln had called up 75,000 men in the state militia for a ninety-day term of service. It was McDowell's thankless task to whip these men into something that resembled a fighting force. Russell, however, was not impressed with what he saw, for he ". . . had expected to find upwards of 100,000 men in the highest state of efficiency, whereas, there were not more than a third of the number, and those in a very incomplete, ill-disciplined state."[33]

[153]

The General confided that ill-organized soldiery was the least of his problems. It seemed that his staff were inadequate to do even the simplest of tasks. McDowell took Russell to a railroad station in order to "trace the whereabouts of . . . [a] . . . single errant battery, because he had no staff that . . . [could] . . . do it for him."[34] Furthermore, McDowell told Russell that his intelligence services were nonexistent. A decent map of Virginia was not procurable and he himself knew little or nothing about the main roads or the surrounding country. Moreover, he had no cavalry officer capable of riding a reconnaissance.[35]

It was an unenviable state of affairs. The Confederates were massed at Manassas, and Russell was sure that McDowell "did not like the look of them."[36] But there was no going back if the people cried for action and the President had to obey. As he rode back to the city, Russell heard the occasional shot. When he asked what they were, the engineer officer replied, "They are volunteers shooting themselves."[37] Evidently, inexperience and carelessness were responsible for the deaths that were reported daily in the newspapers. In Russell's estimation, this was ". . . not an army."[38]

The evening of July 9, Russell dined in the company of General Scott. Also present was John C. Fremont. Of the "Pathfinder", Russell wrote:

> [He was] . . . a man with a dreamy, deep blue eye, a gentlemanly address, pleasant features, and an active frame, but without the smallest external indication of extraordinary vigour, intelligence, or ability; if he has military genius, it must come by intuition. . . .[39]

In his private diary, Russell was even more blunt. Fremont was "no great shakes—& is said to be unpopular in California. . . ."[40]

During dinner the guests forbore from discussing military or political issues. General Scott's tone was apprehensive, while General Fremont's was far more confident. Evidently, the troops in Virginia were getting restive. Some of them were looting and plundering, a state of affairs that Scott deplored. Fremont, however, had no compunction in pointing out that Russell was, no doubt, familiar with such scenes in Europe, and the reporter had to agree. Russell noted with dismay that General Scott continued to grow weaker. He needed more rest than before. Russell, however, had confidence that if the need arose, he could conduct a campaign ". . . with precedents of great military commanders . . .,"⁴¹ who were equally infirm.

The following day, Russell rode over to the House to hear Clement Vallandingham speak. He noted in his diary entry that Vallandingham, the ultra-Democrat and Secessionist, had enormous oratorical power. He also reported that a man standing next to him had said, "Deem me ef I wouldn't just ride that Vallandiggaim on a reay-al."⁴² This rather inarticulate man, with his wish to run Vallandingham out of town on a rail, echoed the sentiments of many Northerners regarding the famous "Copperhead"—the name the Union used for Northern Democrats who were against the war.

After hearing Vallandingham, Russell called on Simon Cameron, the Secretary of War. A typical political appointee, Cameron was promised a cabinet post if he supported Lincoln. However, he was forced to resign in 1862 because of corrupt practices. The reporter needed Cameron's authority to draw rations, should the army finally move. His errand wasn't particularly successful since Cameron felt he might be allowing Russell privileges that the other members of the press did not have.

As the days passed, Russell wrote about the whispers and news tidbits he garnered. One, in particular, and of great interest, concerned the movements of Major General George McClellan. He had advanced into western Virginia with some success. Russell, however, likened these skirmishes to the Highland clans fighting one another.

The journalist spent the next several days riding through the camps of different regiments stationed on the Potomac. What he saw made him doubt seriously that the army was capable of actual fighting. In his opinion, the size of the army was overestimated. The newspapers had given the numbers as somewhere between 50,000 and 100,000 men. Russell's trained eye, however, told him that it was more like 30,000 at best. They were ill-equipped, and seemed completely disorganized. The men were ill-kept, the uniforms were haphazard and they were mostly all "three-month men." Even there, he saw no decent horseflesh. The word "inadequate" best described what he saw, sorely and tragically so. He marveled that the reality of the army was so different from that described in the newspapers. Perhaps, in all fairness to the press, if they were making up the news it was because they had agreed not to print military dispatches not cleared by General Scott. The press had agreed that the government should publish all official accounts of the battles. Russell doubted that either side would keep their word, and railed at a government that, in order to save the republic, was taking away freedoms guaranteed by the Constitution.

On July 13, Russell left Washington, in the company of the Sanitary Commissioners, to visit Fortress Monroe in Baltimore. They arrived at the city early the next morning. The journalist noticed that Monroe itself had altered considerably since his last visit. The most visual change was the considerable presence of the military. With the Commissioners, he entered the Hygeia Hotel, which housed the wounded. Though it was early in the war, several small actions had taken place, and there were an inordinate number of wounded. The mission of the Sanitary Commissioners was to assess the situation and obtain permission from the Commander to inspect the facility. For this purpose, they sought out General Benjamin "Spoons" Butler. An orderly told them that the General had just gotten up and would see them after breakfast. Russell thought ruefully that he wished the General would see them for breakfast, since it had been a long time since he had eaten.

After waiting for what seemed quite a while under a shady tree, their host appeared. Russell described Butler as ". . . a stout, middle-aged man, strongly built . . . his features indicative of great shrewdness and craft. . . ."[43] He was given his nickname "Spoons", and worse, "Beast", for his activities, only a few months later, as the Union Commander in charge of the occupation of New Orleans. Once among his company, the General was hospitable. He told Russell and the Commissioners that they were welcome to visit the hospital at their leisure. He invited the reporter to return to the fortress, where he would personally escort him and show him everything.

As they had already seen, the hospital was full of wounded men. Russell went from bed to bed asking questions. Apropos of the shots that he had heard in the camps around Arlington House, Russell had the following exchange:

> "Where were you hit?" I inquired of the first. "Well," he said "I guess my rifle went off when I was cleaning it in camp." "Were you wounded at Bethel?" I asked of the second. "No, Sir," he replied; "I got this wound from a comrade, who discharged his piece by accident in one of the tents as I was standing outside." "So," said I, to Dr. Bellows, "whilst the Britishers and Germans are engaged with the enemy, you Americans employ your time shooting each other!"[44]

The journalist observed female nurses, whom he hoped were following the teachings of Florence Nightingale and her *Notes on Nursing*. He noticed one in particular, a very pretty young lady, feeding a young Scotsman, who had his arm around her waist. It was obviously, Russell thought, so that she wouldn't get too tired.

Russell returned to the fortress with General Butler, and was given a thorough look at the guns and the armaments. He pronounced them, in his Letters, to be old-fashioned and inadequate. Butler had also, notoriously, begun to employ "contraband" slaves. "Just to think", said the General, "that every one of these fellows represents $1,000 at least out of the pockets of the chivalry yonder."[45] Not all, however, shared his enthusiasm. One of his staff wished them to the bottom of the Chesapeake, for they were far more trouble than they were worth.

After the tour, Butler, Russell and the Commissioners boarded a steamer to Newport News, Virginia, which was situated further inland, there to visit another Federal encampment. The Commissioners thought this camp filthy, but Russell considered it to be in good order. For once, the men seemed respectful, and when the General walked by, they jumped up to salute.

That afternoon, the steamer returned to Fortress Monroe, and Russell was invited to dine with the General and his wife. Afterwards, the two men, with various adjutants, rode around the encampments. Russell was extremely happy with the General's horses, but not impressed by any of the companies they visited. He heard many complaints about the contractors, who were extorting money for supplies by charging over 100 percent more than the usual prices.

Later on, sitting in the General's study, Russell was more impressed with Butler's military acumen than he had expected to be. Though a lawyer in civilian life, General Butler echoed Russell's sentiments that Fortress Monroe was the best base of operation for an attack on Richmond. They agreed that to attack from bases on the peninsula made much more sense than troops traveling overland from Alexandria. The supply lines would be shorter and much more defensible. Although the two men agreed, they talked far too long and the steamer left without Russell, who had wanted to return to Baltimore to send out his Letters. Butler made sure that another steamer, the *Elizabeth*, was procured for the journalist's use. Together, they walked back to the Hygeia Hotel for Russell's knapsack and waited together for the boat to steam up. The journalist was off to Baltimore by eleven that evening.

It was a miserable trip. Russell was "stewed, boiled, baked and grilled"[46] on the unhappy boat. He should have added "eaten," since the insects continued to win their war against the hapless gentleman. Worse still for Russell, the captain was a shy man, the ship's vibration made writing almost impossible, the meals were not to be believed and there was no good company to be had. Resourceful as ever, he decided to disembark at Anapolis rather than suffer another horrendous night aboard the *Elizabeth*. He proceeded to the only hotel, and there was told that the train to Washington had already departed. The next one would be at such a strange hour that Russell resigned himself to remaining overnight. He noticed unpleasant looks from some of the people in the lobby; apparently, they had read his comments that were hostile toward States Rights and slavery.

Russell had no wish to rise, either for breakfast the next day, or for dinner. He caught the train late in the afternoon to Washington. When he arrived, the first person he saw on the platform was General McDowell. The General seemed worried and asked Russell where he had been. He then asked if he had seen several batteries that had "gone astray."[47] Russell, bemused, shook his head. After informing Russell that he and his troops were advancing, General McDowell offered to drive Russell back to his lodgings. The General was very concerned about the fact that he could not do an adequate reconnaissance of the probable field of battle. He could not ascertain even the most rudimentary information about the enemy; ". . . he has not a trustworthy map of the country; no knowledge of their position, force or numbers."[48] He complained, once again, that he had no cavalry, or even an officer that was capable of doing such a task. As McDowell left the reporter at his quarters he warned him to equip himself for what lay ahead, and assured him that he would see him in a few days.

Russell began to inquire around for a mount and other supplies, as they were "fast churning up a great fight—no doubt of it."[49] The other supplies were not so difficult, but the mount, again, posed enormous problems. Various members of the cavalry, as well as other personnel, had grabbed up all the horseflesh, and even the worst-looking nags were not to be had for any price.

On July 17, Russell reported that Federal troops would advance from Fairfax down to the Manassas Junction, where the Confederate troops were encamped. That day, he visited the Arlington headquarters and noted, with surprise, the complete inactivity. Some men were reading maps and writing memoranda in a rather desultory manner, while others loitered about. Russell not only saw no military order, but no order at all.

Russell's search for a horse continued. He was offered gigs and wagons galore, but, unfortunately, no horses. Washington was less full of loitering soldiers than it had been just days before. Now, they had a purpose, but they hoped it would be a short one. Many were "three-month men," and soon their terms would be finished. That evening, Russell received positive news that McDowell's troops would move the next day. Thankfully, the General was able to carry out a reconnaissance and would advance after he was satisfied that his battle plans could be carried out.

Russell walked along Pennsylvania Avenue that evening, catching snippets of the most outrageous and ridiculously false stories as he passed the bars, pubs, and even the public rooms of Willard's. One tale described how the fighting had already begun, and it was bitter, but the rebels were being whipped. Another reported that General Scott, though the old gentleman could not mount a horse, was going to lead the army personally. The officers, in their inebriated state, were bragging about the battle to come and about the great victory that would be theirs, and which would, most certainly, be written in the New York papers.

There is no doubt that, throughout his diary and Letters, Russell was unfailingly critical of both American armies, their men, their discipline, their total ignorance of war and their attitudes. Indeed, there are times when such criticism seems patronizing and unfair. The journalist, however, had fallen victim to American bombast, and the swaggering proved to be an irritant he could not ignore. He did, nevertheless, write:

> It is not fair to ridicule either officers or men of this army, and if they were not so inflated by a pestilent vanity, no one would dream of doing so; but the excessive bragging and boasting in which the volunteers and the press indulge really provoke criticism and tax patience and forbearance overmuch.[50]

The air crackled in Washington the night of July 18; the battle would not be long in coming.

→ *Chapter Ten* ←

"... the magnitude of the disaster ..."

BULL RUN, JULY 21, 1861

ON THE MORNING OF July 18, Russell woke up hearing the sounds of battle. The conflict had begun, and Russell urgently continued his own preparations. He persisted in the hopeless quest for a suitable mount. The reporter scoured Washington and, again, no horse could be obtained, he wrote, except for blackmail prices. The cost of a rig and horse was quoted as a thousand dollars. Further, he was told to:

> ... take it or leave it. If you want to see this fight a thousand dollars is cheap. I guess there were chaps paid more than that to see Jenny Lind on her first night, and that battle is not going to be repeated, I can tell you.[1]

Nevertheless, in this case, Russell decided to leave it.

In addition to his transportation problems, Russell's attempts to gain standing as an accredited war correspondent were in vain. He was told that "... there was no means a neutral correspondent could be licensed ..."[2] by the war department. Unless, they continued, he was willing to take an oath of loyalty to the United States and promise not to reveal military secrets, he would be refused correspondent status and the right to draw rations. Russell, as a British subject, refused to take the oath and was, therefore, on his own.

Meanwhile, all Washington was scurrying in hundreds of different directions. Messengers and orderlies were running to and from the

War Office, the Senate and the White House. They were jubilant with excitement. Russell met Senator Sumner, who told him: "We have obtained a great success; the rebels are falling back in all directions. General Scott says we ought to be in Richmond by Saturday night."[3] Later, Russell heard from another source riding past his lodgings, "You have heard we are whipped; these confounded volunteers have run away."[4]

That evening, Russell dined at the British Legation, where everyone calmly exchanged stories of the day's happenings. Russell had seen President Lincoln "striding like a crane in a bullrush swamp,"[5] hurrying to the White House. However, gentlemen from the other legations were content to discuss the events as though they were observing them from afar. Later that evening, however, Russell received word that the battle proper had been delayed. The reconnaissance had not produced satisfactory results, and McDowell was busily changing plans.

Russell wandered over to Willard's, where the "battles" were being discussed at length. The reality was, of course, that they were exchanging exaggerations and rumors. After listening to tales of great victory, one gentleman was able to corner Russell and told him, "'They were whipped like curs, and they ran like curs, and I know it.' 'How?' 'Well, I'd rather be excused telling you.'",[6] and he went on, no doubt to tell his tale to a more sympathetic listener.

The following day, the heat continued to be fierce. Russell rose early to continue with his preparations. Because of the unbearable heat, some officers in the field, he was told, actually suffered sunstroke. To Russell, soldiers marching back from positions in Virginia looked so tired that he pictured them being knocked down with a ball like a row of ten-pins. Russell's first stop that morning was at the headquarters of General Scott, in order to hear all the gossip. However, not much of interest was said and, afterward, Russell continued in his seemingly endless search for a horse, which, once again, was fruitless. He saw a group of rebel soldiers sitting on the pavement outside the quarters of General Joseph Mansfield. Russell called on the General to pay his respects, and was told that the General had no idea as to what he should do with the prisoners. Moreover, he did not want to be bothered with them.

A truly bad meal that afternoon did nothing to lift Russell's spirits. The hunt for transport, and the lack of any official sanction to draw rations or pay for equipment at military prices, was beginning to cause him endless frustration. He "dined on flies at old Frenchman's Boulanger's . . ."[7] restaurant and listened to men at the next table tell fantastic war stories. "No incredulity in the hearers—all swallowed: possibly disgorged into the note-book of a Washington contributor."[8] That evening, he sat on a porch with a nice family, whom he neglected to name, with particularly lovely daughters. They could see the flashes from the artillery, which caused no end of excitement. Russell chatted with the daughters of the house, and came away with the impression that "American women [sic] very free."[9] He contrasted them to his own wife, Mary, who, evidently, was not.

On July 20, Russell wrote that McDowell had somehow managed to complete his reconnaissance of the terrain around Manassas, and felt confident that he would be in possession of that territory by the evening of July 21. "The great battle which is to arrest rebellion, or to make it a power in the land, is no longer distant or doubtful,"[10] he wrote dramatically. It was getting closer, and they had positive information that the rebels were entrenched along the lines at Bull Run.

Going over to the Senate to see the affects of the day's events, Russell saw no great excitement there. He found the Congress "not listening"[11] to the Senator from California, who was delivering a long-winded political speech. Instead, the members were writing letters, reading newspapers, chewing tobacco and whispering among themselves. All this desultory activity was interrupted when Russell received a message stating that General McDowell would advance early the next morning, the 21st, and hoped to engage the enemy by noon. Others in the Senate evidently received similar messages and, whispering to one another, the news quickly spread along the floor. Senator Sumner told Russell that "McDowell has carried Bull Run without firing a shot."[12] Russell was suspicious since Sumner was proving a most unreliable source. After making inquiries, he ascertained that no one, not even the President, knew anything about this supposed success.

After the "senatorial antics" were concluded, Russell quickly left the building, wondering how he could transport himself to the action. Senate members, hoping to do the same, were wild to find <u>any</u> kind of transportation in order to join the army, and "see the fun." Besides mounts and rigs, food and wine hampers were being hawked at extravagant prices. The cooks in the hotels, for reasons best known to themselves, were charging three times their usual prices for hampers and all edibles.

Having "failed utterly"[13] in his attempts to get a riding horse, Russell eventually obtained a rig with two less than prime pieces of horseflesh. It wasn't particularly satisfactory, but it was the best he could find. He made arrangements to start early the following morning and return the rig late the same night, or pay double. From the livery stable, the journalist returned to the Legation to inform Fred Warre, the young member of the Legation who had accompanied him South, of his plans for the next day. Warre was interested in accompanying Russell, but Lord Lyons hesitated to give permission for him to go because he worried that the American press would not look with favor on a member of the British Legation present at the battle. He eventually consented, on condition that Warre went no further than Bull Run and would return that same evening.

Deciding it might be best to start that same night, the two men walked over to General Scott's headquarters to obtain passes. The passes were handed over with alacrity, until the officers learned that the two men wanted to leave that very evening. There was much discussion and advice from the officers since the sentries had orders not to let anyone cross the Long Bridge over the Potomac during the night. Since there was no way to wake the General to get special permissions and countersigns, the men had to change their plans and leave for Bull Run the following day. Russell used the extra time that night to return to the stable where he was, at last, able to secure a riding horse, though, as he noted, it was at an exorbitant price. This was a great relief to the reporter, as he knew it would be extremely difficult to see any of the action from a gig. Without seeming to care that he had obtained no official recognition or countersigns, Russell rushed back to his room. There he "laid out an old pair of Indian boots, cords, a Himalayan suit, an old felt hat, a flask, revolver, and belt."[14]

After some strange dreams, which left him with a restless night, Russell met with Warre and their driver early the next morning and the party set out. Washington was very quiet as they drove through the streets. Russell was still feeling particularly annoyed since the Secretary of War, Mr. Cameron, had never given him the permissions he needed for rations and equipment. After several meetings, Cameron had said that there was a lack of precedent; this was the first time that an Englishman wanted to follow an American army in the field. Also, it did not help Russell that he was now seen as the representative of a pro-Southern journal, as *The Times* now seemed to many. The correspondent was beginning to see that the great, nearly obsequious, welcome that he had originally received was now but a distant memory.

By nine o'clock, with a lunch of less than fresh bologna sandwiches and a bottle of Bordeaux, they were finally on their way out of Washington and driving towards the Fairfax Courthouse. The sentries at the Long Bridge were a "loafing"[15] group of men who handled their firearms like pitchforks. They studied Russell's and Warre's papers, and then told them, "You'll find plenty of congressmen on before you."[16]

It was a strangely lovely and peaceful day as they drove through the Arlington woods. After two hours of riding, they had not met a single soul. Eventually, they had to cross a constant line of pickets, who continually asked for their papers and passes. Then, as they left the beautiful woods, they saw farms, broken-down or deserted, with the occasional child, woman or old person staring out to see who was driving by. All the men, except the black ones, were away, probably at the battle site. Suddenly, explosions could be heard. The pickets along the way said that the cannon fire had been going on since around seven that morning. As they neared the scene, Russell heard gunfire and eagerly urged his young driver, "They are at it. We shall be late! Drive on as fast as you can."[17]

They came upon a man and woman standing in front of a farmhouse. They were watching clouds of dust on the horizon. Russell took the opportunity to ask, "'How long have the guns been going, Sir?' 'Well, ever since early this morning,' said he."[18] The carriage continued on still until they met a group of armed men, looking so cheerful, laughing and talking. Russell concluded that they could not be members of any defeated army. It seemed, however, that they had not been in the fighting at all, but that was all they would say.

As Russell and Warre traveled closer, they began to run into straggling troops. Many wagons passed, filled with camp furniture and baggage. Russell asked an officer who was sitting with his men:

> "Where . . . [is] . . . your regiment going to?" "Well, I reckon, Sir, we are going home to Pennsylvania." "This is the Fourth Pennsylvania Regiment, is it not, Sir?" "It is so, Sir . . ." "I should think there is severe fighting going on behind you, judging from the firing?" "Well, I reckon, Sir, there is." I paused for a moment, not knowing what to say. . . . "We are going home because . . . the men's time's up, Sir. We have had three months of this sort of work, and that's quite enough of it."[19]

By eleven that morning, traces of Confederate camps could be seen. By noon, they had reached the Fairfax Courthouse.

Fairfax was a poor village of about thirty to forty sad-looking wooden or brick houses. The residents, who appeared to be Secessionists according to Russell, did not look happy about the Federals, who were lounging around in the shade. The sun was boiling and the reporter and his companions were famished, but there were no meals to be had, except at the proper mealtime, as they were informed by a lady in black, who ran the local public house. However, they were in a hurry and could not wait so, unhappily, they continued without sustenance.

As they passed through the burned-out village of Germantown and onto the road to Centreville, the heat became more intense, and sounds of battle could be heard. The smoke, the musketry, ". . . the gleam of arms and the twinkling of bayonets . . .,"[20] exclaimed Russell, were in evidence everywhere. There were also wagons full of spectators, and they all headed toward the hills, which were covered with men, carts and horses. They had their backs to Russell. His driver said, rather unnecessarily, "There's Centreville", a mere twenty miles from Washington. They finally reached the hill, and Russell sent his driver down to the village for food and water.

The landscape thereabouts was beautiful. The area was extremely hilly, being near the Blue Ridge Mountains. Russell admired the flowers, which were still in spring bloom. They gave the area a pastoral woodsy look, but the noise and sounds emanating from the battle below were "in terrible variance with the tranquil character of the landscape."[21]

At that point, there were four Federal divisions amassed at Bull Run. The force amounted to about 30,000 men, who were all under the command of General McDowell. On the other side, there were two somewhat small armies, the Confederate Army of the Potomac, under the command of General Beauregard, and the Army of the Shenandoah, under the command of General Joseph Johnston. The forces in number were nearly equal.

Strangely enough, both forces had virtually the same attack plan. It was simply to go after the enemy on one side, while feinting an attack on the other.

What had actually happened was that the Union Army had arisen at two o'clock that morning, and marched to Sudley Springs on the south bank of Bull Run, a small river. Other forces, further down the bank, crossed over what was called the Stone Bridge to draw attention away from the first group. The Confederate left was overwhelmed by

Union troops pouring down from Sudley Springs. The Union might have triumphed had not Thomas Jackson brought in fresh troops. Another General cried, "Look! There is Jackson standing like a stonewall! Rally behind the Virginians!"[22] Thus, the General got his nickname, "Stonewall" Jackson.

It was about noon as Russell and his friends approached the hill. Behind Russell and Warre were spectators, crowded in ". . . all sorts of vehicles, with a few of the fairer, if not gentler sex."[23] The two men joined many of the audience in taking a vantage point on a hill. A few of the officers and stragglers had moved to the group of spectators, mingling among them and pretending "to explain the movements of the troops below, of which, of course, they were profoundly ignorant."[24] While watching, a lady with opera glasses remarked to Russell, "That is splendid. I guess we will be in Richmond this time tomorrow."[25] This was accompanied by coarser speech from the politicians and congressmen, who had arrived earlier for the great show. Typically, Russell was most irritated by the seemingly constant requests to loan his spy glass, and the unmitigated nerve of one soldier who, seeing his flask, had asked for a drink. Russell assented, and noted that the soldier was much more cheerful after a swig, feeling that he could lick at least ten "seceshers."

Sadly, the driver could find no provisions, and they were forced to eat the stale sandwiches. The saddle-horse, however, was provided for down in the town. After their less than satisfactory repast, Russell and Warre returned to the hill.

At this point, reason gave way to contradictory reports and rumors. The crowd rallied to a young man in uniform, riding a horse and waving his cap, who told them, "We've whipped them on all points. We have taken their batteries. They are retreating as fast as they can and we after them!"[26] Everyone, naturally, was elated. Second-hand communications, however, were useless to Russell, and he decided to take his mount for a closer look while Warre and the driver proceeded straight down the hill.

Russell now was far to the rear of the action, which was raging around Henry House, and continually ran into stragglers. After riding several miles, he came upon wagons and horses riding away from the scene. Some cried, ". . . turn back! Turn back! We are whipped."[27] In the confusion, an officer ". . . confirmed the report that the whole army was in retreat, and that the Federals were beaten on all points. . . ."[28] The rout was utter and complete. Everywhere was mass chaos: "The scene on the road had now assumed an aspect which has not a parallel in any description I have ever read."[29] Russell asked one retreating soldier if he knew where to find General McDowell, and the soldier answered "No! nor can any one else."[30] In the confusion, the reporter was unable to ascertain what had transpired. He continuously asked men, dirty, hungry, and thirsty from battle, for information but they usually waved him away as though he were a fly. When pressed, one soldier finally told him, "We are pursued by the cavalry; they have cut us all to pieces."[31]

Indeed, after midday, the Union advantage had slowly evaporated. Fighting had continued to rage for several hours around Henry House. It did not help that, at certain points, the multiplicity of uniforms, in this case Confederates in blue, caused a great deal of confusion and casualties.[32] The Confederate Commanders had gained better charge of their men by late afternoon and, with the addition of reinforcements, had been able to stabilize their lines. At that point, the rebels had charged, forcing the disorderly retreat that Russell was now observing. In the end, Bull Run was a victory for the South. However, they, made a grave mistake by not pursuing the retreating army right into Washington, D.C. Like their Union counterparts, they were exhausted and slightly confused and, possibly, just more lucky.

Russell decided to turn and head back toward Centreville. He noted that many of those retreating were in the last stages of exhaustion, and were staggering to the sides of the road in order not to be trampled. He saw, too, that the way was cluttered with clothing, firearms, musical instruments, bayonets, and even edibles and water.

He realized that there was nothing he could do but ride with the large tidal wave of men moving back toward Washington.

As he rode back with the defeated Union troops, Russell attempted to establish what on earth had happened. Most merely told him that they were falling back since the attack had not succeeded; naturally, with others, there were many exaggerations and tall tales. Despite the confusion, Russell found it extremely strange that, as soon as they got out of harm's way, many of the men told him how they were going back tomorrow to fight. The officers, however, seemed to feel the defeat. Russell was mystified. He continuously asked where people were going, watching as they continued to drop anything that might impede their progress away from the frightening scene. But, at this point, no one answered; they just kept going.

As the journalist headed toward Centreville, he was appalled at the panic everywhere. "Such scandalous behavior on the part of soldiers, I should have considered impossible. . . ."[33] Upon encountering several men with carts full of baggage:

> "Stop", cried I to the driver of one of the carts, "everything is falling out." ". . . If you stop him", shouted a fellow inside, "I'll blow your brains out." My attempts to save Uncle Sam's property were then and there discontinued.[34]

Russell had no idea how complete the defeat was. He thought, as he rode toward the town, that there were reserves there who would rally the exhausted and disheartened men. The crowds thinned somewhat as he neared Centreville; he even saw men laughing and talking. Some began to ask him for information, which he provided as best he could. He reached the town and began to look for Warre, remembering that he had promised Lord Lyons that the young man would be back in Washington that very night, likewise the horses and conveyance. Alas, driver, rig and Warre were nowhere to be found. Russell attempted to find them, even going back to the hill where all had viewed the proceedings. He was, however, disappointed and, in all events, abandoned. He eventually found out that his companions had left several hours before.

Beyond Centreville, the guns commenced firing again. Though Russell sensed a constant fear of pursuit by Confederate cavalry, those soldiers whom he saw were Union officers and men on horseback frantically beating a retreat. He questioned one soldier:

> "What on earth are you running for? What are you afraid of?" He [exclaimed] "I'm not afraid of you", presented his piece and pulled the trigger so instantaneously, that had it gone off I could not have swerved from the ball.[35]

This frightening incident illustrates the unreasoning panic that had become the rule since the early afternoon. The evidence of untrained troops, totally disorganized in their retreat, was more than a seasoned campaigner like Russell could bear. It was a ". . . sight as can only be witnessed in the track of the runaways of an utterly demoralized army."[36]

The prospect of an eighteen-mile ride to Washington precluded more such chats with the retreating soldiers. Russell saw scenes of alarm, with men panicking while others, it appeared, agitated just for the sake of it. He eventually came upon some slightly more dignified-looking men, who turned out to be officers. He respectfully touched his hat and, referring to the agitators, said, "I venture to suggest that these men should be stopped, Sir. If not, they will alarm the whole of the post and pickets on to Washington."[37] This advice seemed to have some effect, though Russell was not about to wait around to observe the results.

Thereafter, Russell noticed that the stream of retreaters had slowed down appreciably. As he rode further, he was stopped by a soldier who held a rifle to his forehead. The man had been told not to let anyone pass. With admirable calm, Russell bowed to the nearest officer and said, "I beg to assure you, Sir, I am not running away, I am a civilian and a British subject. . . ."[38] The officer was hardly paying attention, and would not allow him to pass. Then, he thought of the letter he had from General Scott and showed it to another officer. This, thankfully, was more successful, and Russell was able to continue the long ride back to Washington.

Further up, he ran across a mail agent in semi-military garb, who was looking for the 69th New York Regiment. Russell could tell him nothing, though he did say that Centreville was probably a safe place to wait for the army. It turned out that the man was an Englishman who lived in Washington. Much later, he told Russell that he would definitely vouch for the correspondent's account of the rout from Centreville. Stopping briefly to water his horse, Russell answered the same questions he'd heard from civilians along the way. Why are they running? Were you at the fight? Will there be more? Retreating, frightened armies were never easy on civilians.

It was evening by then, and, armed with directions to the Long Bridge, Russell pushed on. As he trotted along in the moonlight, he came across plenty of people willing to discuss the day's events. With the sound of fire fading in the distance, Russell met up with a young officer who was escorting a colonel back to Washington, wounded and, Russell suspected, a little worse for the drink. He gave the journalist a fairly accurate account of the battle, without any embellishment, although with a lot of bitterness. Soon, having passed pickets, patrols and others wanting accounts of the battle, and losing his way several times, Russell at last caught sight of the lights of Washington. People continued to be hungry for any scrap of news, which was eagerly passed down the lines and which never arrived in the same condition as it had started.

After crossing the Long Bridge, Russell was, once again, accosted by people wanting news. Had he been to the battle? As he nodded yes, a crowd gathered while he gave his "stereotyped story of the unsuccessful attempt to carry the Confederate position, and the retreat to Centreville to await better luck next time."[39] He continued trotting along, and, as he wearily passed Willard's Hotel at about eleven, he saw crowds of people within and spilling out onto the pavement. All were waiting for news. They had heard rumors of defeat, but with all that they knew and read in the past months, they could not credit such accounts. Indeed, as Russell finally reached his rooms that night, he wondered about what he would write in his Letter to *The Times*. As he gathered his thoughts, he began to understand just what had happened that day. In a letter to his friend Bancroft Davis, he put these ideas together:

> I attribute the disaster first to deficient morale of officers, & want of discipline of men—ie. inferiority to their opponents. Second to the superiority of Confederates in their position. They led the attack to the very points they had selected for defence. Thirdly— want of judgment in delaying the reinforcements too long & deficient arrangements as to ammunition.[40]

At that point, he firmly believed that McDowell would retreat only as far as Centreville or the Fairfax Courthouse. This would prove not to be the case.

He wearily climbed the stairs to his sitting room, just after eleven, and immediately sat down to write his Letter. Even after the day's events, ". . . little did I conceive the greatness of the defeat, the magnitude of the disaster. . . ."[41] Constant questions swirled around his head as he attempted to set down what he had seen. What army had ever retreated in such an ignominious and chaotic manner? Why didn't the Confederates chase the Federals into Washington? It seemed so obvious to Russell that a swift end to the war would have resulted. The truth of the matter was that the men had been overworked, according to the correspondent's observations, they had been in the sun too long and badly advised by their officers. To withdraw such a large army successfully, when it became necessary to do so, would have been little short of a miracle for the most battle-hardened officers. The alarm turned into panic, which was unfortunately uncontrolled. McDowell did all that he could, and Russell would never waver in his support of this man, who never shirked the responsibility of the defeat.

Completely exhausted, and despite efforts to the contrary, Russell fell asleep over his blotter before he could complete his Letter. He was roused by a messenger from the Legation. Lord Lyons was concerned that he had gotten back safely. It turned out that Warre and the rig had returned several hours before. Russell was relieved, but refused an invitation for a very late supper since he wanted desperately to write. However, when the messenger left, he fell sound asleep.

→ *Chapter Eleven* ←

"Bull Run Russell"

WASHINGTON, D.C., JULY—AUGUST, 1861

THE FOLLOWING MORNING, July 22, saw a heavy rain. Russell, exhausted, pulled himself out of bed and padded over to the window. He saw the multitudes of disorganized, retreating men. Their immediate intent, as far as the journalist could see, was to place as much as possible of the Potomac River between themselves and the enemy, and to do this as quickly as they could. Again, in the light of day, Russell wondered why Beauregard did not give chase. He had expected the sound of Confederate cannon to begin, since Washington was currently vulnerable.

Russell rushed down and watched the men shuffle by. They were in various states of exhaustion, and their faces were sadly dispirited. He stopped a pale young man and asked where they were all coming from. "Well Sir, I guess we're all coming out of Virginny as fast as we can and pretty well whipped too."[1] He told Russell that he'd had enough fighting to last a lifetime and was going home. The reporter tried to discover whether there was any pursuit by the rebels, but a straight answer was not forthcoming.

Russell was facing a dilemma. Should he write his Letter, or continue to bear witness to the retreat? After some deliberation, and the realization that there was an imminent deadline, he opted for the Letter. He put a cardboard sign on his door, announcing that he was "out," and sat down to write.[2] As his pen scratched over the pages, he heard the sound of the tramping soldiers in the pouring rain. He introduced his Letter by making it emphatic to his readers that this was not an account of the action itself (which he had not witnessed), but of the retreat (which he had). What followed was the recounting of the experiences of the previous twenty-four hours. The narrative omitted many of the more unsavory incidents, but enough remained to convey to the British reader a very negative picture of the armies, both Union and Confederate.

Contemporary critics made many excuses for Russell's unflattering Bull Run Letter. The *New York Herald* accused him of being a Confederate agent.[3] Moreover, as the Special Correspondent of the pro-Southern *Times*, it was naturally assumed that he held the same views as the journal. Therefore, since ". . . [the paper] . . . was assailed everywhere as the chief secessionist organ . . .,"[4] Russell was judged accordingly.

As the situation worsened, Russell's objectivity was appreciated by neither side. The South became increasingly disillusioned with him as his accounts of Southern proclivities for violence trickled back into the Southern papers. The North was far more than chagrined by the Bull Run Letter. In any case, it was most likely that his motivation was a strong distaste for military incompetence. This he expressed often enough during his stay. He concluded that the panic was disgraceful and completely unnecessary. The irony, of course, was that both sides still waited with baited breath to read Russell's accounts. Mary Chestnut chortled: "I long to see Russell's letter in *The Times* about Bull's Run and Manassas. It will be rich and rare."[5]

Russell ended his Letter with an ominous portent of the future, when the outcry against his reporting would be virulent: "Let the American journalists tell the story their own way. I have told mine as I know it."[6]

Despite his "out" sign, friends from the embassy, the military and other acquaintances still knocked on the journalist's door, wanting to gossip about the events of the previous day. However, Russell resisted the temptation to be sociable and would not answer. By evening, he slowly put down his pen. The rain had abated somewhat, and he decided to take a stroll to see and hear the latest news. As he walked along, he continued to see the stragglers, with and without arms, wearily stumble by. Passing shops, he saw many merchants and shop-keepers giving the demoralized hordes a distinctly jaundiced eye. There were no military police about or patrols delegated to keep order, as the circumstances were completely unforeseen. It was obvious to the reporter that there was a justified uneasiness with the presence of what he called a semi-armed mob. He walked by Willard's, which had become, among other things, a barracks for some of the officers.

As Russell later learned, the men in charge, Generals Scott and Mc-Dowell, were either overwhelmed by the affair, or not yet back from the battlefield. The politicians, it seemed, were temporarily chastened and, for once, quite speechless. Mr. Lincoln and Mr. Seward were, to all appearances, calm but momentarily paralyzed by the catastrophe and, for a breathless moment, the government appeared at a standstill.

The papers either talked of victory or were cautious in their negative reporting. The evening press said that McDowell would be marching on from Centreville. What was evident to anyone who simply looked outside his window was that "The grand army of the Potomac is on the streets of Washington, instead of being on its way to Richmond."[7] As was not unusual, Russell found his own name mentioned in the press reports. Someone on the spot, no doubt, was quoted as saying, ". . . Mr. Russell was last seen in the thick of the fight, and was not yet returned. Fears are entertained for his safety."[8] Russell sighed when he read this report. He knew that he would be extremely uneasy about such a report, if he gave the slightest credence to most American journals.

Having spent nearly all that night writing before finally falling asleep, Russell woke very late the next morning and, again, took in the view outside his window. The wagons and soldiers continued to pass by in a seemingly endless procession. The city was in grave disorder because of the disheartened soldiers who clogged its streets; no other traffic was visible. Like everyone else, the reporter would have had great difficulty trying to reach any destination.

News, however, was beginning to trickle in. Russell duly noted that the Washington papers castigated the officers for not being at their posts. They were exhorted to "forego one day's duty at the bars and hotels"⁹ and return to their deserted troops. In addition, retribution was instantaneous for those who had taken part in the disaster. General Patterson, whose men had left because they had fulfilled their three months of service, was honorably discharged. McDowell, however, was not so lucky. In his entry for July 23, Russell wrote that McDowell had been swiftly punished for his defeat ". . . or rather for the unhappy termination to his advance."¹⁰ The General was removed from command of the Army of the Potomac, and General George B. McClellan took his place. To aggravate the insult, after the battle Russell reported that rumors circulated that McDowell ". . . who never tasted any thing stronger than watermelon in his life . . . was dead drunk during the battle."¹¹

The new commander was thirty-six years old and, as were so many other top officers on both sides, a graduate of West Point. Russell was acquainted with him because of his visit to the Crimea. The Secretary of War at the time, Jefferson Davis, had sent McClellan and several other officers to study the operations of the war. Judiciously, Russell commented, they were sent when the war was quite over.

The prime news of the day was that Mr. Lincoln and Mr. Seward had gone to see the disarray of the army. They rode to Arlington House, McDowell's headquarters, which just days before had been the scene of great calm. They now "beheld despair."¹² At nearby Fort Corcoran, the volunteers were threatening to murder an officer of the regulars, who was doing his best to restore order and efficiency to the group. When the President appeared, the men demanded a hearing. They wished the officer to be punished, and the President asked the officer why he used "such violent language towards his subordinate. 'I told him, Mr. President, that if he refused to obey my orders I would shoot him on the spot.'"¹³ And he reiterated this conviction to the

President several times. The mutineers were impressed and completely convinced of his intention. They backed down. The officer concerned was General William T. Sherman.

On July 24, Russell met with McDowell, who ". . . displayed a calm self-possession . . . which could only proceed from a philosophic temperament. . . ." Russell felt that the General had been sacrificed to the ". . . vanity, self-seeking, and disobedience of some of his officers. . . ."[14] McDowell was intent on explaining to Russell exactly why Bull Run was lost. They had difficulty turning the enemy's right, which, naturally, needed heavy columns on their extreme left. To accomplish this, they needed to move quickly before the Confederates became aware of their design, which, unfortunately, due to their slowness, they could not do. Having been on the move since two that morning, by the afternoon the Federals were at a point of exhaustion. They stopped at the streams to drink under the baking sun and, unfortunately, exposed themselves to Confederate fire. The rebels also had the advantage of the fresh reinforcements brought up by Jackson and, later, General Johnston. McDowell then ordered a retreat, and that was when disorder broke out.

Later that month, McDowell told Russell that he was much rejoiced to find that the journalist was as much abused as he had been. Bull Run, he continued, was an unfortunate affair for them both, for ". . . had I won it, you would have had to describe the pursuit of the . . . enemy, and . . . you would have been the most popular writer in America. . . . I would have been lauded as the greatest of generals."[15] Russell never lost his admiration for McDowell, his "philosophical temperament" and his great sense of duty. He was convinced that the General was sorely wronged for his part in the battle.

As the days passed, and Washington slowly regained its equilibrium, Russell reckoned that the Confederates had lost their chance to pursue. In fact, in their own disorder, they had not even attempted to do so. The city's population began to relax. All seemed well, and ". . . the Senate, the House of Representatives, the Cabinet, the President, are all at their ease once more and feel secure in Washington."[16]

In his Letter of July 24, Russell discussed American concern of what Europe would think of Bull Run. He included a sort of post-mortem of thoughts and feelings. In all the President's cabinet, Mr. Chase was the only man who realistically bore up under the defeat. Mr. Seward and the rest were recovering their spirits as they found that their army was ". . . more scared than hurt."[17] Flagging spirits were bolstered as the press fuelled rumors of Northern victory with such headlines as "We have successfully outflanked the enemy"; "Greatest battle ever fought on this continent"; "After a terrific fight each and every rebel battery was taken"; "The rout of the enemy was complete"; and finally, as imaginations worked overtime, it came easily to the pens of journalists to write "Victory at Bull Run."[18]

As the days sped by, the city, the country and the army began their recovery. Many cooler heads opined that, despite the hyperbolic press reports, it was a good thing that the Union had been defeated since it meant that it would have to redouble its efforts in order to be victorious. Others, conversely, felt that it showed once and for all that the North should let the South go in peace.

During the latter part of July, Russell became ill with what he called "Potomac Fever." He wrote that powders and mint juleps were prescribed for the malady, which sounded something like a mild form of malaria. He was to take these powders every two hours to make six a day, along with the juleps, which were mostly whiskey. It was obvious to Russell that he would feel no pain. The remedies were, nevertheless, successful, and by the beginning of August, Russell ". . . returned to life."[19]—just in time, it seemed, to witness a great change in the attitude of the Northerners. There were no drunken soldiers in the streets or begging ones, either. There were patrols and an extremely strict system of passes. They "begin to perceive their magnificent armies are mythical, but knowing they have the elements of making one, they are setting about the manufacture."[20]

McClellan was the man to do this. After all the uncomplimentary remarks that were made about his dismissal after the Battle of Anti-etam, it was only fair to credit him with the formation of a tough, organized fighting force. Russell wrote:

> McClellan is . . . very squarely built . . ., broad-chested . . . under middle height. His features are regular and prepossessing; the brow small . . . and furrowed; the eyes deep and anxious looking. A short, tick, reddish mustache conceals his mouth; the rest of his face is clean shaven. . . . Everyone, however, is willing to do as he bids: the President confides in him and "Georges" him; the press fawn upon him, the people trust him, he is "the little corporal". . . .[21]

The first invitation that Russell accepted after his illness was to a reception at the White House. It was a comparatively casual affair, with no one in formal attire. People from the streets seemed to be walking in and out at will; surely not the best of security at that tense moment in history. The President, in his customary suit of black, was in much better spirits, and shook hands with everyone in his usual genial manner. Russell conversed with all his acquaintances in the room, and noted the absence of Mr. Seward. It seemed that the Secretary of State was at home in New York, ascertaining the feelings and willingness of the population to continue the fight. Russell was privy to little tidbits of gossip. It was said that all the commanders at Bull Run were drunk, having stayed up all night drinking and playing cards. That was, of course, complete nonsense, though it probably would have been quite fair to say that some of the volunteers were inebriated.

The anger against General Patterson, who, as he stated, had nineteen out of his twenty-three regiments leave the minute their three months were up, continued unabated. The reality of the situation was that he had led his remaining patrols, as well as the "three-month men," away from fire, so that they could disband out of harm's way. Nonetheless, he remained one of the main scapegoats of the entire fiasco.

Amazingly enough, despite the failure at Bull Run, the volunteers were pouring into regiments and filling up the city. These men were ready to fight, though they were not trained to do so. Russell understood this, and, more importantly, so did McClellan. Feeling this would be of great interest to his readers, Russell began a very detailed observation of the army, its training and its eventual "whipping into shape." McClellan was often mentioned. He ordered ". . . regular parades and drills in every regiment . . . [and Russell began to see] . . . some improvement in the look of the men."[22] To add substance to the army, military men from all over the world and mercenaries of every stripe were converging upon Washington. "The news of the Civil War has produced such an immigration of military adventurers from Europe that the streets of Washington are quite filled with medals and ribbons."[23] It seemed that the regular officers did not like them, though the politicians encouraged them, so that "Garibaldians, Hungarians, Poles, officers of Turkish and other contingents . . . surround the State Department and infest unsuspecting politicians with illegible testimonies in unknown tongues."[24]

Though it hardly seemed possible, the August days became even hotter. The roads to Washington were, again, choked with volunteers, and General McClellan was drilling and training his men vigorously. At one point, the General met with members of the press in order to hammer out some rules under which everyone could live. The gentlemen of the press agreed that they would print nothing that would give the enemy aid and comfort. In return, the military would cooperate, giving the press as many details of battles as was possible, considering that certain actions could not be divulged.

One of the more famous of the arrivals from abroad was Prince Napoleon, cousin of Emperor Napoleon III. Russell wrote that the politicians were suspicious, because they could not figure out why he had come. The Prince applied for a pass to look at the battlefield at Bull Run, which made the authorities extremely uncomfortable. It seemed as though France, too, might recognize the belligerent status of the Confederacy, just as England had done. Russell met the Prince at a reception at Mr. Seward's home on the evening of August 7. The Prince was extremely interested in Russell's experience of the roads around Alexandria down to the Fairfax Courthouse. The Prince had visited Mount Vernon, and he and Russell talked about the dilapidated condition of Washington's home in Virginia. At this point, Russell remarked that General Scott admonished the troops against any sort of looting or destruction of the General's house, though it was in a rebel state. The Prince wanted to know whether General Beauregard spoke good French. The reporter deduced that the Prince had come over to decide in which combatant's headquarters he would serve. When he later returned from Bull Run, he had decided for the Union Army, having not been favorably impressed by Beauregard's Creole French. The unbearable heat continued in the reception rooms, and the Prince perspired profusely. Russell was impressed with his bearing, saying that "he moved off long before the guests were tired of looking at him."[25]

The following day, Russell drove with Mr. Olmsted over the Long Bridge into Alexandria. A large building, which had once been a school, was now a hospital, and many of the wounded from Bull Run were convalescing there. Russell praised the skill of the care and the conditions of the hospital. The entire town was now occupied with Federals, and Russell went over to see where poor Colonel Ellsworth had been shot by the innkeeper, who had been so offended when the Colonel attempted to remove the rebel flag from atop of his inn.

To avoid the dog days of summer in sweltering Washington, and, more importantly, to make some inquiries about an entirely personal issue, Russell made a diversion to Baltimore. The issue was about a young man, Meyrick Beaufoy Feild, who had served in the Crimea and had presented himself to Russell several days previously. He was interested in getting letters of voucher so that he could serve in the Union Army. Several days later, Russell heard that he had suddenly dropped dead of a seizure in Baltimore. Seeking to do the decent thing for a fellow British subject, Russell betook himself to Maryland.

When he arrived, he found that an inquest and burial had already taken place. He was annoyed at the cavalier treatment given to the young man, and wrote, "Little value indeed has human life in the new world. . . ."[26]

As a reporter, Russell noted that the citizens of Baltimore, chafing under their "border state" status, disliked Lincoln, his cabinet and the entire section of New England as much as they always had. The city continued to be in a state of martial law. However, in Russell's eyes, it was nothing more, or less, than a dictatorship. Citizens were subject to unwarranted searches and arrests, as well as suppression of journals that were anti-Union. He did, however, like the look of the Baltimore men. They dressed in such a way, and had such a style, that marked them as similar to upper-class Englishmen.

Soon, reports came in from the Battle at Wilson's Creek, Missouri. Russell, who had known General Lyon, the Federal Commander, was genuinely saddened at the news of his death. He remarked that he was one of the very few officers who combined military skill and personal bravery with political sagacity and moral firmness.[27]

On the 15th, Russell returned to Washington. Lincoln had proclaimed it a day of prayer and fasting. Russell's Baltimore friends told him that the President would not have made such a proclamation if his cause was prospering. In other more favorable news that day, the bankers of New York and Philadelphia decided to lend the Federal government fifty million dollars in return for treasury notes.

The following day, Russell dined with Seward. He found the Secretary, who had now returned from his home state, much comforted in the will of the people to fight, and in the willingness of the bankers to lend fiduciary sustenance. Seward talked to Russell at length about the necessity of creating a strong navy. He thought if they could really organize a fleet, the rebels would be lost.

As August wore fitfully on, Russell was grateful for an opportunity to leave the sweltering city. A fortuitous invitation had arrived to stay at Drohoregan Manor, the home of the Carrolls. He was off to Baltimore. The Carrolls were descendants of one of the signers of the Declaration of Independence, Colonel Charles Carroll of Carrollton. Russell boarded the train at Washington station, noting that guards were posted all round lest unauthorized persons get in or out. The country through Maryland was wooded and hilly. The presence of the military was both seen and felt during the entire trip. Russell observed that Maryland, unlike the Southern states, had a substantial population that worked in factories. These people were inevitably Unionists. Their richer fellow citizens, with large tracts of land, tended to be Secessionists. The Carrolls, naturally, fell into the latter category.

The grounds of Drohoregan Manor were reminiscent of the old country houses that the journalist had seen in Ireland, except for the presence of black slaves. Having been followers of Lord Baltimore's brother, Leonard Calvert, the Carrolls were a Catholic family. Russell's host, another Colonel Carroll, showed him around his home, pointing out the room where General Washington and old Colonel Carroll plotted out their "splendid treason."[28] Despite the efforts of his ancestor, this Colonel Carroll did not blanche at disunion.

At chapel the following morning, Russell noted that the slaves attended along with the family. They obviously knew something of Christianity. In addition, their quarters were far better than the slave huts Russell had seen down South, and certainly better than the huts of the laborers in Ireland. The slaves appeared to have more spirit and were less cringing and servile than they had been in the deeper Southern states. Afterward, the family and Russell sat on the veranda, discussing the war. The local priest joined them, and Russell noted that he talked intelligently and seriously about events, having just returned from the North. The priest felt that the native-born Americans would not fight the war, but would have foreigners, such as the Irish and the Germans, do it for them. He admitted, along with many Marylanders, that slavery was evil, but excused it, as they and their Southern kindred did, by asking, what could they possibly do about it?

The following morning, the news was that McClellan might move forward. But, then again, as Russell was learning quickly, he might not, for this was constantly being reported, he complained, and was in the headlines nearly everyday. This time, the reporter was determined not to take the newspapers' bait and, instead, he stayed and rode with his host, touring the beautiful and verdant estate. He gave it no greater compliment than that it resembled the countryside around Hampshire.

On the 20th, Russell took the train to Harper's Ferry, Virginia. He wanted to see the spot of "old John Brown's" raid on the Federal arsenal. Harper's Ferry was located at the intersection of the Potomac and Shenandoah Rivers. As the train neared the town, Russell was able to see how the buildings of the city had been blackened and ruined, though, thankfully, not all. In some places, the railroad tracks had been torn up, in others, the arches of bridges destroyed. Nevertheless, looking up and down the river, he found the landscape picturesque, though he was sure that John Brown cared little for scenery. At the moment, however, the town was a dangerous place. It was officially Confederate property, though Unionists continued to live there. It was surrounded by Federals on the Maryland side of the Potomac. It would not officially become West Virginia, and part of the Union, until 1863. Therefore, Russell thought it prudent to get the next train to Washington, which is what he did. More importantly, however, in his entry for the evening of August 20:

> . . . the New York papers came in with the extracts from the London papers containing my account of the Battle of Bull's Run. Utterly forgetting their own version of the engagement, the New York editors now find it convenient to divert attention from the bitter truth that was in them, to the letter of the foreign newspaper correspondent.[29]

Russell could have accepted this storm of invective if the New York journals' original accounts had not far surpassed his own in severity. On August 21, he wrote of the gathering storm. Could it really be a month since the soldiers had dragged themselves back from Manassas in such disarray? The editors, Russell wrote, were "weeping, wailing, and gnashing their teeth . . ."[30] just four weeks previously. Now, he complained, these scenes were all forgotten. What they read of Russell's account, now thirty days in the past, was presently a "rebuke to their pride."[31] He wrote that he was not

> aware that any foreigner ever visited the United States who was injudicious enough to write one single word derogatory to their claims to be the first of created beings, who was not assailed with the most viperous malignity and rancor. The man who says he has detected a single spot on the face of their sun should prepare his winding sheet.[32]

Most aggravating was the *New York Times*. While finding that, alas, they could not criticize his account, they were, nevertheless, attributing some fictional quotes to the journalist. He was supposed to have said that he ". . . had never seen such fighting in all my life, and that nothing at Alma or Inkermann was equal to it."[33] Mr. Russell was in no doubt as to the truth of Alexis De Tocqueville's remark ". . . that a stranger who injures American vanity, no matter how justly may make up his mind to be a martyr."[34] Throughout the North and South, abuse was heaped on Russell's Letter so that it was ". . . difficult to describe or exaggerate the force of the shock which Russell's Letter produced."[35] Though the American journals had been even more scathing than Russell, a backlash of inconsistency set in. The press had begun to forget what had been said by its own journalists thirty days before, and became affronted by Russell's comments. Because of his objective reporting, Russell had earned the hatred of both sides.

One officer asked the reporter if he intended to stay in the face of the denunciations that were piled upon him. He replied, "'But is what I've written untrue?' 'God bless you! do you know in this country if you can get enough of people to start a lie about any man he would be ruined, if the Evangelists came forward to swear the story were false?'"[36]

Voicing the opinions of the South, Mary Chestnut wrote that Russell, in his capacity as an Englishman, despised both sides and derided them both equally, attributing Bull Run to ". . . Yankee cowardice rather than to Southern courage. . . . After all, we are mere Americans!"[37] Further, she wrote, ". . . the licensed slanderer, mighty Russell of *The Times* . . .," said that Bull Run was fought at long range, and with Confederates steadily retreating. When a commotion in the Union wagon trains frightened the Yankees, ". . . they made tracks. . . . And . . . we were too frightened to follow them. . . ." Nevertheless, she conceded that, in spite of this insult, ". . . there are glimpses of the truth . . ."[38] in his Letter.

Catherine Cooper Hopeley, an Englishwoman blockaded in the South, overheard a group of disgruntled Southern ladies sneering that ". . . these itinerant reporters of whom no one has ever heard before come and partake of our hospitality, and then. . . ."[39] The ladies delicately left off at this juncture, implying that the ill-mannered English scribbler was bereft of the finer feelings of gratitude.

In the North, the press took this opportunity to pay Russell back for the constant snipes he had taken at their "good name." It was as if each reporter tried to outdo the others in thinking up descriptive names for the hapless Russell. Titles such as "London Stout Russell", "Bombast Russell", "that Cassandra in breeches, Dr. B.R. Russell", "this bilious LL.D.", "the snob correspondent of *The Times*", were invented simply because he had offended the fragile national pride.[40] Sir George Otto Trevelyan, author of the poem "Horace in Athens", wrote:

> Stain not a spotless name with useless crimes,
> O, save the correspondent of the *Times*.[41]

The *New York Times*, which, perhaps, felt itself more dignified than to resort to name calling, nevertheless labeled him, "Bull Run Russell." His ". . . terrible epistle has been read with quite as much avidity as an average President's message." The *New York Times* scarcely felt that it exaggerated when it further stated that the thought ". . . first and foremost . . . on the minds . . ." of the American reading public was, "what will Russell say?"[42] He gave, they continued, a clear, fair, just and accurate account, ". . . discreditable as those scenes were to our Army. . . ."[43] However, in between finding justification for Russell's account, they were able to attribute the aforementioned fictional quotes, about the Battles of Alma and Inkermann in the Crimea, to the reporter. Despite the ill feelings and the fanciful quotes, it seemed that the *New York Times* could not bring itself to discredit the English journalist completely.

Unfortunately, his Bull Run Letter managed to alienate Russell from the Lincolns. He noted, in his diary entry of September 9, that the couple were not nearly as affable to him as they had been during the spring. Bitterly, he attributed this to the fact that he would ". . . not bow . . . [his] . . . knee to the degraded creatures who have made the very name of a free press odious to honorable men . . .,"[44] in other words, the Northern press.

There were those in the North who were indignant at the wanton slander of an honorable English journalist. Horace Greeley wrote that Russell had written nothing to justify such offensive attacks. Senator Charles Sumner was also appalled at the vicious treatment meted out to Russell. In a letter to the correspondent, dated September 16, 1861, Sumner wrote: ". . . I have been astonished at the minuteness of criticism directed against your account of the panic. . . ."[45] John Bigelow, in his memoirs, defended his friend. He stated that Russell gave his paper a highly realistic and accurate description of the action.[46] A modern historian, Allan Nevins, said it best, however, when he observed that Russell wrote a ". . . graphically true description of the Bull Run panic." In vain, Nevins continued, did honest officers, such as Sherman and Keyes, endorse his account: ". . . Russell . . . [was] . . . fair and expert, the ablest reporter the war had found. . . ."[47]

Fortunately, Russell's sense of humor prevailed in the face of the most virulent attacks and the most half-hearted defense. He wrote to Bigelow:

> It is not true that I commanded the Confederates in person or let off the Federalist centre; neither did I lie on my stomach disguised as Raymond of the . . . [New York] . . . *Times* and kill Beauregard with a pistol tooth pick . . .; neither did I say that I had never seen such slaughter at Solferino (where I wasn't) or at Inkermann where I was. . . .[48]

He wrote later: "I'm not kilt yet, tho' the *Herald* is doing its best to get me assassinated. . . ."[49]

Russell spent relatively little time defending himself in his Letters of August and September. The one notable exception was the answer to his critics in his Letter of August 31. Russell wrote that he had never impeached the courage of those who fought, but only endeavored to describe the terror and panic of those who ran.[50] Nevertheless, he noted in his diary that August was a "month during which I have been exposed to more calumny, falsehood, not to speak of danger."[51]

The unfair situation filled Russell with indignation. These feelings stemmed not only from the point of view that Russell, a British journalist, had dared to criticize the American armies, but also because, as the representative of *The Times*, he felt himself to be a martyr to their pro-Southern policies. In an agitated letter to Delane, his editor, Russell wrote: "If I am ever in another Bull Run, you may depend upon it I shall never get out alive. . . ."[52] Undoubtedly, too, the journalist felt unsafe in Washington, for he had received hate-mail and even death treats. While walking, ". . . [a] German soldier on guard . . . thrust a loaded rifle at him shouting, 'Pull Run Russell! You shall never write Pull Runs again!'"[53] Mowbray Morris, the foreign manager of *The Times*, momentarily feared for Russell's safety. In a letter, he told the reporter that when his description of the battle appeared in *The Times*, everyone said, "Russell will be lynched." Londoners, it seemed, felt great concern for Russell's security.[54]

Despite all, Delane was thrilled with the Bull Run Letter. In his reply to Russell, he wrote that he could barely describe the delight with which all had read the vivid account of the repulse; he added that ". . . it is only for you that I have any fear."[55]

In the sum and substance, neither Delane nor Morris must have worried overmuch regarding Russell's well-being. In response to the journalist's pleas to return to England, supposing he might have outlived his usefulness and welcome, Morris wrote that he did not find any difficulty in advising Russell to remain in America. Further, if he abandoned his post at this critical juncture, it would be said that ". . . the New York press had succeeded in intimidating you. . . ."[56] Delane also urged him to stay, writing that the "great danger of a bitter resentment upon the receipt of your letter . . . is well over, I should hope there was no more to be feared on that account."[57] Neither man being on the scene, they had no difficulty either making these assumptions or advising these actions.

As August came to its tumultuous close, Russell received further threats from "Bowie knives and revolvers." He was even advised by a friend not to go about unarmed and to apply for the protection of Lord Lyon's legation walls. Russell rejected all such advice. With admirable tenacity, he resolved to put the tempest behind him. But, there is little doubt that his objectivity suffered in the face of the bitter denunciation to which he was subjected. Nevertheless, his determined adherence to duty in times of adversity held him fast in America—at least for the time being.

Chapter Twelve

"Mint Juleps and Prairie Dogs"

WASHINGTON, D.C.—WISCONSIN
AUGUST—OCTOBER, 1861

BILLY RUSSELL, fearless reporter of the abuses of the Crimea, would hardly allow the American press to bother him. He was determined to keep busy, in order to avoid thinking about, or responding to, the continuous and rancorous criticism of which he was the target. To this end, he maintained a constant stream of detailed Letters to his readers in England.

In his Letter of August 10, 1861, Russell described at length the 37th session of the United States Congress. In addition to the usual business that occupied these meetings, the Congress passed copious wartime legislation. Among these resolutions were, "An act to punish certain crimes against the United States", "An act to indemnify the states for expenses incurred by them in defense of the United States", and scores of others. Curiously enough, after passing all these measures providing for the emergency situation, ". . . it was not without opposition at last that the resolution of Congress approving and confirming the acts of the President for suppressing insurrection and rebellion, was passed before the House adjourned. . . ."[1] Strangely, the gentlemen of the Congress seemed reluctant to acknowledge officially what was actually happening.

The atmosphere in Washington had the foreboding calm of the "phony war" of Europe in 1939. The circumstances after the Battle of Bull Run were fraught with tension as the opponents, stunned at the reality of what they had done to one other, retreated to their corners. In their confusion, they licked their wounds, all the while growling and snapping at their rivals.

The North, particularly, was at a loss. As seen in the Congressional sessions, it had not yet embraced its cause as firmly as had the South. Indeed, Russell wondered exactly which course the Northerners would choose to follow. Ideas, which the journalist busily recorded, floated around the capital like pollen on a spring day. Many of them, for good or bad, died painless deaths, while others took root to grow and flourish. In the Letter of August 20, Russell speculated, mistakenly as it turned out, that the President would most likely free all the slaves behind Union lines. In addition, he told his readers that Washington was once again rife with rumors, puzzlement and a plethora of causes. Socialism, he wrote, was rearing its "ugly head" in the Northern cities. Indeed, one day ". . . we may yet hear re-echoed the terrible cry of French revolution by the masses whom the war has plunged into poverty."[2]

Out of this cacophony of rumors, Russell wrote to his friend Bigelow in Paris:

When you left America last, you left also
A free Press—Prosperity—A Constitution
Habeas Corpus
Peace
I hope you may come back and find them. There is now—
No freedom of the Press—A passport system—Domiciliary visits—
Police surveillance—Fort Lafayette—a bastille—
No freedom of the person—
War calamity and distress—
Irresponsible Govt.[3]

Ominous indeed; however, Russell was oversimplifying and certainly not making allowances for the wartime situation.

In the later days of August, Russell continued to receive death threats and anonymous letters. Some of the exotic weaponry suggested for Russell's imminent demise were the Bowie knife, rifles and revolvers. However, the harassed reporter saw quite clearly that the prevalent weapon of his persecutors was to verbally abuse him to death.

The good news, however, was that the Army of the Potomac was shaping up. The drilling and training of the men was, at least, not an uncertainty. Russell continually rode with McClellan to inspect the ever-improving body of men. Normally, such expeditions were what Russell needed; however, he exclaimed ruefully that "... these little excursions are not the most agreeable affairs in the world, for McClellan delights in working down staff and escort ... and not returning til passed midnight."[4] Later, Russell wrote comments on McClellan's strenuous reviews. The General rode and reviewed indefatigably. More difficult, for those who accompanied him, there was scarcely a day when he did not cover at least twenty to thirty miles of men and camps.[5] As critical as he had been before, Russell was just as sincere and fair-minded when he discussed the improvement of the army. In a letter to his friend Bancroft Davis, he wrote that there was no real news, but that McClellan was "working to get his army into shape and he is *succeeding*."[6]

Hard as the inspection rides were, Russell never faltered. On one particular day, when they planned to inspect McDowell's division, the journalist rode over the Long Bridge with McClellan's aides and showed his pass to the sentry. The sentry called to his sergeant, who looked at the pass, examined it very closely, turning it around and around, and said, "'Are you Russell of the London 'Times'?'" Russell replied, "'If you look at the pass, you will see who I am.' . . . at last, with an expression of infinite dissatisfaction and anger upon [the sergeant's] face, handed [the pass] back, saying to the sentry, 'I suppose you must let him go.'"[7] Once over the bridge, Russell met with General McDowell. As they were talking, an escorted carriage arrived, carrying the President and Mr. Seward, accompanied by General

McClellan. After the "Star-Spangled Banner" was played, the troops marched past the assembled dignitaries. Russell was more than complimentary at the improvement in the look of the men. They were, he thought, far superior to the "three-month men," but still had a way to go to look like battle-ready soldiers.

Russell shared the camp dinner that evening with the officers at Arlington House. Among those attending were General William T. Sherman and General Erasmus D. Keyes. While discussing the debacle at Bull Run, Sherman told Russell point-blank:

> . . . I can endorse every word that you wrote; your statements about the battle, which you say you did not witness, are equally correct . . . though some of the troops did fight well. . . .[8]

General Keyes corroborated Sherman's statements, saying further:

> I don't think you made it half bad enough. . . . [W]e drove them easily at first . . . but when they did come on I could not get the infantry to stand, and after a harmless volley they broke.[9]

The Generals, nevertheless, complained loudly and long about the press. Their editors, Russell was told, were not gentlemen, and they cared only about advertisements and circulation—not truth. This must have been cold comfort considering all the denunciation that Russell had suffered because of his Letter. The compliments, however, were astonishing in light of the fact that General Sherman, in particular, loathed war correspondents. He once said: "Reporters print their limited and tainted observations as their history of events they neither see nor comprehend."[10] Sherman truly felt that all war correspondents should swing from the nearest tree, and would have been delighted to perform the task himself.

Russell's now sparse popularity continued to spiral downward. People turned to stare at him on the street, and women turned up their noses. After chatting with a clerk at Willard's, saying that he, Russell, thought the clerk was no longer working at the hotel, the other shook his head. He replied that if he had no longer been there, gone with him would have been the last man to support the journalist. Curiously, however, the clerk was not the last man at Willard's to speak up for what Russell had written. Walt Whitman, in his *Battle of Bull Run, July 1861, Memoranda During the War*, could not have been more accurate when he wrote:

> There you are, shoulder straps, but where are your companies? Where are your men? Incompetents! Never tell me of chances of battle, of getting stray'd and the like. I think this is your work, this retreat, after all. Sneak, blow, put on airs in Willard's sumptuous parlors and bar-rooms, or anywhere.
>
> No explanation will save you. Bull Run is your work; had you been half or one-tenth worth your men, this would have never happened.[11]

Since Russell faced the continuing fallout of the Bull Run Letter, his friends continued to urge him to seek physical protection. He and his companions whiled away many an hour wondering which brutally described demise would be the death of the reporter. All tried to make light of it, but Russell was extremely unhappy and longed for letters from Mary and a quick return home to the warmth of his family. Protection was there for him only if he stayed inside the walls of Lord Lyons's legation. To hide behind the British Ambassador, however, was not Russell's style. He continued reporting events in the capital, but it became more and more difficult . . . and dangerous.

* * * *

On the evening of August 31, Russell dined with U.S. naval officers and met Captain Andrew H. Foote, USN. Foote, along with General Grant, was charged with clearing the Western rivers, and, most importantly, the Mississippi River, with his flotilla of steam and gunboats. Russell described him as a ". . . calm, energetic skillful officer." He said, further, that the Confederates would have a hard time with such a man, for he knew his business well. Later, it would be Foote and Grant who would give the North its first resounding successes, indeed, clearing the Western rivers. Foote, Russell wrote, ". . . was an able and experienced seaman. His wife . . . [however,] . . . was taken into custody for treasonable practices."[12] Russell did not elaborate on this curious statement, saying only that the lady was under house arrest with another lady, and, strangely, that there were many fires in that area.

Toward the end of the month, Russell went to the Department of the Navy. His purpose was to secure passes on steamers, should there be any naval expeditions. He walked through the halls of the building, noting the bad engravings on the walls and the portraits of naval men such as Decatur and Perry, whose claim to fame was that they had triumphed over Britain. Russell was very much impressed, however, by the courtesy of the functionaries in the department. They were much nicer, he thought, than their British counterparts.

Soon, Russell fell ill again, as he had been at the end of the previous month. Whether it was from watermelons, as General McClellan speculated, or a repeat of Potomac fever, this time, the reporter chose to dose himself with quinine rather than drink himself senseless with prescribed mint juleps. As usual, this illness did not prevent him from receiving guests—usually friends from the various legations, who inevitably wished to discuss the situation. Now, most felt that the war would be over within the next two years, although only on the condition that the Union accept Southern independence. They all agreed that the Union Navy was most definitely the most formidable branch of the military and would give the South the most trouble.

Remembering his trip south, Russell wrote that, though he'd met many men to whom he had taken a great liking, he could not honestly find any sympathy for their cause. Nevertheless, such introspection made no impression on his critics, which only served to anger the reporter further against the press. In his opinion, the North, in general, fared no better. It seemed to make little impact on the Northerners that Russell wrote these thoughts. They felt that the reporter was pro-

South simply because he was not praising the North to the rooftops. These embittered reflections were characteristic of Russell's feelings as well, and continued to be so.[13]

* * * *

In his Letter of September 2, Russell mentioned General Fremont's proclamation of martial law in Missouri. Now, the reporter speculated, the war must be one between abolitionists and slave owners. In another Letter, Russell explained the situation by discussing Fremont's proclamation, insofar as ". . . freeing the slaves of all Confederate sympathizers in Missouri . . .,"[14] and how it had split Lincoln's cabinet. It was a reckless proclamation at best since, at that point, it only served the border states with notice that martial law or, indeed, staying in the Union would ultimately mean freeing their slaves, something many were not yet prepared to do. Further, in a Letter published later in England but written days before, on August 30, Russell wrote of Fremont's expedition down the Mississippi. The journalist described Fremont as ". . . displaying zeal, judgment, and vigour in his preparations. . . ."

Events just days later, however, proved the reporter wrong, and his initial assessment of Fremont's behavior in Missouri was revealed as the more accurate: "In all events, it is embarrassing. Fremont is an ambitious, bold and enterprising man, but it will surprise me to find he proves a very great man."[15] A sentiment echoed by history. Russell's opinion of Fremont and his excesses had reason to decline even more sharply in the following months. He discussed the General's dismissal with very little regret in *The Times* Letter of November 2. His pronouncement, several days later, was positively scorching: "The part of his career which most becomes him seems to have been his retirement and his conduct on taking leave of his troops."[16]

That day, the 2nd, Russell had occasion to see General Scott leaving the War Office. He was walking between two aides, his pace slow and hesitant. The journalist had heard several people discussing the possibility of Scott's stepping down. Several months ago, he thought, people could not honor the General enough; now, men in uniform did not salute him on the streets. In fact, one soldier remarked almost in the General's hearing, "'Old Fuss-and-Feathers' don't look first-rate today."[17]

In addition to discussing General Scott and Fremont's activities, the Letter of September 2 praised General McClellan on the continued improvement of the troops. However, Russell was not happy about the fact that McClellan was beginning to refuse passes to correspondents. Nevertheless, the reporter felt that ". . . McClellan is rapidly becoming the master of the situation."[18] Having written such a statement in his Letter, it was most surprising to his readers that Russell began to express certain doubts about McClellan. In his diary entry of that day, he wrote that ". . . McClellan does not appear to me a man of action, or, at least, a man who intends to act as speedily as the crisis demands."[19] In his entry of September 11, he stated that ". . . it is now quite plain McClellan has no intention of making a general defensive move against Richmond. He is aware his army is not equal to the task."[20] Several lines later, he wrote that ". . . I am satisfied that he does not intend to move now and possibly will not do so til next year."[21] His Letters and diary entries are marked by impatience, juxtaposed with admiration for McClellan.

That evening, Russell went to General McClellan's headquarters accompanied by a friend. There were officers lounging about, smoking, reading and writing. Russell and his companion were escorted to McClellan's room to find the General sitting in shirt sleeves on his camp bed. Russell described him as calm, with clear eyes and great energy. Rarely did he smile, but when he did, it animated his entire face. The reporter noted the telegraph lines running throughout the house and constant dispatches being sent and received. They spoke of many things, least of which was the current situation. Like most career officers, McClellan understandably did not have much use for volunteers. He explained to Russell that they didn't understand the precautions a career soldier knew by heart, and were too rash and credulous. After studying the lists of officers, the journalist commented that many of the West Pointers, such as McClellan, had remained on the Union side. The men talked also about the Crimea, which they had in common, and about other places and subjects. McClellan implied that he was determined to regain lost ground or, at least, try to reconnoiter enemy headquarters to find out what was afoot. He promised that if he went on such an expedition, he would send an orderly to fetch Russell.

Late the following evening, Russell heard movements in the streets. Dragging himself out of his sick-bed, he went to the window to see troops marching by. As he was puzzling over their purpose, he received information that McClellan was sending off several brigades for reconnaissance. Feeling that there might be a battle on the morrow, Russell retired, only to be wakened by voices asking to speak with him in order to ascertain the troop movements. These voices expressed concern about getting their affairs in order and wondered, too, if they should be hoisting the Confederate flag. They were also apprehensive as to when the looting was set to begin. Russell tried to reassure them that it was simply a reconnaissance mission. Nevertheless, they were skeptical.

Later that morning, Russell rode over the Chain Bridge, a bridge about five miles above Washington, but he could not get through despite his pass. His horse, Walker, behaved most abominably, kicking and jumping nervously, possibly, Russell thought, because the noise reminded the hapless animal of Bull Run. The morning, as it had been during the entire summer, was incredibly hot. The reporter, again, rode over to the Long Bridge to see if he could cross but, again, could not get through. It seemed that all passes had been suspended. Undaunted, Russell rode to the Navy Yard in order to get a look at Munson's Hill, the area of McClellan's reconnaissance, where the fighting would no doubt take place. He was told by a lookout that nothing was happening. After returning from a quick visit to headquarters where he was told that there was positively no fighting, his landlord gave him a different story. The landlord's friend, a hospital steward, "had seen ninety wounded men carried into one ward from over the river, and believed the Federals had lost 1,000 killed and wounded and twenty-five guns."[22]

On September 6, Russell continued to feel "seedy." He refused several invitations from McClellan to ride inspection and, instead, stayed in his rooms. It remained hot and humid. Russell wrote in his private diary, "there is no chance of our side moving . . .,"[23] then remonstrated with himself for saying "our side" when he was supposed to be a neutral. Such a statement belied accusations that he was pro-Southern— things he had heard since his Southern Letters trickled back to the United States. In his misery, he also berated himself for not being a better human being. This was Russell's usual response to his guilt at having to leave Mary, and his anxiety about whether she could handle their eldest daughter, Alice, whom he called a "wild child."

Russell roused himself enough to go over to General Scott's headquarters in order to pay his respects. The General had finally decided to hand in his resignation. Russell wrote in his diary that Scott was headed for retirement in Europe, while ". . . McClellan takes his place, minus the large salary."[24] Russell's opinion was that Scott had his faults, but ". . . meanness and underhanded dealing can not be among them."[25] Faint praise, indeed. In the spirit of discussing pecuniary recompense, Russell made a note that Scott would receive £3,500 a year for a pension, at that time an impressive sum.

At the headquarters, Russell met several important generals. He described General Ambrose Burnside as ". . . a soldierly, intelligent-looking man . . . [who] . . . spoke like a man of sense and a soldier of action . . .";[26] Henry Hallack, a West Pointer, known to his men as "Old Brains", was a man ". . . of great ability, very calm, practical, earnest, and cold, devoted to the Union . . .";[27] and Joe Johnston was the Union's "best strategist."[28] In discussing their opponents, these men told Russell that they considered Lee to be ". . . the best man on the

Confederate side, but he is slow and timid."[29] Undoubtedly, this astounding pronouncement came back to haunt these military men after Lee's audacious performances at Fredericksburg and Chancellorsville.

In the evening papers, there were rumors of the death of Jefferson Davis, and the following day, there were lamentations and obituary notices. The journalist, knowing how misleading American newspapers tended to be, knew this to be quite untrue.

Russell's Letters of September and October were peppered with items about Kentucky, passport information, further inspections of troops and men, and conversations with Union officers. In his Letter of September 13, he showed concern about the neutrality of Kentucky. The pressure from both sides on this state seemed to foil a ". . . strong party for peace and neutrality. . . ."[30] In a later paragraph, Russell warned Englishmen who were planning to visit the South not to do so. Any passport that they might obtain would be signed by Seward, and would state ". . . it is expected that the bearer will not enter any of the insurrectionary states."[31]

In further excursions through the camps, Russell remarked that he ". . . had never heard in America more enthusiastic and vigorous cheering than marked . . . [his and McClellan's] . . . return to camp, and their reception of . . . General . . . [McClellan] . . ., who has evidently become most popular with the men in spite of, or in consequence of his strictness."[32] Having spoken with several Northern officers, Russell wrote that they loved the Union but not the government. Particularly, they told Russell that they would not fight a war against slavery. In further discussions, Russell observed that there was, indeed, a class system in America. It seemed that ". . . all men are equal, but it by no means follows that the man who sells tobacco behind a counter is equal to the man who grows tobacco for sale on his estate."[33]

With a clearer head, and beginning to feel his old self, Russell continued riding around the countryside inspecting camps. He was often regarded with hostility, mixed with a great measure of curiosity; he was, after all, the now infamous Russell of *The Times*.

On September 10, Russell was writing at his desk when he heard the unmistakable sound of cannon. He drove towards the Chain Bridge and joined a crowd of curious people staring at the smoke in the distance. The uproar was another of McClellan's reconnaissances into Virginia. This time, it was a town called Lewinsville. The noise abated, and the people eventually calmed down and disbursed. As he drove back to his lodgings, Russell concluded, once again, that McClellan had no intentions of marching to Richmond or, it seemed, anywhere, at that moment. Though the reporter in no way thought that the army was ready for major campaigning, the months of waiting after Bull Run were wearing on him, his acquaintances and, indeed, on both sides of the conflict. His friends would gather in his rooms, discussing non-events, becoming impatient with each delay, mostly McClellan's, and then leaving "with a hope that tomorrow would be more lively. . . ."[34]

Russell made some notes in his diary in order to combat the tedium in the capital. A petition was drawn up by certain people in Philadelphia to be presented to Mr. Seward. They accused Billy Russell of "treasonous practices and misrepresentations. . . ."[35] On the calendar, there would be a lecture at Willard's Hotel, in which the subject would be Russell himself. On the social scene, the Prince of Joinville and his nephews, the Count of Paris and the Duke of Chartres, arrived in Washington. The Prince intended to attach his nephews at the Federal headquarters. They were received happily by the White House and the army. Russell suspected it was because the Emperor of France showed no inclination towards the Union, the family of the Pretender would.

In a letter to Delane, Russell decided to be absolutely blunt. He pointed out that anyone who wrote for *The Times* in a spirit of moderation would be lambasted by both sides. He was at a loss and held himself aloof from men like Lincoln and Seward, who just months earlier had received him so warmly. Now, he was being snubbed by these gentlemen. In the end, he told Delane, the North was getting very strong, and the neutrality of *The Times*, which had gained the ill will of both parties, would put England on shaky ground when their quarrel was mended. He concluded by saying that if his presence were a disadvantage to the paper, then Delane should "withdraw me altogether if necessary tho' I confess I should not like to give all the rascals in the U.S. such a triumph over me and you."[36]

At the infamous lecture at Willard's, a member of the British Legation staff attended out of curiosity. He reported that it was a terrible affair, which no one would admit to having attended. The orator used such abusive language that "the respectable portion of the audience left the room."[37] The orator's coup de grâce was to produce a gentleman who swore that he had accompanied Russell during the entire day of the Bull Run fiasco, and who would swear, too, that everything the Englishman wrote was a falsehood. To his credit, President Lincoln, who certainly had better things to do, did not attend.

Despite such events, the reporter continued to lament the dullness of life in Washington. If it were not for the hospitality of Lord Lyons, the time spent there would have been intolerable. Smoking, drinking and talking were, at present, the only amusements afforded the gentlemen who waited and waited. With the hot, humid weather, the sudden rains and thunderstorms, Russell's monotony was complete.

In late September, the journalist, thankfully, made an additional trip to Baltimore. The situation, he wrote, was explosive. The Union was determined not to let Maryland leave:

> They cry out loud, "Why do you treat us as if we were enemies? We are still part of the Union. We are not out of it." . . . [and Unionists reply] . . . "We regard you as people who would be open enemies of the Union if you had the means. . . ."[38]

The majority of the landowners in the ". . . respectable classes of Maryland are in favor of secession principles. . . ."[39]

On his two previous visits to Maryland, much had transpired to impress the journalist. On the first, Sumter had been fired upon, and the ". . . feeling which displayed itself was certainly not one of regret."[40] On the second, when Russell visited Fortress Monroe, ". . . Baltimore had the air of Warsaw, pickets at the street corners, patrols in the thoroughfares, camps on the hills, soldiers cooking in the public places, the people sullen and angry."[41] Now, Russell wrote, Maryland feels like a man who is in manacles, waiting for liberation.

After the Maryland visit, Russell assured his readers that no movement was yet forthcoming from the armies around Washington. Therefore, he decided to take this opportunity to escape from the continuing attacks of various journals, and visit where ". . . Union sentiment burns brightest . . ."[42]—the Northwest. In his present mood, Russell could not resist throwing several barbs while traveling westward. He remarked that the Westerners were fighting on the Union side to liberate the slaves whom they would not permit into their own territories. He further accused Lincoln and other abolitionists of wanting to free the slaves in order to force them to emigrate from the country. Again, Russell was letting his anger and bitterness cloud his usually excellent judgment.

In his Letter of September 23, originating from Racine, Wisconsin, he waxed rhapsodic:

> The place from which this Letter is dated is one of the wonderful creations of the grain harvest and immigration in the vast prairie tracts which lie on the western shore of the Michigan Inland Sea. It looks like a Russian settlement.[43]

Nevertheless, he did fear that it was not, perhaps, quite civilized. In any event, his pen beautifully described the lands he visited and their resources, topography, climate and agriculture. Here, the naturalist's voice was heard over that of the cynic—at least, some of the time. At others, he again complained about the American need for the visitor to exclaim at some beauty of nature, and say that he had never seen anything like it in his life.

Russell's travels took him through Maryland, Pennsylvania, Indiana and on to Illinois and Wisconsin. On the prairies, the correspondent and his party of friends did their quail shooting. However, even in the sylvan peace of nature, Russell managed to court controversy. Despite his protests to them, members of Russell's party decided to shoot on a Sunday. This put the locals out to no end. That evening, at dinner, a constable rushed in from a rainstorm that had stopped the sport and ordered Russell to identify himself. He then proceeded to arrest him: "Then I arrest you . . . in the name of the people of the commonwealth of Illinois."[44]

It seemed that a citizen had complained about Russell and his companions disturbing the peace of a Sunday. After accepting a glass of liquid refreshment, the constable explained that the man who had lodged the complaint was himself known to go out shooting on Sundays and he had seen the group. Russell was sure that this man had decided to make a reputation for himself by persecuting the best known, and least liked, member of the party. Ironically, the accused was the one person who had, himself, complained about his own party having their sport on Sunday.

Russell agreed to appear to answer charges. The following day, he and his friends went to the Courthouse in Dwight, Illinois. Russell chose not to defend himself, and Colonel Foster, a member of his party, felt that he must "do the honors." The Colonel made an impassioned plea in Russell's defense, but to no avail. The reporter was fined seven dollars, to the dismay of many in the courtroom, who thought the whole thing was ridiculous—to the point that many of the gentlemen in the room offered to pay the small fine themselves. Russell thanked them, and paid his own fine.

That evening, with the receipt of mail and newspapers, Russell felt that it was, perhaps, time to get back to the front.

→ *Chapter Thirteen* ←

"The *Trent* Affair"

WASHINGTON, D.C.—NEW YORK CITY
OCTOBER—DECEMBER, 1861

AFTER HIS SPORT, and day in court, Russell reached Washington on October 3. The reporter hoped that his writer's instinct, which was telling him that something was brewing, would hold true. His next Letter, however, belied that hope, as it expressed the frustration and impatience many continued to feel at the stagnation of McClellan's command. It was apparent to Russell that in the public's present temper, on hearing that "... a great battle will take place immediately ...," some forward movement was most assuredly expected. He quickly emphasized that there was none of the ignorance or arrogance which had led to Bull Run. It was just that the fighting season had arrived, and most were becoming intolerant with inaction.[1]

Russell wrote that now, interestingly enough, the rank and file of the Army of the Potomac was ready for battle, while it was the officers who remained unfit. He railed in his Letter of October 4 about the inferior condition of the officers.

> Talk of the system of purchase in our army! If any one will turn to the New York's papers, he will see plenty of advertisements which show that purchase of commissions of such a sort as never should be tolerated is not unknown in the United States.[2]

Russell's readers were impatient for action, and the reporter doggedly tried to placate them by predicting that, by the end of the month, ". . . land and sea will resound with the tumult of battle."³ And none too soon, since the army's main condition for complete discipline, Russell told his readers, was total abstinence from hard drink. "Never has Bacchus in all his forms and poor John Barleycorn been so persecuted in any army in the world."⁴

Russell often endeavored to keep his readers amused with notes and tales of small incidents that took place during the month. At the beginning of October, after supper one evening, Russell's friend, Sam Ward, told him that Mr. Seward complained that the reporter never visited him anymore. His complaint was valid; it had been quite a long time since the two men talked. However, the truth was that Russell had visited, but, as stated earlier, he had been snubbed by the Secretary. Seward, it seemed, had joined the group that railed against Russell. He had received the petition from the good people of Philadelphia, complaining bitterly about the reporter, and had agreed that the allegations against Russell were true. The journalist, in Seward's opinion, had grievously abused Northern hospitality.

In order to talk things over with General McClellan, Russell often went to military headquarters. Though his Potomac fever had, once again, returned, the journalist was determined to drag himself around town and glean whatever bits of information that he could. One evening, he and a friend found themselves in the parlor of McClellan's headquarters. In walked a tall man in an ill-fitting suit. He inquired of the General's aide if he were in.

> "'Yes sir. He's come back, but is lying down, very much fatigued. I'll send up, sir, and inform him you wish to see him.' 'Oh, no; I can wait. I think I'll take supper with him. . . .'"⁵

After witnessing this exchange, Russell quickly ushered his friend out of the parlor. Upon being asked why they had left so precipitously, and why Russell had stood when the tall man had walked in, Russell replied:

"'Because it was the President.' 'The President of what?' 'Of the United States.' 'Oh! Come, now you're humbugging me. Let me have another look at him.'"[6]

The friend returned, shaking his head, indicating that he had certainly expected a much finer-looking gentleman. Russell wrote that Lincoln might, indeed, have suffered a lack of elegance and finery—and that there may well have been better-dressed and "more courtly presidents who, in a similar crisis, would have displayed less capacity, honesty, and plain dealing than Abraham Lincoln."[7]

Relieving the boredom, William Butler Duncan, Russell's New York banker friend, arrived in Washington. Though he stayed for only two days, it provided a welcome diversion. The two men, and several other of Russell's British acquaintances, rode around the Arlington area and up to the now infamous Munson Hill of McClellan's reconnaissances and noisy puffs of smoke. From the hill, Russell remarked, one could see a lovely view of Alexandria. After breakfast the following day, Duncan was on his way back to New York, and Russell was again feeling "seedy."

The journalist commented on the banker's short visit in a letter to John Delane. He wrote that riding around the countryside, Duncan was satisfied that "Washington is safe & they are getting value for their money."[8] In that same letter Russell makes a telling observation: ". . . our consuls do lay themselves open to charges of favoring Secessia by words & deeds."[9]

On the 22nd of the month, Russell was pleased to write about actual battles again: the Battle of Harper's Ferry, that took place on October 17, and, closer to Russell, the Battle of Ball's Bluff, which had taken place the night before. The results of Harper's Ferry were reported as positive; however, Ball's Bluff was unfavorable to the Union. Russell resolved that very afternoon to ride to the scene. At last, he could report on the spot. However, before he was able to approach the location, night was falling, and, to his frustration, it was necessary to turn back, without any interesting news. Doggedly, however, he rode out the next day, determined to ascertain the turn of events. As he approached, he met some returning orderlies who told him that he would have to return the following day. When he did, he was informed that it was all over, and there was nothing to report. Russell's frustration can only be imagined.

Tired of military reviews, wet weather and complete boredom, Russell made another trip to Maryland—this time for duck hunting.

During the month of October, both North and South began to realize that the articles written by such correspondents as Russell were, perhaps, not the best promotion for their causes. Both sides began to mount massive propaganda machines designed to influence British public opinion. The North, in particular, felt that what was needed was

> . . . some gentlemen of intelligence and experience, possessing a good knowledge of all circumstances preceding and accompanying the rebellion . . . to disabuse the public mind, especially in England and France, where numerous and active agents of secession and rebellion have been at work.[10]

Many, however, thought that in order to disabuse the British public, at least, of anti-Northern proclivities, the United States had better stop abusing Mr. Russell. *The Times* scornfully wrote:

> The Americans have been conspicuous from the beginning of their troubles for an almost childish irritability. . . . [They] seem totally unable to bear the check in their career with anything like manly fortitude.[11]

The waiting, however, went on for everyone.

> Day follows day and resembles its predecessor. McClellan is still reviewing, and the North is still waiting for victories and paying money, and the orators are still wrangling over the best way of cooking the hares which they have not yet caught.[12]

Yet, still, by the end of October, nothing had happened. Russell told his readers that ". . . something must be done, for the country is fretting and fuming at the inaction or the slow progress of affairs. . . ."[13]

November came with the comment, "again stagnation. . . ."[14] Mc-Clellan continued training his troops, General Scott's resignation was made public, and it was announced that he would probably go to Europe for his retirement. Russell's homesickness and boredom threatened to overtake him altogether, so he resorted to repeating gossip. He noted several newspaper reports mulling over the loyalty of Mrs. Lincoln. Some of the press called her true blue, while other writers were positive that she was susceptible to influences from bad quarters. Perhaps they were thinking of her Southern relatives, or of her sister, a dyed-in-the-wool Confederate, who would live with her for most of the war. There was also talk about sending several gentlemen to Europe to promote Federal interests and counteract the Southern Commissioners.

Russell continued his social rounds. Dinners and balls persevered in great numbers in the capital. Since the weather, which had been dreary and wet, cleared up, Russell decided to go to the ball given by the Sixth U.S. Cavalry. The spread, Russell wrote, was lavish, and he met many acquaintances including the Duke of Chartres, one of the Orleans princes, who was now a United States captain. The Duke regaled him with tales of the great hilarity he had experienced when he had been called "Captain Chatters."[15] Russell was extremely impressed that he took the whole thing in his stride, laughing louder than anyone else.

Along with the gossip and social whirl, there was some other news. Russell, most inconveniently, had to move. The landlady at his lodgings had been too greedy with her bill, and a change of quarters was viewed as a necessity in order to keep down expenses. The reporter idly speculated about some statistics he had gleaned from James Lesley, the Chief Clerk in the War Department.[16] As of November 11, the United States had "600,000 infantry, 600 pieces of artillery, 61,000 in the field,"[17] but, nevertheless, they had not conquered the South or even,

Russell noted, the Southern ladies. He mentioned that some of the people with whom he had stayed in the South had now been arrested for their sympathies; or, in the case of the British consuls, they had been recalled. He noted this, together with the growing dislike of Britain that he felt everywhere.

It seemed as though Seward's snubs of the previous few months were finished, and, in mid-November, Russell was once again invited to join him for dinner. The talk turned to the problems with Britain. Many were angry that the British appeared to be aiding and even abetting Southern blockade-runners. Conversely, as General McDowell told Russell, "There is no nation in the world whose censure or praise the people of the United States care about except England. . . ."[18]

On another evening spent with Seward, the President came to play whist, and the talk turned to Bull Run. Seward's cryptic comment was that "civilians sometimes displayed more courage than soldiers, but perhaps the courage was unprofessional."[19] Russell thought this a strange concept of courage.

November wore on, fulfilling the promise of being even more tedious than the preceding month. Indeed, on November 16, just when Russell thought nothing truly newsworthy was ever likely to happen again, he learned that the Southern Commissioners, Mason and Slidell, had been seized and removed from the HMS *Trent* by Captain Charles Wilkes of the *San Jacinto*. With the air of a Sherlock Holmes crying to Watson, "The game is afoot!", Russell regaled his readers with continuous coverage of what is now known as the "Trent Affair."

Captain Charles Wilkes of the USS *San Jacinto* had stopped and boarded a British West Indian mail packet, called the HMS *Trent*, off the Bahamas. The British steamer was carrying the Southern Commissioners, James Mason and John Slidell, both of whom Russell had met and dined with the previous spring in Washington.

Mason was a contentious figure. He had been a senator, and had helped to pen the Fugitive Slave Act of 1850 that had so upset Harriet Beecher Stowe. He was also a minister to England, and, during Parliamentary debates, had typically chewed tobacco and spat the juice, only some of which reached the spittoon. Slidell had been President James K. Polk's envoy to Mexico before the Mexican War.[20] These two gentlemen had been sent to England to take advantage of whatever pro-Southern favor existed there, and to try to win recognition. President Jefferson Davis felt that after the victory at Bull Run, this was the opportune moment.

Captain Wilkes, Russell wrote, was returning from Africa and knew that the rebel emissaries were on board and thought he would create a little sensation, ". . . being a bold and daring fellow with . . . a great love of notoriety. . . ."[21] Henry Adams, a member of the prestigious Adams family, commented that if the Atlantic cable had been working, the United States and Britain would surely have gone to war over this unfortunate incident. As it was, the cable, which had been operational but had broken in 1858, would now not be entirely in working order again until 1868.[22]

A Navy Department official, whom Russell did not name, told the reporter that, naturally, they would apologize and rake Wilkes over the coals, but they would never give up the two men. The journalist took an unofficial poll of the legations of Russia, France, Italy and others, since they had all called on Lord Lyons. They were all in accord and on the side of England.

Wilkes brought on ". . . a storm of exaltation . . . over the land . . . [and] . . . Wilkes is the hero of the hour."[23] He was already the subject of biographies, and there was great demand for his photograph. The "hero of the hour" and the potentially incendiary incident he precipitated comprise the bulk of Russell's November and December Letters. As the days passed, each side was endeavoring to conceal their next move. Lawyers were walking the halls of the State Department, looking for legal precedents and arguments as hand-outs for the press. The journalist roamed the offices and headquarters listening to the murmured comments and asides. McClellan, he wrote, was in favor of immediate surrender of the prisoners, but public opinion would not have that. The talk from the Navy Department was that now that the deed was done, they would stick to their guns. Russell even heard from the Prince of Joinville, whose opinion was that it was an unfortunate turn of events for which there was no justification.

The reporter also discussed the conduct of Wilkes, for which he said there was no excuse. He wrote of the insult of the seizure and the questions that would most likely be asked; for example, ". . . what will the people say in England? How will they take this I wonder." [24] He scoffed at the American journalists who were writing as if it ". . . is the most natural and ordinary thing in the world to board a mail steamer and take . . ." Mason and Slidell.[25] He reported, later, that the papers ". . . are full of arguments, invectives and declamation concerning the seizure of the Confederate 'ambassadors', who have, I observe, become 'rebels' since they were sent to Fort Warren . . ."[26] in Boston.

The American Thanksgiving took place on November 28 that year and was celebrated, Russell said, by great drunkenness and fighting in the army. This was only an aside, as the debate of the *Trent* continued at a furious pitch. Russell attested to the legality of Mason and Slidell aboard the *Trent*, since they were lawful passengers on a neutral ship. Perhaps, had Russell known that they had letters from the Confederate government, he might have thought differently.

As the month drew to a close, Union successes, and in particular, the blockade, were noted. The President, who had been so downcast after the battles of the summer, was cheered enough to indulge in "quaint speculations."[27] For example, Mr. Lincoln calculated that "there are human beings now alive who may ere they die behold the United States peopled by 250 millions of souls."[28] Russell thought this fanciful observation extremely diverting.

The month of December opened with nothing new so far as the *Trent* situation was concerned. Captain Wilkes continued to be a hero. The Belgian Ambassador told Russell of an occasion during the Crimean War when a similar incident occurred. A United States ship received a Russian Ambassador in the Bay of Piraeus. Also in the bay were English and French ships, who were obviously in a state of war with the Russians. The captain of the U.S. ship hoisted and saluted the Russian flag when the Ambassador boarded. The French admiral suggested that the English admiral board the American ship and seize the Russian Ambassador. The Englishman, however, refused to do this.

The days passed, with Russell visiting back and forth and dining with various prominent individuals. He attended balls with sundry regiments which he complimented. He visited the Garabaldian Guard for dinner, a meal which he pronounced excellent. He thought it an incredible company, filled as it was with Spaniards, Poles, Hungarians and Frenchmen.

The unanimity of the South, he wrote, was forcibly brought home to the people of the North by "the very success of the expeditions."[29] Russell said that any positive gains in battle the North made turned against them. This was readily evident in the hatred in the eyes of the women; the villages and crops that were burned; and the curses that rang out as the soldiers passed. Instead of persuading the South back to the Union, as Seward vainly hoped, they were having the opposite effect.

Ever in the minds of Americans (both North and South) was England's reaction in the face of the crisis. Russell wrote that the press was confident ". . . that the *Trent* business was quite according to law, custom, and international comity, and that England can do nothing. . . ."[30] Yet, Americans waited with ears cocked across the Atlantic, and in his entry of December 15, Russell recorded that ". . . the first echo of the *San Jacinto's* guns in England reverberated in the United States and produced a profound sensation."[31]

These reverberations were very strong. It seemed that England exalted in a euphoric war fever. Delane, in a letter to Russell dated December 11, wrote that there was real and honest desire to settle old scores, namely ". . . the foul and incessant abuse of Americans. . . ." If the British were foiled by a surrender of the prisoners, there would be a universal feeling of disappointment. They were confident, however, that they would ". . . give them such a dusting this time. . . ."[32] Even Karl Marx contributed to the war fever, writing later: ". . . the call for war with the United States resounded from almost all sections of society."[33]

Russell, on the other hand, was puzzled by the reactions of the Americans around him. It appeared that they were angry that the British reacted negatively to the seizure. Meeting Mr. Seward at a ball, Russell found him taking pains to tell all how disastrous a war with the United States would be for the British: "We will wrap the whole world in flames"[34] was his extravagant pronouncement. One of the guests drew the reporter aside and explained that when Seward was most extreme, he was really his most amenable. It seemed that had he been calm and quiet, there would have been serious cause to worry.

In the face of such martial excitement, Mowbray Morris, again, expressed concern for his Special Correspondent. Morris, in communication with Russell, detailed what he must do in the eventuality of a war. Presuming that his base of operations would be Canada, Morris told the reporter that his first duty was to place himself in the safety of the British Legation on board a British ship.[35]

Meanwhile, Lord Palmerston, the Prime Minister, had called a meeting of the cabinet, making it quite clear that he had no intention of waiting for the situation to change. As tempers simmered and rumors flew, Lord Lyons was instructed by Lord John Russell, the Foreign Minister, to make the following demands: reparations, the immediate release of the prisoners and a formal apology. If these conditions were not met, the Ambassador was told to break relations and return home, or, at least, to move on to Canada. The truth, however, was that since the cables were not working, mail took a very slow two weeks to get across the ocean. Hence, the hot tempers were already beginning to cool, especially as each adversary eventually learned of the reactions of the other.

Russell wrote that Lord Lyons came to Mr. Seward to read out Lord Russell's letter. Mr. Seward made no immediate response, though it was understood, through the letter, that the United States could admit to no wrongdoing. During the days before a formal answer was given, many in the capital were sure that it would mean nothing less than war. Rumors of war gave way to speculation. Some said General Scott ought to bring his "old bones" back from Europe in order to lead a campaign into Canada. Lincoln, however, on behalf of his government, refused to be coerced in the matter. In his Letter of December 19, Russell wrote that Lincoln had put his foot down on the questions of surrender, saying that "he would die sooner than submit to the humiliation of his country; whereupon it was observed that it would be better to lose a President than see the ruin of the republic."[36]

The war frenzy died down, however, when the ". . . Prince Consort . . . professed willingness to believe that Wilkes' act was unauthorized or a result of a misunderstanding of orders. . . . [He] . . . hoped that Americans of their own accord would make redress."[37] The letter was obviously worded in such a way so as to give Washington an "out." They could simply agree, even if it were not the case, that Captain Wilkes had, indeed, acted as specified in Prince Albert's letter.

In a letter to John Delane, dated December 20, Russell wrote his assessment of the situation. Though Seward was confident that the matter would be peaceably resolved, Russell told Delane that it would be a difficult resolution as long as the press and public continued to laud the seizure of the two men as a bold act. Lord Lyons, he continued, was "a very odd sort of man & not quite the person to deal with this crisis."[38] Though Lyons was diligent, Russell felt that he was nervous and afraid of responsibility. In addition, he had no great influence in Washington circles because he did not mix very much with them, preferring his fellow Englishmen and gentlemen from the other legations.

The time limit for these "explanations" came and went, since it was all overshadowed by the report that the Prince Consort had died on December 14. The journalist noted this lamentable event, saying that it cast the deepest gloom over the English colony in Washington. As it did with much news of this sort, the colony waited, hoping that the report was false. Sadly, it was not. They were informed of the melancholy event ten days after it occurred. Therefore, Christmas celebrations were unusually subdued. After Christmas had passed, there was still no answer from Seward to Lord Lyons. However, on the 27th, the answer came, stipulating that the North would, indeed, give up the prisoners. Russell was extremely surprised, not to say put out, with this outcome. All his dire prophecies had been completely wrong. Mr. Seward had given a letter placing the Commissioners at the disposal of Lord Lyons. They would leave by steamer for Europe immediately. Russell decided to go to Fort Warren to see the detainees released. In this context, he wondered what a particular friend of his, an unnamed general, would think, since that general had said that he would "snap his sword, and throw the pieces into the White House, if they were given up."[39]

The truth was that Russell felt insulted on behalf of his government by the way in which the circumstances concluded. Putting the men quietly on board a steamer gave the government and people of Great Britain no satisfaction whatsoever. Russell fumed that it was "exigent, imperious . . . ."[40]

Offended as he was, Russell must have known that the history of maritime relations between the two nations had been shaky at best. This relative victory for the United States must need put all these issues finally to rest. Seward had stated that when Wilkes took Mason and Slidell off of the *Trent* that he was, in a way, impressing them. Since the United States had freed them, and the British had approved of the freeing, it then followed that the British, themselves, could no longer justify impressment. In addition, this issue finally settled the question of any British intervention in the conflict between the states. To the Americans, it appeared that the roaring of the British lion had all been just a lot of talk.[41]

The prisoners were released, and Russell wrote with irony that

. . . the hate of Britain is at least twice as strong as the love of Union among many millions of Americans. . . . Some of the regiments were rejoicing over the prospect of war with Britain, whom, perhaps, they think more easy to be beaten than Confederates.[42]

The irony ceased as the journalist, in a complete about-face, also communicated to his readers the estimable way in which the American public had received the sad news of the death of the Prince Consort. Their genuine expressions of sympathy were a credit to them, and gratifying to all Englishmen. All the American papers, reflecting public opinion. expressed deepest condolences for the grief-stricken Queen.

Russell proceeded to New York with the Queen's messenger, Mr. Conway Seymour. Seymour's instructions from the British admiral allowed for the removal of the prisoners from Provincetown. From there, they were to continue their interrupted journey to England, where they were received, by all accounts, in a "blaze of apathy."

Russell, not anxious to return to Washington, which would probably "close down" through the holiday season, spent New Year's Eve at the New York Club with several friends. These friends were berated by the other members for inviting the Englishman to the club. The reporter's popularity, which had rebounded slightly before this latest incident was, once again, in the cellar.

* * * *

Russell's next Letter from Washington showed effects of the backlash of the "Trent Affair." Regrettably, the journalist resorted to sarcasm. He described the idle boasting of the newspapers that the United States could have taken care of two enemies at once. Again the oft-repeated refrain was heard that after they had beaten England, because of her insults, the United States planned to annex Canada, and possibly make a move down to Mexico. Russell then harangued the press for its versions of the incident, saying that the statements, which appeared in the papers, had not even the smallest credence and less foundation.[43] Since the press took New Year's Day off, Russell wrote with a pen oozing with venom:

> The papers having suspended their circulation for one day in order to enable their printer to enjoy New Year's day, however, reappeared this morning with some expression of gratification at their finding the world had been able to survive their absence.[44]

It is stating the obvious to say that, once again, Russell was beginning to lose his objectivity. The journalistic high-jinks and elated American spirits were positively irksome to him. During the "Trent Affair," Russell's writing indicated just how personally the reporter was beginning to take these events, as well as his great offense and disappointment at its resolution. Hence, his assessment of the press and the events, themselves, begins to smack of overreaction.

During the "Trent" days, Russell's column and diary focused on little else. He did, however, manage to squeeze in the news that ". . . Federal General [Don Carlos] Buell is represented to be making preparations for the invasion of Tennessee, with the design of attacking Nashville . . . but the idea is in a crude state as yet."[45] Another item that came through, between grumblings that the ". . . march of events are the only things that march at Washington . . .,"[46] was one concerning General Sherman:

> General Sherman is believed to be rather too much of a Southerner in his views . . . because he will not permit the cotton to be taken and sent to New York . . . but I doubt the fact very much.[47]

Events in Tennessee would prove the truth of the first report and as for General Sherman's Southern proclivities, little space should be wasted in denying such a preference.

* * * *

Russell contracted typhoid in New York and spent most of the month in bed, complaining about the American press and continuing his letter writing. Largely, his letters were filled with concern for his family —making arrangements for them, and making sure that bills were paid. Russell, however, continued to ponder his usefulness at this point. The antipathy against him, which had abated during the fall months, was once again at a high pitch. Even McClellan had cooled toward him.

Adding to the hostility he was again experiencing, Russell's friend Bancroft Davis had resigned from *The Times*. It seemed that his strongly pro-Northern views were severely out of synch with the paper's implied editorial policy. For Russell, it was like losing his only ally.

Fretfully, he decided it was time for a break.

Chapter Fourteen

"Ave atque vale . . ."

IN THE LATTER PART OF JANUARY, desiring some kind of relief from his various maladies, and from the antipathy of the public, Russell decided to make an extensive trip to Canada instead of returning to Washington. He was concerned with his recuperation and thought a change of air would help recover his strength. Moreover, he was hoping, at a later point, to add a Canadian volume to his United States diaries. He planned to spend ten days there and "see how things are going on . . ."[1] north of the 39th Parallel. He would then, he told his readers, return to Washington, with the hope of getting back into the field. More importantly, he sincerely hoped there was something happening in the field when he returned. Russell's mood was such that he was sure, and reiterated this thought to his readers, that should he encounter another Bull Run, he would not come out of it alive. In spite of his plans for a short sojourn, he spent more than a month visiting the United States' northern neighbor.

Telling his readers he was widening the scope of his field, while availing himself of the inaction of the Army of the Potomac, he stated further that, when he left Washington, there was an obvious improvement in the appearance of the men. Discipline was much better and the ". . . hand of command was gradually hardening, contracting and closing its fingers on the yielding body."[2]

On the train to Toronto, Russell was able to observe what he termed the "republican simplicity" of the passengers. The windows were all closed, he wrote, and everyone huddled around the stove. He marveled that all sat together, rich and poor. He assured his readers that only those who have ". . . gone in third class Parliamentary train from London to Aberdeen . . ."[3] can imagine such a trip.

Arriving at Niagara Falls, Russell went again, with tourist-like fervor, to the British side to stand behind the falls. Returning to his train, he mentioned how the influence of the United States had crept into the Dominion. Without the Union Jack, one would have almost imagined oneself on an American train. While Russell was committing such idle thoughts to paper, the train ran through Hamilton and reached Toronto.

Russell, as already mentioned, intended to gather material for a Canadian companion to his diaries, North and South.[4] Away from the controversies and disquietude of Washington, he was able to regain some of the tattered shreds of his objectivity. He sat down and wrote Mowbray Morris a long and disheartening assessment of his stay. Having been in the United States for a year, he felt himself enormously unpopular, both politically and publicly; there was even a point when he blamed himself for the bad relations between England and the United States. The tone of *The Times* was regarded with anger and bitterness, and ". . . I am looked upon as the main agent in producing that disposition on the part of the paper."[5] Russell went on to explain his position, saying how tenuous his very life had become, and the death threats to which he was exposed. The disarray of his domestic matters bothered him tremendously, and he wrote about them in a most despairing way. He worried endlessly about how his wife would handle his older children in England. Along with the financial difficulties, resulting from a prolonged stay in the United States, he had two questions. What was his future in America, and, more importantly, what was his future with *The Times?*

These questions and concerns, however, were not answered satisfactorily by return mail. Instead, both Delane and Morris had made hasty replies, with definite views on where Russell should be. Ignoring Russell's depression, Morris told him to leave Canada, and that he must ". . . either go to the front or come home."[6] Delane relayed much the same message. The editor was not happy with Russell's move so far afield, and told him bluntly that he wanted ". . . letters from the Potomac . . .,"[7] not from Canada.

In a Letter from Montreal, Russell remarked that ". . . with new victories, the New York journalists begin their swaggering threats that England is next; that they will annex Canada, Cuba and all the islands of the West Indies."[8] The American press, he continued, told their readers that since there will be three-quarters Northern and one-half Southern troops who will surely no longer be fighting one another by the next 4th of July, rather than be disbanded, they will take the opportunity to rid the continent of every single foreign influence.[9]

Related to the above matter, Russell wrote about Canada's defenses in Toronto, and said that though they, too, were not sufficient, he believed that they were much improved since the troubles and threats of their southern neighbors.[10] He talked of Canada's train system and felt that it could not carry soldiers at high speed during the winter. However, perhaps because of the fierce Canadian winters, that would logically not be a problem.

He could not resist a final complaint about the United States press:

> The low price of the newspapers compels the proprietors to seek a large circulation, and to appeal to the passions, ignorance and prejudices of the multitude as the only means of doing so.[11]

Russell mentioned the death of Willie Lincoln, the Lincolns' eleven-year-old son, with great compassion. "There seemed a great deal of sympathy for the loss sustained by the President who is tenderly attached to his little boy. . . ."[12] Willie died on February 20, and it must have given Russell a slight shudder to know that the cold that Willie was said to have was, in actuality, typhoid.

Taking Delane and Morris's mandate to heart, Russell returned to

Washington on March 1, 1862. Several events of importance were recorded by the journalist. Firstly, owing to the fair spring weather and the good clean condition of the roads, war councils were in progress. The officers, the heads of the medical, transport and commissariat "have been warned and in a short time the Army of the Potomac will be in the field."[13] Secondly, the Secretary of War, Mr. Simon Cameron, having been dismissed and sent to St. Petersburg as Ambassador,[14] was now replaced by a lawyer from Ohio named Edwin Stanton. In fact, those who were contented with Mr. Cameron's dismissal were also hoping for the dismissal of Mr. Seward, so that there would be "a reasonable chance of obtaining a hearing for their pleas of reconstruction."[15]

Stanton, appointed in January of 1862, was a Democrat and a harsh critic of President Lincoln. After the war, he was a Radical Reconstructionist, who pushed for acrimonious measures in the treatment of the former rebel states. He so angered the current President, Andrew Johnson, that Johnson summarily dismissed him. The furor over this and others of Johnson's unpopular policies brought the country to its first impeachment trial.

Stanton was a great favorite in the capital, wrote Russell in his Letter of February 23. People liked his ". . . clear-cut manifestos."[16] Russell met Stanton who, ". . . without making any positive pledge, used words which led me to believe he would give me permission to draw rations and undoubtedly promised to afford me every facility in his power."[17] This was Russell's last positive statement from Stanton concerning the necessary passes. From this point, his difficulties with the Secretary would begin.

Reporting that Donelson and Henry, forts on the Western rivers, were successfully taken by U.S. Grant and Andrew Foote, Russell's war news took a much more positive turn. In addition, Captain David Dixon Porter was massing a mortar flotilla, ready to menace New Orleans and Savannah. Russell, having spoken to a gentleman of Savannah, warned his readers that New Orleans would very likely capitulate, as had the forts in the Western rivers.

Preparations began in earnest for the Army of the Potomac to move, and Russell was eager to report all that occurred. To this end, at his next meeting with Stanton at Lord Lyons's, Russell asked point blank for a pass; Stanton got a pen and paper and wrote him one on the spot, putting a handwritten copy in his own pocket. This was authorization to accompany the army to Manassas, and only to Manassas. Unfortunately, the army had moved to Alexandria, so the pass was useless.

The problem with passes, as Russell wrote to Morris in mid-March, was that his were dated on a weekly basis, and no other journalist was subject to this treatment. He would constantly have to reapply for permissions, and this could easily be at most inopportune times, say in the middle of a crucial battle. Needless to say, it was an impossible situation.

Many of the officers who had befriended Russell during his stay were anxious for him to accompany them on various campaigns, but only if he could obtain the necessary passes. They were not willing to brave the displeasure of the press, and wanted all the responsibility to fall on the government. Each invitation stipulated "You will, of course, get written permission from the War Department. . . ."[18]

Despite problems with the War Department and the local press, Russell continued to concern himself with slavery and the affects the war was having on that institution. It seemed that the freed slaves, who were now working for the Federal government, were not in much better condition than they had been before the war. They were "in want of clothing, forced to work, [and] kept under strict surveillance."[19] Still, Russell's pen sighed, "they are free."[20] The reporter quoted Mr. Greeley's paper, the *Tribune*: "The manner in which a portion of this Northern army allows itself to act and speak toward the negroes is a disgrace to the civilisation it assumes to represent and defend."[21]

Before proceeding to Manassas, Russell was concerned with returning to Fortress Monroe. He had received information that the ironclad *Merrimac*," . . . was coming out again . . ."[22], and he was interested in seeing the results of her expedition. However, he was unable to get the specific pass needed, and had to be content, in his Letter of March 11, to send the account by the *Baltimore American* of the famous first battle of two ironclads, the USS *Monitor* and the CSA *Merrimac.* Russell felt that the Confederates lost yet another opportunity in this battle. The captain of the *Merrimac,* Captain Buchanan, formerly the head of the Washington Naval Yard, could have pushed his successes by destroying the whole fleet of transports and wooden ships at Fortress Monroe. He did not do this. Nevertheless, even with the *Monitor,* the U.S. Navy was constantly uneasy about the Confederate ironclad until it was scuttled in May of 1862.

In the "Monitor" Letter, Russell mentioned McClellan and predicted that

> . . . unless he speedily achieves some signal success by the troops under his direct personal command, he is not likely to retain the confidence of the Nation. . . . But General McClellan can never lose the credit of having taken the Volunteer masses in hand and formed them into an army, of inspiring them with confidence and instilling into them the principles of soldierly life and discipline. . . .[23]

Probably gratified by this praise, McClellan invited Russell to join the army, which was preparing to march to the York and James Rivers. Russell went, once again, to Stanton to obtain the proper passes and documentations, but this time he was directly refused. Stanton's excuse was that he could not treat Russell differently than he was treating the other journalists. Russell had received a pass from McClellan, and when the Secretary of War heard about this, he flew into a rage. This was a most curious reaction in view of the fact that Russell noted in his Letter of February 23 that Stanton and McClellan had a good relationship, and that Stanton praised the General. Strangely enough, in his diary entry, Russell says just the opposite. Russell felt that Stanton's animosity toward McClellan was due to a lack of confidence in the General's abilities. Stanton, according to Russell, was not a man of courtesy or delicacy of feeling. He was heady with the power of his office and let his personal feelings get in the way of the business he conducted. In a letter to Morris, he was much more blunt; he said that Stanton was "coarse vigorous ill tempered dyspeptic of the most inordinate vanity & ambition & his jealousy of McClellan is almost a mania for he thinks he sees in him ye next President. . . ."[24] Scholars, too, have speculated that the rage and refusal of a pass were due to Stanton's jealousy and dislike of McClellan, rather than enmity towards Russell.[25]

None of this helped the reporter much, since the guards would not honor McClellan's pass without further documentation from Stanton. Russell quickly walked to the Secretary's office. The Secretary, however, refused to see him. The journalist wrote him a letter, expressing his grave disappointment over the situation, and asked for an explanation. He never had the satisfaction of receiving one. Russell, then, appealed directly to President Lincoln. The President replied that it was *The Times'* pro-Southern attitude that was the problem. Therefore, the Union was no longer able to grant special favors to its correspondent.[26]

On April 2, the press was thrown into confusion because all passes for newspaper correspondents with the army were revoked. Further, those who had gotten passes to Fortress Monroe were told to leave or be arrested. Two days later, the order was rescinded. It seemed that ". . . it had been framed exclusively to prevent the London *Times* correspondent . . . Russell, from going to the peninsula."[27]

Russell's frustration can only be imagined, especially in view of the fact that he had once been so free to go everywhere and see anything that he chose. He felt that without this first-hand position, with the necessary official sanction, he could not report properly. It was plain, he wrote, that he had only one course open to him. His mission had been to describe the events and operations of the war. He had visited the South, come back north, and had the misfortune to witness the failed march to Richmond by McDowell. Russell assured his readers, perhaps defensively, that he had been an impartial witness to all these events, even favoring the nation trying to suppress a rebellion against a people by whom he was by no means impressed. Interestingly enough, the Confederacy now invited him to travel with the Southern armies. However, he felt that having stayed so long in the North, it would have been dishonorable to have done so. Besides, it would have been tremendously difficult to send letters from the Confederacy to England with the Union blockade solidly in place.

The notorious Bull Run Letter, he concluded, hurt every American's feeling, and, above all, "his vanity and his pride. . . ."[28] Billy Russell had known that no foreigner would be free from scorn when he wrote truthfully of the United States and its people. He had also known how his articles would be received and was prepared for the calumnies that were heaped upon his head. In the end, however, if he could not do his job, traveling with the army, there was little point in remaining. It was as simple as that.

Russell decided to terminate his mission and return to Britain.

On April 4, he arranged his passage, and on April 9, 1862, he sailed, with little regret, on the *China*.

> . . . I saw the shores receding into a dim gray fog, and 'ere the night fell was tossing about once more on the stormy Atlantic, with the head of our good ship pointing, thank Heaven, towards Europe.[29]

"... so illuminating a record ..."

1862–1907

NEITHER DELANE NOR MORRIS were pleased at what they could only see as Russell's impetuous return to Britain. Delane wrote, in a "... brief note of regretful greeting ...,"[1] that he was not sure that Russell had done right in returning so precipitately.[2] However, the reporter himself was thrilled to come home. His personal life was about to take a turn for the better since he wrote "... *The Times* had settled 300 a year on me for life. ..."[3] In addition, Russell, being only human, was relieved to be free of the tensions of Washington, D.C.

In 1863, the journalist published the United States portions (Vols. 1 and 2) of *My Diary North and South*. Upon reading the volumes, Russell's friend, John Bigelow, wrote a complimentary letter from Paris:

> I wish I could feel sure that leading members of the American Press visiting England in a period of great national trial would prove as fair witnesses.[4]

... and later on in the letter: "You have made a book which I found exceedingly readable, and I think it will prove so generally to Americans."[5]

Modern appraisals are even more complimentary. Allan Nevins called the diary "... so illuminating a record that all students of the war must regret that he could not continue to the end."[6] As a diarist, Nevins described Russell as "... indefatigable, perceptive and impartial."[7] Fletcher Pratt, who presented the first edited version of the di-

ary in 1954, described the work as ". . . a book of pictures in movement. . . . No one has left anything comparable"[8] and its value was ". . .
its objectivity at a time when almost nobody was being objective. . . ."[9]
Russell undoubtedly would have made his place in American history
had he stayed the entire course of the Civil War. American schoolchil-
dren would have known him for his possible pronouncements on the
Battle of Gettysburg or the Emancipation Proclamation, as English
children do for his dispatches from the Crimea.

Employing hindsight, there is little doubt that Russell's immense
unpopularity in America, after the Bull Run Letter, was due to the
widespread resentment towards an Englishman's criticism of the country and its inhabitants. It wasn't only because, as de Tocqueville and as
Russell himself observed, Americans couldn't "take it"; it was also because

> . . . Russell was an alien, writing for a paper that was partisan in its
> views on the American conflict and for an audience that was accus-
> tomed to being entertained by the crudities and absurdities of the
> American scene.[10]

Nevertheless, one must admit that some of the fault was Russell's,
since, along with adopting some of the stereotypes, there were additional facets of the American character that he failed to understand.
He tended to put too much emphasis, in his own mind, on the cari-
catures and vulgarities of habit, while omitting the proper emphasis
on the ideological zeal and the infinite worth that Americans put on
freedom, liberty and Union. Perhaps, had he stayed longer, those less
tangible "peculiarities" might have become more evident.

The result of Russell's departure was ". . . a serious reduction in the
quality of *The Times'* American reporting and the removal of the last
effective counterweight to the paper's pro-Southern editorial authority."[11] Subsequently, Charles Mackay, a journalist and poet, was sent to
America. Politically, his bias was clearly pro-Southern, and he made no
claims to objectivity. Ultimately, he became so obvious in his predis-

positions that his editors had to instruct him to moderate his tone. Russell's return also convinced the British reading public of the "illiberality"[12] of the Union, and cast a shadow on the veracity of further Northern military reporting.

Several other diary entries and Letters concerned the American conflict. These words were written after the first two volumes of *My Diary North and South* were published. The entry, for September 28, 1863, showed that Russell had recovered his equilibrium regarding the United States. He wrote that the British journals still went on as if the North were going to lose the war: "Such rubbish!" Billy Russell declared that "John Bull" was distracted by jealousy to such a great extent that they had ceased to be even moderately reasonable.[13]

In a letter dated March 8, 1865, Russell complained:

> As I from the first maintained the North must win, I was tabooed from dealing with American questions in *The Times* even after my return to England.[14]

And, on June 12, 1865, in his last entry pertaining to the civil conflict, he confided that, in view of four years of abuse, *The Times* was committing an enormous blunder in threatening the North with the loss of good British opinion. Things might have been quite different had they followed Russell's sage advice. Nevertheless, he ended smugly:

> Why, we have been abusing them for four years, and cannot think worse of them! But had *The Times* followed my advice, how different our position would be—not only that of the leading journal, but of England. If ever I did a state service, it was in my letters from America.[15]

There was, indeed, at the end of the Civil War, little for which Russell need reproach himself. He had maintained objectivity, until bitterness and anger overtook him after the unfair reaction to the Bull Run Letter. Moreover, even in such a state of resentment, most of his attacks had been limited to the American press. As a result, those final seven or so months of reporting had afforded the reader some fascinating insights and beautifully drawn pictures of nearly every major figure on the Union and Confederate scene, with the very regrettable exception of General Robert E. Lee. Significantly, his writings, in both Letters and diary, had maintained a sense of humor and drama, along with an imaginative and, in some instances, uncanny foresight. Added to that were his wonderfully detailed descriptions of flora and fauna, and the ability to convey the unparalleled beauty of this immense and pristine land.

Contending with all the influences and obstacles that a man of warmth and compassion, and with such a great ability to make friends, might have to overcome, Russell never flinched at what he believed to be his role as a correspondent: "All that a newspaper correspondent wants is to see what is done, and to describe it to the best of his ability."[16]

* * * *

The man who tells the truth as he sees it is not usually appreciated until after his death has smoothed out the controversies of his life. The amount of recognition that Russell received during his productive and declining years, however, belies this axiom.

The Times continued to use Russell's services as a painter of word pictures. In March of 1863, Delane pleaded with Russell to write the Letter describing the wedding of the Prince of Wales to Princess Alexandra of Denmark. After all, Delane said, he had done such a good job with the coronation of Alexander II. Besides, since he, Delane, would rather be at the bottom of the Castle well than at the Castle wedding, Russell was reluctantly compelled to take the assignment. The Prince of Wales was so pleased with the account that he asked Russell to render it into book form. It was the beginning of a great friendship between the reporter and His Royal Highness.

In 1865, with the end of the American Civil War, Delane had the excellent idea that Russell ought to go back in order to describe the settlement and after-effects of the long and harrowing conflict. Russell considered the idea, actually eager to return to the United States. He wanted to see what had resulted from the cruel and horrifying war, and personally wished to justify himself to his American friends. In the end, seeing a stronger obligation to his wife and children, he demurred, writing: "I have sacrificed my own strong personal feelings to go to the States and wipe off the mud with which I have been encrusted there."[17]

However, Russell could not resist new adventure, when, in 1866, he was asked to report the Austro-Prussian War. Once again, he hesitated momentarily because of Mary's continued bad health; nonetheless, in the end, he went. He traveled with the Austrian army, and witnessed their retreat in July of 1866, and the armistice on the 18th of that month. In October, Russell returned home to find Mary deathly ill. Her condition was so serious that he was required to limit his own visits, as they tired her out.

Mary died January 24, 1867. Delane wrote to Russell: "There has been no more devoted husband than you."[18] Considering her state of mind and health for the previous ten years, one has to wonder according to what standard Delane was making this tender assessment.

On a more positive note, despite the publication of Russell's American diary, which clearly underlined his lack of decisiveness, General McClellan, nevertheless, eagerly sought out the journalist during his visit to London in 1867. Disappointed in not finding Russell at his office, McClellan wrote this short, regretful note:

> I called at your office this morning and was much disappointed to find that you are not in town, for I had hoped to renew the acquaintance begun some years since in Washington, and to express the regret I have always felt that the Secretary of War did not permit you to accompany the Army of the Potomac to the Peninsula.[19]

After Mary's death, Russell felt an uncharacteristic need for solitude. It was during this period that he decided to finish a novel he had been working on in a desultory fashion for quite some time. He retired from public life, but found that he could not work under those circumstances; his need for company impeded his ability to concentrate. He did eventually produce a novel entitled *The Adventures of Dr. Brady*, which was serialized in a magazine and printed in three volumes. It was the story of a man's life from boyhood onward in Ireland. By no means a bestseller, even Russell thought it was "bosh."

The journalist continued working closely with the two publications with which he had so long been associated. His post as editor on the *Army and Navy Gazette* lasted from its founding in 1859 until about 1900. In 1868, he tried dabbling in politics when he decided to stand for Parliament—he lost. He continued both on assignment and as a frequent contributor to *The Times*. His subsequent assignments included the various military conflicts, and some interesting junkets with the Prince of Wales. For example, he joined the Prince on a tour of Egypt and the Near East in 1869, then back to India in 1875. It was at this point that Russell was drawn closely into the Prince's circle, receiving invitations to tour with him, as well as to Sandringham, the Prince's country home, for weekends and to Marlborough House.

The reporting of the Franco-Prussian War of 1870 became Russell's last major military outing, though he did cover the Zulu War in South Africa in 1879. He had initially thought about traveling with the French army, but was eventually posted with the Prussian armies. More specifically, the journalist accompanied both the Crown Prince Frederick William and Bismarck during the campaign. He had the opportunity to meet the Crown Prince's wife, Queen Victoria's oldest daughter, Vicky, and was invited to their youngest daughter's christening.

It was during this assignment that Russell observed changes in the profession of war correspondent, to which he regretfully could not agree. As a result of modern methods, the speed in covering the news seemed more important than the accuracy of reporting. Therefore, acute judgment or writing skills were pushed aside for the ability to quickly "scoop" a story.

In 1879, Russell went on his last campaign, spending six months in South Africa. He had applied to *The Times*, but they were no longer interested in his services. The *Daily Telegraph*, however, was, so Russell traveled to the continent of Africa to report the Zulu War. The war was being fought for control of South Africa, and continued for a long time after Russell returned to England. It was during this campaign, on November 22, 1879, that Russell's long- time editor, John Delane died. Russell, who considered him an extremely close friend, was devastated. "The pain I feel now is incurable. It is now more than thirty years since he began the friendship. . . ."[20] Most importantly, Russell felt that the last link with the past was gone.

The trip to which he looked forward with greatest anticipation, in the later years, was his return to the United States and Canada. His group traveled by way of Canada, through to California, then back east to New York. The reception that Russell received on his second visit in 1881 must have provided him with a source of immense satisfaction.

In the company of his good friend, the Duke of Sutherland, and others, Russell spent the spring and summer in North America. After arriving in Washington, Russell noted a ". . . vast change for the better."[21] Moreover, he was happy to report that spitting and chewing of the hated tobacco quid was definitely on the decline.

During his visit, Russell found that the bitterness and resentment of his reporting during that fateful year had, for the most part, dissipated. He found himself fêted and received with the same enthusiasm that had marked his pre-Bull Run months. He was much sought after, interviewed and described by the American press. They recognized that ". . . no one could dispute his right to be regarded as the most remarkable member of the profession."[22]

As before, Russell met with many notable figures on the political scene. At a dinner, President James Garfield remarked, when the subject of the notorious Bull Run Letter inevitably came up: "You brought us very bad news but we have since discovered it was true. I guess you were very sorry to be the bearer of it."[23] Later, at the same function, a cartoon was handed to Russell, which showed a man running madly, with a hint of cavalry in the distance. The caption read: "Russell at Bull Run." With good humor and tact, Russell drew, in front of the first man, a pair of legs and a disappearing body with a caption reading: "The last man of the Federal Army on that occasion." Everyone laughed, and the tension abated.[24]

Russell, again, wrote diaries of this new expedition. They were published in the following year, constituting several volumes and called *Hesperothen: Notes from the West.* In the book, he had many positive things to say about the progress of the United States. It was an apolitical writing, describing a meeting with Jefferson Davis, among many others, and a transcontinental train journey. He was also fascinated by the "Wild West" aspect of the towns that they visited: the outlaw gunslinger, the saloons and the Indians. Russell was able to see San Francisco, Yosemite, the Southwest, Leadville, and even stopped in Las Vegas. As before, he commented on the diversity of the citizenry, especially the Irish, the Germans and, now, the Chinese. He was most impressed and captivated by the members of the Pueblo tribe, whom he met outside of Santa Fé.

Perhaps the last word on Russell's American experience came from his friend Bigelow, in a letter written in the early 1890s:

> I think Seward regretted the necessity of your leaving the United States when you did. . . . [You were] . . . a victim of the Army for revealing its shortcoming to the world.[25]

* * * *

In 1883, Russell, rather surprisingly in view of his first experience, became engaged to marry. He had met the Countess Antoinette Malvezzi of Bologna, a Catholic lady from a very old family. His friends would view her as a much more amenable companion for Russell than Mary had ever been. She loved to travel, and, as evidenced by rotund figure, she also loved to eat, making them a pudgy couple. The Countess was also wise, charming, capable and a good money manager—everything poor Mary was not. However, the differences in their ages, Russell was sixty-three and the Countess thirty-six, as well as the differences in their backgrounds and religions, must have been very trying. They were married at the British Embassy in Paris in February of 1884. Afterwards, there was a large reception, among the invited guests Lord Lyons, who was now British Ambassador to France.

Russell spent the remainder of his life traveling to where the news was happening. He journeyed to Egypt and Palestine in 1882, and to South America, in 1889. He returned home via New York and took this opportunity to visit his friend John Bigelow. He returned to Egypt in 1892 and voyaged up the Nile. During, and in between, his trips, Russell was writing and publishing books, correspondence and several more unremarkable novels.

The conditions in Ireland continued to be an object of great concern, though his last diary entries show that he was becoming less and less optimistic about the possibility of an equitable solution to the problem. Moreover, in his later years, Russell became positively vituperative on the subject of the British press. No doubt, his American counterparts would have felt somewhat vindicated if they could have read diary entries like:

> The bitterness of *The Times* is unbounded. It is the most violently partisan paper in England or for that matter in the three kingdoms.[26]

or:

> I am disgusted with *The Times*. It now represents the worst side of the Saxon character—greed, selfishness, arrogance, intolerable conceit—chauvinism in excelsis.[27]

The journalist's last word as a war correspondent, however, was an article written on the Boer War for the *Daily Telegraph*. Although Billy Russell was eighty years old and could not go himself, he followed this conflict closely through the newspapers, and showed great concern for the initial poor showing of the British army. He was no more sparing of the British government, in its imperialistic posturing, than he had been at the interminable boasting of the Confederate and Union governments. He wrote: "We seem to imagine that we are not only actually, but naturally and permanently, the greatest country in the whole world."[28]

In 1895, on the recommendation of Lord Roseberry, Russell was knighted, and most people felt that it was a long time coming. Apart from England, five other European countries bestowed honors upon the world-famous journalist. In 1902, Edward VII presented Russell with the Commander of the Royal Victorian Order (C.V.O.). During the ceremony, the King whispered "to the veteran of eighty years, who had been his intimate friend, 'Don't kneel Billy, stoop', . . . giving him a warm grasp of the hand."[29]

The last years of his life saw Russell affected by many physical infirmities. By 1904, his writing was stilled, his hand too shaky to put pen to paper. He was also crippled in his legs from rheumatism. Nevertheless, he and his wife kept up their travel schedules, going to Ireland and various parts of England, looking for sea and water cures. He died in 1907, and was buried in St. Paul's Cathedral. The memorial inscription read:

SIR WILLIAM HOWARD RUSSELL, LL.D

THE FIRST AND GREATEST OF WAR CORRESPONDENTS

CRIMEA, 1854. INDIA, 1857.

UNITED STATES OF AMERICA, 1861

FRANCE, 1870. SOUTH AFRICA, 1879.

BORN MARCH 28, 1821. DIED FEBRUARY 10, 1907.

* * * *

It was extremely unfortunate that Russell was unable to stay in America for the full four years of the Civil War. His astute and often acerbic writing would have been a tonic to a nation and press often mired in self-delusion. Russell, like a Greek chorus, commented on the tragedy of war, but generally kept sentiment and emotional involvement out of the scene. The journalist was, however, in the United States long enough to write about the major events of the first year: Bull Run and the "Trent Affair."

Sadly, the impact of those writings on the American and British public (excepting the meteoric Bull Run "controversy") was, of necessity, rather slight. Knowing the intense impression that Russell made on his readers during the Crimean War and other events, it is interesting to examine the reasons for this lack of impact. Primarily, Russell was sabotaged by *The Times'* dogged pro-Southern stance. It was mainly because of this position that Russell was denied his safe conduct pass for the Peninsular Campaign of spring, 1862. Secondly, Russell's impartial reporting was making him enemies in both the North and South. During a war, positive propaganda is often more important to national morale than the truth. And, finally, Russell did not stay long enough to make a lasting impression on the American mind. Indeed, the unfortunate circumstances of his departure provided us with a diary of great value, but deprived us of one that might have been priceless.

* * * *

Russell's dedication to the truth and his ". . . absolute independence of judgment . . ."[30] made him, on the one hand, vastly unpopular and, on the other, positively inspirational. Nevertheless, Russell always told the truth, insofar as he saw and knew it. In the Crimea, this meant criticizing the leadership of the army, and, thus, becoming the conduit for improving the conditions of the men. It meant writing the kind of harrowing and graphic articles that inspired the tireless Florence Nightingale to bring her band of intrepid nurses to the ghastly horror of Scutari. It also meant carefully analyzing both American armies in the spring of 1861, and seeing in them only slight potential as fighting forces. It meant that Russell saw nothing glorious in the dubious victory at Bull Run, and virtually none of the heroics of that afternoon that the American press had busily manufactured a scant month later. However, to be fair, as Russell himself said again and again, he had not seen the battle.

His foundation for telling the truth was his acute powers of observation. He was able, from a good position, to ". . . see the changing shape of a battle. . . ."[31] In addition, his judgments were made always on the basis of an observer and not a participant. They ". . . sprang from . . . a realistic view, based on . . . [Russell's] . . . reading of history and his . . . experience . . . and high standards of what constituted decent, civilized, humane conduct."[32]

In addition to military acumen, his Letters showed an amazing feel for assessing and comprehending the convolutions of a particular political situation. In his travels, he was able, with reasoned intuition, to gain rapid insight into whatever forces were influencing the governments and people of a specific place. Moreover, he understood how these forces might affect those persons closest to the situation, and yet be least understood by the reading public. In India, this comprehension made him sensitive to the plight of the Sepoy during the mutiny; in the Crimea, it made him fight for better conditions for the common soldier; and, in the United States of 1881, it made him particularly concerned about the fate of the American Indian.

In the totality, Russell was extraordinarily lucky. From his vantage point, he saw virtually all of the Victorian Age. He reported most of its wars, saw all of its progress and recoiled at its mistakes. He had a chance to meet and observe most of the major figures of the era and count a sprinkling, such as Thackeray, Dickens and, later, Edward VII, as his friends.

It was said that he was the "first and greatest of war correspondents." This statement is, perhaps, an exaggeration, for there were certainly others. There is no doubt, however, that if he was not strictly the first, he was certainly the greatest, the most original and the most innovative war correspondent of his age. This is true not only because he had the opportunity to report nearly all the significant clashes of the nineteenth century, but also because of the intellectual and visceral manner in which he reported those conflicts.

Even when Russell lost the most valuable attribute of his profession —objectivity—a day never passed when the English-speaking world did not wonder "what Russell would say" about this event or that. Based on his outstanding reputation, what Russell said is still a most valuable resource of what really happened during the many events and conflicts of the age. Russell was never a chauvinist or a propagandist; his strength was, and is, that his readers knew that for him, at least, "great is truth and mighty above all."[33]

Notes

Abbreviations

MD Russell, William Howard. *My Diary North and South*. London: Bradbury and Evans, 1863.

TT *The Times* of London

Chapter One

1. *MD*, p.7.
2. Alan Hankinson, *Man of Wars: William Howard Russell of the "Times"*. London: Heinemann, 1982, p.268. Most biographical information comes from Mr. Hankinson.
3. Fletcher Pratt (ed. and intro.), *My Diary North and South*. New York: Harper & Brothers, 1954, p. vii.
4. Oliver Woods and James Bishop, *The Story of the Times*. London: Michael Joseph, 1983, p.98.
5. Hankinson, *Man of Wars*, p.7.
6. R.J. Wilkinson-Latham, *From Our Special Correspondent: Victorian War Correspondents and Their Campaigns*. London: Hodder and Stoughton, 1979, p.36.
7. Sir Sidney Lee (ed.), "Sir William Howard Russell" *Dictionary of National Biography*. (Supp.), Oxford: Oxford University Press, 1966, p.241.
8. Hankinson, *Man of Wars*, p.14.
9. Wilkinson-Latham, *From Our Special Correspondent*, p.36.
10. *Ibid.*, p.37.
11. *Ibid.*
12. Hankinson, *Man of Wars*, p.28.
13. *Ibid.*
14. Rupert Furneaux, *The First War Correspondent*. London, Toronto: Cassell & Company, 1944, p.12.
15. Pratt, *My Diary*, p. x.

16. Woods and Bishop, *The Story of the Times*, p.67.

17. Hankinson *Man of Wars*, p.2.

18. *Ibid.*, p.43.

19. Joseph J. Mathews, *Reporting the Wars*. Connecticut: Greenwood Press, 1957, p.66.

20. Nicolas Bentley (ed. and intro.) William Howard Russell, *Russell's Dispatches from the Crimea 1854–1856*. New York: Hill and Wang, 1967, p.13.

21. *Ibid.*, p.242.

22. Mathews, *Reporting the Wars*, p.66.

23. *Ibid.*

24. Lee, "Sir William Howard Russell", p.242.

25. Russell to Mary, November 8, 1854, as quoted in Hankinson, *Man of Wars*, p.76.

26. Furneaux, *The First War Correspondent*, p.12.

27. Letter from Russell to Morris, dated February 16, 1862. *Ibid.*, p.154.

28. Woods and Bishop, *The Story of the Times*, p.99.

29. Hankinson, *Man of Wars*, p.128.

30. *Ibid.*

31. Martin Crawford (ed.). *William Howard Russell's Civil War: Private Diary and Letters, 1861-1865*. Athens, Georgia: The University of Georgia Press, 1992, p.xxiii.

32. *The History of the Times: The Tradition Established*. London: Written, Printed and Published at the Office of *The Times*, Printing House Square, 1939, p.360.

33. Hankinson, *Man of Wars*, p.152.

34. John Bigelow, *Retrospections of an Active Life*, Vol. 1 (1817–1863). New York: The Baker & Taylor Co., 1909, p.346.

35. Hankinson, *Man of Wars*, p.2.

36. *Ibid.*, p.156.

37. Belle Becker Sideman and Lillian Friedman (eds.), *Europe Looks at the Civil War*. New York: Houghton Mifflin Company, 1931, p.80.

38. Donaldson Jordan and Edwin J. Pratt, *Europe and the American Civil War*. Boston and New York: Houghton Mifflin Company, 1931, p.80.

39. Sideman and Friedman, *Europe Looks at the Civil War*, p.38.

40. C. Van Woodward (ed.), *Mary Chestnut's Civil War*. New Haven, London: Yale University Press, 1981, p.227.

41. Alan Brinkley, *The Unfinished Nation*. New York: McGraw-Hill, Inc., 1993, p.251.

42. James McPherson, *Battle Cry of Freedom: The Civil War Era*. New York, Oxford: Oxford University Press, 1988, p.73.

43. "The Terror of Submission", *The Charleston Mercury*, October 11, 1860, http://members.aol.com/jfepperson/mercury.html.

Chapter Two

1. *TT*, www.spartacus.schoolnet.co.uk/PRtimes.htm, p.3.

2. *TT*, www.britannica.com.

3. Bigelow, *Retrospections*, Vol.1, p.348.

4. Philip Knightley, *The First Casualty: From Crimea to Vietnam*. New York and London: Harcourt Brace Jovanovich, 1975, p.34.

5. Bigelow, *Retrospections*, Vol.1, p.345.

6. Leslie Stephen, *"The Times" on the American War: A Historical Study*. London: William Ridgeway, 1865, p.1.

7. *Ibid.*, p.6.

8. *Ibid.*, pp.105-106.

9. *Ibid.*, p.106.

10. *Ibid.*

11. Hankinson, *Man of Wars*, p.155.

12. *The History of the Times*, p.359.

13. *Ibid.*, p.366.

14. *Ibid.*

15. Knightley, *The First Casualty*, p.34.

16. James Spence, *On Recognition of the Southern Confederacy*. London: Richard Bentley, 1862, p.2.

17. *The History of the Times*, p.360.

18. Wilkinson-Latham, *From Our Special Correspondent*, p.77.

19. Ephriam D. Adams, *Great Britain and the American Civil War*. New York: Russell & Russell, 1925, p.56.

20. *Ibid.*

21. Martin Crawford, "William Howard Russell and the Confederacy" *Journal of American Studies*, 15 (2), 1981, p.200.

22. Furneaux, *The First War Correspondent*, p.147.

23. Jordan and Pratt, *Europe and the American Civil War*, p.17.

24. The average Englishman saw Americans as having a distinct sympathy for rebellions. The Polish, Hungarian and Irish conflicts seemed a threat to the

Britons' very existence. (G. Smith, "Great Britain and the Civil War" *Nation*, 84 (January 31, 1907), p.304.)

25. Donald Bellows, "A Study of British Conservative Reaction to the American Civil War" *Journal of Southern History*, 51 (4), 1985, p.509.

26. *The History of the Times*, p.365.

27. Jordan and Pratt, *Europe and the American Civil War*, p.59.

28. Furneaux, *The First War Correspondent*, p.146.

29. G. Smith, "England and the War of Secession" *Atlantic Monthly*, 89, March 1902, p.23.

30. Knightley, *The First Casualty*, p.33.

31. Wilbur D. Jones, "The British Conservative and the American Civil War" *American Historical Review*, 58, 1953, p.543.

32. Hankinson, *Man of Wars*, p.155.

33. From R.K. Webb's *Modern England from 18th Century to the Present*, and quoted in Eugene H. Berwanger, Jr., (ed.), *My Diary North and South*. New York: Temple University Press, 1988, p.8.

34. William Howard Russell, *My Diary North and South*. Boston: T.O.H. Burham, 1863, p.3.

35. Edwin G. Burrows and Mike Wallace, *Gotham: A History of New York City to 1898*. New York, Oxford: Oxford University Press, 1999, p.867.

36. Crawford, *William Howard Russell's Civil War*, p.7, entry for March 8, 1861.

37. *MD*, p.5.

38. Crawford, *William Howard Russell's Civil War*, p.8, entry for March 9, 1861.

39. *MD*, p.4.

40. Crawford, *William Howard Russell's Civil War*, p.5, entry for March 5, 1861.

41. *Ibid.*, p.7.

42. *Ibid.*, p.28.

43. *Ibid.*, p.9.

44. Burrows and Wallace, *Gotham*, p.867.

45. *MD*, p.13.

46. Berwanger, *My Diary*, p.30.

47. *MD*, p.17.

48. John Black Atkins, *The Life of Sir William Howard Russell*. 2 Vols. London: J. Murray, 1911, Vol.2, p.7.

49. Hankinson, *Man of Wars*, p.157.

50. *Ibid.*

51. *MD*, p.14.

52. *Ibid.*

53. *MD*, p.4.
54. William Howard Russell, *The Civil War in America*. Boston: G.A. Fuller, 1861, p.3-4.
55. Crawford, "William Howard Russell and the Confederacy", p.192.
56. *MD*, p.25.
57. *MD*, p.24.
58. *MD*, p.26.
59. Crawford, *William Howard Russell*, p.24.
60. *MD*, p.14.
61. *Ibid.*, p.27.
62. Crawford, *William Howard Russell*, p.23.

Chapter Three

1. *MD*, p.32.
2. Richard M. Lee, *Mr. Lincoln's City: An Illustrated Guide to the Civil War Sites of Washington*. McLean, Virginia: EPM Publications, Inc., 1981, p.13.
3. Margaret Leech, *Reveille In Washington*. New York: Time Incorporated, 1962, p.11.
4. Knightley, *The First Casualty*, p.20.
5. . . .almost outnumbering the army of prostitutes which also descended on the capital. (Rupert Furneaux, *News of War: Stories and Adventures of the Great War Correspondents*. London: Max Parrish, 1964, p.29.)
6. *MD*, pp.33-34.
7. Hugh Brogan (ed.), *The "Times" Reports the American Civil War*. London: Times Books, 1975, p.9.
8. *Ibid.*, p.9.
9. *Ibid.*, p.10.
10. *Ibid.*
11. *MD*, p.51.
12. J. Cutler Andrews, *The North Reports the Civil War*. University of Pittsburgh Press, 1985, p.35.
13. Russell, *The Civil War in America*, p.12.
14. *Ibid.*, p.15.
15. With the exception of the Bull Run Letter, dated August 6, 1861, and published as *Mr. Russell on Bull Run*. New York: G.P. Putnam, 1861.
16. *MD*, p.34.

17. *The History of the Times*, p.365.
18. Crawford, *William Howard Russell's Civil War*, p.22, entry for March 26, 1861.
19. *MD*, p.36.
20. *Ibid.*, pp.37-38.
21. *Ibid.*, p.39.
22. *Ibid.*, p.40.
23. Russell, *The Civil War in America*, p.17.
24. *MD*, p.41.
25. *Ibid.*, p.42.
26. Amy Lafollette Jensen, *The White House and Its Thirty-three Families*. New York: McGraw-Hill, 1962, p.83.
27. *MD*, p.42.
28. *Ibid.*, p.48.
29. William Seale, *The President's House: A History*. Washington, D.C.: White House Historical Association, 1986, p.367.
30. *MD*, p.51.
31. *Ibid.*, p.49.
32. *Ibid.*, p.55.
33. *Ibid.*, pp.50-51.
34. *Ibid.*, p.47.
35. *Ibid.*, p.52.
36. Robert W. Johannsen (ed.), *Democracy on Trial: 1845–1877*, Vol. 4 *A Documentary History of American Life*. New York: McGraw-Hill, 1966, p.213.
37. Russell, *The Civil War in America*, p.16.
38. *MD*, p.61.
39. *Ibid.*, pp.60-61.
40. *Ibid.*, p.65.
41. *Ibid.*, p.64.
42. Crawford, *William Howard Russell's Civil War*, p.31 (f2).
43. Allen C. Guelzo, "The Gentleman from the Times" *Civil War Times Illustrated*, 18 (7), 1979, p.6.
44. Crawford, "William Howard Russell and the Confederacy", p.194.
45. Brian Jenkins, *Britain and the War for the Union*, Vol. 1. Montreal: McGill-Queens University Press, 1974, p.37.
46. Furneaux, *The First War Correspondent*, p.126.
47. David Herbert Donald (ed.), *Why the North Won the Civil War*. Louisiana State University Press, 1960, p.53.

48. Seward to Adams, April 10, 1861, from *Foreign Relations*, 1861, pp.71-80. David P. Crook, *The North, the South and the Powers, 1861–1865*. New York, Sidney: John Wiley & Sons, 1974, p.64.

49. Jenkins, *Britain and the War for the Union*, Vol.1, p.37.

50. *MD*, p.61.

51. Johannsen, *Democracy on Trial: 1845–1877*, Vol.4, p.224.

52. *MD*, p.66.

53. *Ibid.*

54. *TT*, April 5, 1861.

55. Crawford, "William Howard Russell and the Confederacy", p.192.

56. Gardner, "Bull Run Russell" *American Heritage*, 13 (June 1962), p.59.

57. Bigelow, *Retrospections*, Vol.1, p.347.

58. Furneaux, *The First War Correspondent*, p.126.

59. Atkins, *Sir William Howard Russell*, Vol.2, p.20.

60. *MD*, p.73.

61. *Ibid.*, p.72.

62. *Ibid.*, p.76.

Chapter Four

1. Russell, *The Civil War in America*, p.9.

2. *MD*, p.78.

3. *Ibid.*, p.84.

4. James McPherson, *Ordeal By Fire: The Civil War and Reconstruction*. New York: Alfred A. Knopf, 1982, p.153.

5. William and Bruce Catton, *Two Roads to Sumter*. New York: Mc-Graw-Hill Book Company, Inc., 1963, p.257.

6. Letter from Beauregard to Anderson, April 11, 1861.

7. "Confederate Military History, Volume 5, Chapter I", web page *The War Begins! Fort Sumter*. www.civilwarhome.com/CMHsumter.htm, pp.7-8.

8. Catton, *Two Roads*, p.269.

9. *TT*, April 15, 1861.

10. *MD*, p.79.

11. *Ibid.*, p.80.

12. *Ibid.*, p.81.

13. *Ibid.*, p.83.

14. *Ibid.*, p. ix.

15. Crawford, *William Howard Russell's Civil War*, p.36.
16. *MD*, p.85.
17. *Ibid.*, p.86.
18. Crawford, *William Howard Russell's Civil War*, p.37.
19. *MD*, p.91.
20. *Ibid.*, p.96.
21. *Ibid.*, p.98.
22. *Ibid.*, p.95.
23. Atkins, *Sir William Howard Russell*, Vol.2, p.23.
24. Crawford, *William Howard Russell's Civil War*, p.20n.
25. Letter of April 20, 1861. Russell, *The Civil War in America*, p.37.
26. *MD*, p.97.
27. *Ibid.*
28. *Ibid.*
29. George C. Rogers, Jr., *Charleston in the Age of the Pickneys*. Norman: University of Oklahoma Press, 1969, p.165.
30. *MD*, p.98.
31. *Ibid.*
32. *Ibid.*, p.99.
33. *Ibid.*, p.100.
34. *Ibid.*, p.102.
35. *Ibid.*, p.105.
36. *Ibid.*
37. *Ibid.*, p.108.
38. *TT*, April 15, 1861.
39. Brogan, *The "Times" Reports the American Civil War*, p.14.
40. *Ibid.*
41. Jordan and Pratt, *Europe and the American Civil War*, p.7.
42. *MD*, p.113.
43. *Ibid.*
44. Crawford, *William Howard Russell's Civil War*, p.40.
45. *MD*, p.116.
46. Crawford, *William Howard Russell's Civil War*, p.42.
47. *MD*, p.122.
48. Crawford, *William Howard Russell's Civil War*, p.43n.
49. *MD*, p.124.

Chapter Five

1. Entries of April, 1861. Woodward, *Mary Chestnut*, p.50.
2. *TT*, April 30, 1861.
3. Arnye Robinson Childs (ed.), *The Private Journal of Henry William Ravenel*. Columbia: University of South Carolina, 1947, pp.80-81.
4. Woodward, *Mary Chestnut*, pp.76-77.
5. *Ibid.*, p.65.
6. *TT*, April 30, 1861.
7. *Ibid.*
8. *Ibid.*
9. James Ford Rhodes, *History of the Civil War 1861–1865*. New York: MacMillan Company, 1930, p.28.
10. *MD*, p.125.
11. *Ibid.*, p.126.
12. Crawford, *William Howard Russell's Civil War*, p.45n.
13. *MD*, p.128.
14. *Ibid.*, p.130.
15. Russell, *The Civil War in America*, p.61.
16. Louis B. Wright, *South Carolina: A History*. New York: W.W. Norton and Company, Inc., 1976, p.171.
17. Wright, *South Carolina*, p.171.
18. *MD*, p.138.
19. *Ibid.*, p.140.
20. *Ibid.*
21. *Ibid.*, p.141.
22. Elizabeth Fox-Genovese, *Within the Plantation Household: Black and White Women of the South*. Chapel Hill and London: University of Carolina Press, 1988, p.104.
23. *Ibid.*, p.148.
24. *MD*, p.154.
25. Entries for May, 1861. Woodward, *Mary Chestnut*, p.59.
26. Crawford, *William Howard Russell's Civil War*, p.47n.
27. *TT*, May 1, 1861.
28. *MD*, p.155.
29. *Ibid.*, p.156.
30. *Ibid.*
31. *Ibid.*, p.157.

32. *MD*, p.157.
33. Letter from Russell to Bancroft Davis, May 1, 1861. Crawford, *William Howard Russell's Civil War*, p.49.
34. Russell to John T. Delane, July 16, 1861. *Ibid.*, p.90.
35. *TT*, May 2, 1861.
36. *Ibid.*
37. Letter from Russell to Bancroft Davis, May 2, 1861. *Ibid.*, p.50.
38. *MD*, p.157.
39. Crawford, *William Howard Russell's Civil War*, p.49.

Chapter Six

1. *MD*, p.159.
2. *Ibid.*
3. *Ibid.*, p.161.
4. *Ibid.*, p.162.
5. *Ibid.*
6. *Ibid.*, p.164.
7. *Ibid.*
8. *Ibid.*, p.165.
9. *Ibid.*
10. *Ibid.*, p.165.
11. *Ibid.*
12. *Ibid.*, p.167.
13. *Ibid.*, p.168.
14. *Ibid.*
15. *Ibid.*, p.169.
16. Russell, *The Civil War in America*, p.67.
17. Orville James Victor, *The American Rebellion*. London: Beadle and Company, (c)1861, p.40. Mr. Victor could not have read the Letter of May 8, 1861.
18. Entry for November 6, 1861. Woodward, *Mary Chestnut*, p.227.
19. Jordan and Pratt, *Europe and the American Civil War*, p.81.
20. Victor, *The American Rebellion*, p.48.
21. Crawford, "William Howard Russell and the Confederacy", p.199.
22. Russell, *The Civil War in America*, p.63.
23. Letter of June 20, 1861. Russell, *The Civil War in America*, p.175.
24. Johannsen, *Democracy on Trial: 1845–1877*, Vol.4, p.214.

25. *MD*, p.172.
26. *Ibid.*, p.173.
27. Atkins, *Sir William Howard Russell*, Vol.1, p.32.
28. Letter of May 8, 1861. Russell, *The Civil War in America*, p.72.
29. *MD*, p.253. This impression is most curious in view of Russell's unfortunate anti-Semitic bias. In his diary entry for May 29, 1861, he makes anti-Semitic remarks regarding the "undue" influence of Jews such as Benjamin, etc., in South Carolina. (Berwanger, *My Diary*, p.172.)
30. Crawford, *William Howard Russell's Civil War*, p.52.
31. *MD*, p.177.
32. *Ibid.*
33. *Ibid.*, p.179.
34. *Ibid.*, p.180.
35. Russell, *The Civil War in America*, p.52.
36. *MD*, p.182.
37. *Ibid.*
38. *Ibid.*, p.188.
39. *Ibid.*, p.189.
40. *Ibid.*
41. Letter for May 11, 1861. Russell, *The Civil War in America*.
42. *The Times*, May 16, 1861.
43. *Ibid.*, p.157.

Chapter Seven

1. *MD*, p.195.
2. Letter for May 12, 1861, *TT*.
3. *MD*, p.200.
4. *Ibid.*, p.203.
5. *Ibid.*
6. *TT*, May 16, 1861.
7. *MD*, p.206.
8. Russell, *The Civil War in America*, p.111.
9. Stewart Sifakis, *Who Was Who in the Civil War*. New York, Oxford: Facts on File Publications, 1986, p.68.
10. Russell, *The Civil War in America*, p.89.
11. *MD*, p.207.

12. *Ibid.*, p.208.

13. *Ibid.*

14. *Ibid.*, p.215.

15. *Ibid.*, p.217.

16. Russell, *The Civil War in America*, p.95.

17. *MD*, p.224.

18. *Ibid.*, p.225.

19. *Ibid.*, p.227.

20. *Ibid.*, p.229.

21. Letter from Russell to Lord Lyons, May 21, 1861. Crawford, *William Howard Russell's Civil War*, p.58.

22. Russell, *The Civil War in America*, p.121.

23. *MD*, p.233.

24. Crawford, *William Howard Russell's Civil War*, p.61.

25. *TT*, May 24, 1861.

26. *TT*, May 28, 1861.

27. *MD*, p.242.

28. *TT*, May 23, 1861.

29. *TT*, May 25, 1861.

30. *MD*, p.242.

31. *Ibid.*, p.244.

32. Entry of July 4, 1861. Woodward, *Mary Chestnut*, p.88.

33. Crawford, *William Howard Russell's Civil War*, p.65.

34. *TT*, June 14, 1861.

35. *MD*, p.257.

36. Russell, *The Civil War in America*, p.150.

37. *MD*, p.260.

38. Russell, *The Civil War in America*, p.147.

39. *Ibid.*, p.155.

40. *MD*, p.274.

41. *Ibid.*

42. *Ibid.*

43. *Ibid.*, p.275.

44. *Ibid.*, p.281.

45. *Ibid.*, p.285.

46. Russell, *The Civil War in America*, pp.167-168.

Chapter Eight

1. Crawford, *William Howard Russell's Civil War*, p.72n.
2. *MD*, pp.295-296.
3. *Ibid.*, p.299.
4. Henry Blumenthal, "Confederate Diplomacy: Popular Notions and International Realities" *Journal of Southern History*, 32, 1966, p.153.
5. *MD*, p.306.
6. Russell, *The Civil War in America*, p.181.
7. *Ibid.*
8. *MD*, pp.311 312.
9. Russell, *The Civil War in America*, p.182.
10. *MD*, p.313.
11. Guelzo, "The Gentleman from the Times", p.41.
12. *Ibid.*
13. *MD*, p.332.
14. Letter to *The Times*, July 15, 1861.
15. *MD*, p.333.

Chapter Nine

1. *MD*, p.323.
2. *Ibid.*, p.324.
3. *Ibid.*, p.327.
4. *Ibid.*, p.338.
5. *Ibid.*, p.340.
6. *Ibid.*, p.346.
7. Letter from Russell to Davis, June 22, 1861. Crawford, *William Howard Russell's Civil War*, p.74.
8. *Ibid.*, pp.74-75.
9. *MD*, p.355.
10. *Ibid.*, p.357.
11. Crawford, *William Howard Russell's Civil War*, p.75.
12. *MD*, p.367.
13. *Ibid.*, p.371.
14. *Ibid.*, p.369.
15. *Ibid.*, p.370.
16. Mathews, *Reporting the Wars*, p.83.

17. Bernard Weisberger, *Reporters for the Union*. Boston: Little Brown and Company, 1953, p.8.
18. *Ibid.*, p.16.
19. Andrews, *The North Reports the Civil War*, p.x.
20. Mathews, *Reporting the Wars*, p.85.
21. Russell to John T. Delane, July 16, 1861. Crawford, *William Howard Russell's Civil War*, p.89.
22. *Ibid.*, p.81.
23. *Ibid.*, p.86.
24. Weisberger, *Reporters for the Union*, p.79.
25. *TT*, November 26, 1861.
26. *MD*, p.377.
27. *Ibid.*, p.381.
28. *Ibid.*, p.382.
29. *Ibid.*, p.389.
30. *Ibid.*
31. Louis M. Starr, *Bohemian Brigade: Civil War Newsmen in Action*. New York: Alfred A. Knopf, 1954, p.42.
32. Crawford, *William Howard Russell's Civil War*, p.82.
33. Atkins, *Sir William Howard Russell*, Vol.1, p.47.
34. Pratt, *My Diary*, p.x.
35. Allen Nevins, *The War for the Union: The Improvised War 1861–1862*. New York: Charles Scribner's Sons, 1959, p.161.
36. *MD*, p.396.
37. *Ibid.*
38. Stewart Beach, "Exonerating Great Britain: a Review of *Great Britain and the American Civil War* by Ephriam Douglas Adams." *The Independent*, July 4, 1925, Vol.155, p.23.
39. *MD*, p.397.
40. Crawford, *William Howard Russell's Civil War*, p.85.
41. *MD*, p.398.
42. *Ibid.*, p.400.
43. *Ibid.*, p.406.
44. *Ibid.*, p.407.
45. *Ibid.*, p.413.
46. *Ibid.*, p.419.
47. *Ibid.*, p.424.
48. *Ibid.*, p.425.

49. Russell to John T. Delane, July 16, 1861. Crawford, *William Howard Russell's Civil War*, p.89.
50. *MD*, p.426.

Chapter Ten

1. Gardner, "Bull Run Russell", p.78.
2. Furneaux, *News of War*, p.30.
3. *MD*, p.428.
4. *Ibid.*
5. *Ibid.*, pp.428-429.
6. *Ibid.*, p.431.
7. Crawford, *William Howard Russell's Civil War*, p.92.
8. *MD*, p.433.
9. Crawford, *William Howard Russell's Civil War*, p.93.
10. *MD*, p.435.
11. *Ibid.*
12. *Ibid.*, p.436.
13. *MD*, p.437.
14. *Ibid.*
15. *TT*, August 6, 1861.
16. *MD*, p.442.
17. Gardner, "Bull Run Russell", p.78.
18. *MD*, p.444.
19. *Ibid.*, p.445.
20. *Ibid.*, p.448.
21. *Ibid.*
22. McPherson, *Ordeal By Fire*, p.208.
23. *MD*, pp.448-449.
24. *Ibid.*, p.449.
25. Gardner, "Bull Run Russell", p.80.
26. *MD*, p.450.
27. *Ibid.*, p.451.
28. *Ibid.*
29. *Ibid.*, p.453.
30. *Ibid.*, p.452.
31. *Ibid.*, p.453.

32. McPherson, *Ordeal by Fire*, p.208.
33. Russell, *Mr. Russell on Bull Run*, p.2.
34. *Ibid.*, p.9.
35. *MD*, p.457.
36. Russell, *Mr. Russell on Bull Run*, p.9.
37. *Ibid.*
38. *MD*, p.459.
39. *Ibid.*, p.465.
40. Letter from Russell to J.C. Bancroft Davis, July 22, 1861. Crawford, *William Howard Russell's Civil War*, p.94.
41. *MD*, p.464.

Chapter Eleven

1. *MD*, p.467.
2. Atkins, *Sir William Howard Russell*, Vol.1, p.64.
3. Gardner, "Bull Run Russell", p.64.
4. *Ibid.*, p.83.
5. Entry for July 30, 1861. Woodward, *Mary Chestnut*, p.122.
6. Russell, *Mr. Russell on Bull Run*, p.11.
7. *MD*, p.470.
8. *Ibid.*
9. *TT*, August 10, 1861.
10. *MD*, p.473.
11. Atkins, *Sir William Howard Russell*, Vol.1, p.69.
12. *MD*, p.474.
13. *Ibid.*, p.475.
14. *Ibid.*
15. *Ibid.*, pp.506-507.
16. *Ibid.*, p.477.
17. *TT*, August 10, 1861.
18. *Ibid.*
19. Atkins, *Sir William Howard Russell*, Vol.1, p.67.
20. *MD*, p.479.
21. *Ibid.*, pp.479-480.
22. *Ibid.*, p.482.
23. *Ibid.*, p.512.

24. *Ibid.*, p.483.
25. *Ibid.*, p.485.
26. *Ibid.*, p.487.
27. *Ibid.*, p.488.
28. *Ibid.*, p.492.
29. *Ibid.*, pp.497-498.
30. *Ibid.*, p.498.
31. *Ibid.*
32. *Ibid.*, p.500.
33. *Ibid.*
34. *Ibid.*, p.499.
35. Andrews, *The North Reports the Civil War*, p.100.
36. *MD*, p.499.
37. Entry for August 23, 1861. Woodward, *Mary Chestnut*, p.159.
38. Entry for August 29, 1861. Woodward, *Mary Chestnut*, p.171.
39. Catherine Cooper Hopeley, *Life in the South: From the Commencement of the War* [by a Blockaded British Subject], Vol. 1 and 2. London: Chapman and Hall, 1863, p.29.
40. Starr, *Bohemian Brigade*, p.56.
41. *Ibid.*, p.57.
42. Adams, *Great Britain and the American Civil War*, p.178.
43. *The History of the Times*, p.368.
44. *MD*, p.528.
45. Edward L. Pierce, *Memoir and Letters of Charles Sumner.* 4 Vols. Boston: 1893, Vol.4, p.42.
46. Bigelow, *Retrospections*, Vol.1, p.344.
47. Allan Nevins, *The War for the Union: War Becomes Revolution: 1862–1863.* New York: Charles Scribner's Sons, 1960, p.3.
48. Letter of July 27, 1861. Bigelow, *Retrospections*, Vol.1, p.358-359.
49. Letter of August 27, 1861. Furneaux, *The First War Correspondent*, p.144.
50. *TT*, September 10, 1861.
51. *MD*, p.516.
52. Furneaux, *The First War Correspondent*, p.152.
53. Woods and Bishop, *The Story of the Times*, p.102.
54. Furneaux, *The First War Correspondent*, p.141.
55. *Ibid.*, p.140.
56. *Ibid.*, p.155.
57. *Ibid.*

Chapter Twelve

1. *TT*, August 24, 1861.
2. *TT*, August 18, 1861.
3. Bigelow, *Retrospections*, Vol.1, p.370.
4. *MD*, p.505.
5. *TT*, October 19, 1861.
6. Letter from Russell to Davis, August 24, 1861. Crawford, *William Howard Russell's Civil War*, p.108.
7. *MD*, p.505.
8. *Ibid.*, p.508.
9. *Ibid.*
10. Wilkinson-Latham, *From Our Special Correspondent*, p.77.
11. Richard Wallace and Marie Pinak Carr, *The Willard Hotel: An Illustrated History*. Washington, D.C.: Dicmar Publishing, 1986, p.33.
12. *TT*, September 16, 1861.
13. *MD*, p.513.
14. McPherson, *Ordeal by Fire*, p.158.
15. *TT*, September 23, 1861.
16. *TT*, November 26, 1861.
17. *MD*, p.520.
18. *TT*, September 18, 1861.
19. *MD*, p.519.
20. *Ibid.*, p.535.
21. *Ibid.*, A prophetic statement.
22. *Ibid.*, p.525.
23. Crawford, *William Howard Russell's Civil War*, p.120.
24. *MD*, p.526.
25. *TT*, November 18, 1861.
26. *MD*, p.526.
27. *Ibid.*, p.525.
28. *Ibid.*, p.526.
29. *Ibid.*, pp.525-527.
30. *TT*, September 28, 1861.
31. *Ibid.*
32. *Ibid.*
33. *Ibid.*
34. *MD*, p.534.

35. *Ibid.*
36. Letter from Russell to Delane, September 13, 1861. Crawford, *William Howard Russell's Civil War*, p.131.
37. Atkins, *Sir William Howard Russell*, Vol.2, p.77.
38. *TT*, October 8, 1861.
39. *Ibid.*
40. *Ibid.*
41. *Ibid.*
42. *TT*, October 15, 1861.
43. *Ibid.*
44. *MD*, p.542.

Chapter Thirteen

1. *TT*, October 19, 1861.
2. *Ibid.*
3. *Ibid.*
4. *TT*, October 26, 1861.
5. *MD*, p.552.
6. *Ibid.*
7. *Ibid.*
8. Letter from Russell to John Delane, October 14, 1861. Crawford, *William Howard Russell's Civil War*, p.151.
9. *Ibid.*
10. From the *Historical Outlook*, May 1928, p.204, quoted in Knightley, *The First Casualty*, pp.33-34.
11. Quoted from *TT*, October 8, 1861. *The History of the Times*, p.369.
12. *MD*, p.319.
13. *TT*, November 18, 1861.
14. *MD*, p.566.
15. *Ibid.*, p.568.
16. Crawford, *William Howard Russell's Civil War*, p.148n.
17. *MD*, p.570.
18. *Ibid.*, p.572.
19. *Ibid.*, p.573.
20. Howard Jones, *The Course of American Diplomacy*. New York: Franklin Watts Inc., 1985, p.181.

21. *MD*, p.574.

22. Stanley Weintraub, *Uncrowned King: The Life of Prince Albert.* New York: The Free Press, 1997, p.409.

23. *MD*, p.575.

24. *TT*, December 3, 1861.

25. *TT*, December 9, 1861.

26. *Ibid.*

27. *MD*, p.577.

28. *Ibid.*

29. *Ibid.*, p.584.

30. *Ibid.*, p.576.

31. *MD*, p.587.

32. Knightley, *The First Casualty*, p.35.

33. *The History of the Times*, p.373.

34. *MD*, p.587.

35. *The History of the Times*, pp.371-372.

36. *TT*, January 8, 1862. It would be interesting to know whether Russell remembered these strange words after Lincoln's assassination.

37. David P. Crook, *Diplomacy During the Civil War.* New York, Sidney: John Wiley & Sons, 1975, pp.48-49.

38. Russell to John Delane dated December 20, 1861. Crawford, *William Howard Russell's Civil War*, p.207.

39. *MD*, p.593.

40. *Ibid.*

41. Jones, *Course of American Diplomacy*, pp.184-185.

42. *TT*, January 10, 1862.

43. *TT*, January 17, 1862.

44. *Ibid.*

45. *TT*, December 17, 1861.

46. *TT*, December 24, 1861.

47. *Ibid.*

Chapter Fourteen

1. Letter from Russell to John Delane, January 27, 1862. Crawford, *William Howard Russell's Civil War*, p.220.

2. *TT*, February 13, 1862.

3. *TT*, February 18, 1862.
4. A third volume of *My Diary North and South* entitled *Canada: Its Defences, Conditions and Resources* was later published.
5. Letter dated February 16, 1861. Furneaux, *The First War Correspondent*, p.153.
6. Letter from Morris to Russell, March 6, 1862. Hankinson, *Man of Wars*, p.180.
7. Furneaux, *The First War Correspondent*, p.155.
8. *TT*, February 23, 1862.
9. *Ibid.*, March 18, 1862.
10. *Ibid.*, February 19, 1862.
11. *Ibid.*, February 23, 1862.
12. *Ibid.*, March 18, 1862.
13. *Ibid.*, March 24, 1862.
14. The Democratic Party was not pleased with the selection of Cameron for this post. They disliked his abolitionist sympathies. In Russell's Letter of February 6, 1862, he declared that, on the contrary, Cameron was dismissed not for abolitionist sympathies but for "... the maladministration of the War Office and to the want of confidence reposed in him. ..." (*TT*, February 18, 1862.)
15. *TT*, February 6, 1862.
16. *Ibid.*, March 18, 1862.
17. *MD*, p.595.
18. *Ibid.*, p.596.
19. *TT*, March 13, 1862.
20. *Ibid.*
21. *Ibid.*, March 13, 1862.
22. *MD*, p.596.
23. *TT*, March 27, 1862.
24. Letter from Russell to Morris, April 4, 1862. Crawford, *William Howard Russell's Civil War*, p.237.
25. Berwanger, *My Diary*, p.339.
26. Atkins, *Sir William Howard Russell*, Vol.1, p.119.
27. Louis M. Starr, *Reporting the Civil War*. Allan Nevins (intro.) New York: Collier Books, 1962, p.195.
28. *MD*, p.600.
29. *Ibid.*, p.602.

Epilogue

1. Atkins, *Sir William Howard Russell*, Vol.2, p.116.
2. *Ibid.*
3. *Ibid.*
4. *Ibid.*, p.117.
5. *Ibid.*
6. Nevins, *The War for the Union: War Becomes Revolution: 1862–1863*, p.3.
7. *Ibid.*, p.245.
8. Pratt, *My Diary*, p.xiii.
9. *Ibid.*, p.x.
10. Mathews, *Reporting the Wars*, p.100.
11. Crawford, "William Howard Russell and the Confederacy", p.205.
12. Jordan and Pratt, *Europe and the American Civil War*, p.81.
13. Hankinson, *Man of Wars*, p.182.
14. *The History of the Times*, p.376.
15. Atkins, *Sir William Howard Russell*, Vol.2, p.120.
16. Hankinson, *Man of Wars*, p.270.
17. Atkins, *Sir William Howard Russell*, Vol.2, p.121.
18. *Ibid.*, 2:146.
19. *Ibid.*, 2:114.
20. Hankinson, *Man of Wars*, p.250.
21. *Ibid.*, p.251.
22. From the *St. Paul Pioneer Press*, dated May 25, 1881. *Ibid.*, p.252.
23. *Ibid.*, p.251.
24. Atkins, *Sir William Howard Russell*, Vol.2, p.314.
25. *Ibid.*, p.114.
26. Entry for March 6, 1893. Hankinson, *Man of Wars*, p.265.
27. Entry for February 8, 1894. *Ibid.*, p.265.
28. *Ibid.*, p.264.
29. F. Lauriston Bullard, *Famous War Correspondents*. Boston: Little, Brown and Company, 1914, p.67.
30. *Ibid.*, p.68.
31. Hankinson, *Man of Wars*, p.269.
32. *Ibid.*
33. Atkins, *Sir William Howard Russell*, Vol.2, p.390.

Bibliography

Primary Sources

Bemis, George. *Hasty Recognition of Rebel Belligerency and Our Right to Complain About It*. Boston: A. Williams & Company, 1865.

Bentley, Nicolas (ed. and intro.), Russell, William Howard. *Russell's Dispatches from the Crimea 1854–1856*. New York: Hill and Wang, 1967.

Bernard, Mountague. *A Historical Account of the Neutrality of Great Britain During the American Civil War*. London: Longmans, Green, Reader & Dyer, 1870.

Berwanger, Eugene H. Jr. (ed. and intro.). *My Diary North and South*. New York: Temple University Press, 1988.

Bigelow, John. *Retrospections of an Active Life*, Vol.1 (1817–1863). New York: The Baker & Taylor Co., 1909.

Brogan, Hugh (ed.). *The "Times" Reports the American Civil War*. London: Times Books, 1975.

Childs, Arnye Robinson (ed.). *The Private Journal of Henry William Ravenel*. Columbia: University of South Carolina, 1947.

Crawford, Martin (ed.). *William Howard Russell's Civil War: Private Diary and Letters, 1861–1865*. Athens, Georgia: The University of Georgia Press, 1992.

Hopeley, Catherine Cooper. *Life in the South: From the Commencement of the War* [by a Blockaded British Subject], Vols.1 and 2. London: Chapman and Hall, 1863.

The Times of London March 1861-April 1862.

Pratt, Fletcher (ed. and intro.). *My Diary North and South*. New York: Harper & Brothers, 1954.

Russell, William Howard. *The Civil War in America*. Boston: G.A. Fuller, 1861.

_____. *Mr. Russell on Bull Run*. New York: G.P. Putnam, 1861.

_____. *My Diary North and South*. London: Bradbury and Evans, 1863.

Pierce, Edward L. *Memoir and Letters of Charles Sumner*, Vol. 4. Boston: 1893

Spence, James. *On Recognition of the Southern Confederacy*. London: Richard Bentley, 1862.

Stephen, Leslie. *"The Times" on the American War: A Historical Study*. London: William Ridgeway, 1865.

Victor, Orville James. *The American Rebellion*. London: Beadle and Company, (c)1861.

Woodward, C. Vann (ed.). *Mary Chestnut's Civil War*. New Haven, London: Yale University Press, 1981.

Secondary Sources

Books

Adams, Ephriam D. *Great Britain and the American Civil War*. New York: Russell & Russell, 1925.

Andrews, J. Cutler. *The North Reports the Civil War*. University of Pittsburgh Press, 1985.

Atkins, John Black. *The Life of Sir William Howard Russell*, 2 Vols. London: J. Murray, 1911.

Brinkley, Alan. *The Unfinished Nation*. New York: McGraw-Hill, Inc., 1993.

Bullard, F. Lauriston. *Famous War Correspondents*. Boston: Little, Brown and Company, 1914.

Burrows, Edwin G. and Wallace, Mike. *Gotham: A History of New York City to 1898*. New York, Oxford: Oxford University Press, 1999.

Caroll, Betty Boyd. *First Ladies*. New York, Oxford: Oxford University Press, 1987.

Catton, William and Bruce. *Two Roads to Sumter*. New York: Mc-Graw-Hill Book Company, Inc., 1963.

Crook, David P. *Diplomacy During the Civil War*. New York, Sidney: John Wiley & Sons, 1975.

_____. *The North, the South and the Powers, 1861-1865*. New York, Sidney: John Wiley & Sons, 1974.

Divine, Robert A., Breen, T.H. et al. *America Past and Present*. (Brief 3rd Edition) New York: Harper Collins College Publishers, 1994.

Donald, David Herbert (ed.). *Why the North Won the Civil War*. Louisiana State University Press, 1960.

Foote, Shelby. *The Civil War: A Narrative; Fort Sumter to Perryville*. New York: Random House, 1958.

Fox-Genovese, Elizabeth. *Within the Plantation Household: Black and White Women of the South*. Chapel Hill and London: University of Carolina Press, 1988.

Furneaux, Rupert. *The First War Correspondent*. London, Toronto: Cassell & Company, 1944.

_____. *News of War: Stories and Adventures of the Great War Correspondents.* London: Max Parrish, 1964.

Hankinson, Alan. *Man of Wars: William Howard Russell of the "Times".* London: Heinemann, 1982.

The History of the Times: The Tradition Established. London: Written, Printed and Published at the Office of *The Times,* Printing House Square, 1939.

Hyman, Harold M. (ed.). *Heard Round the World: The Impact Abroad of the American Civil War.* (1st Edition) New York: Alfred A. Knopf, 1969.

Jenkins, Brian. *Britain and the War for the Union,* Vol.1. Montreal: McGill-Queens University Press, 1974.

Jensen, Amy Lafollette. *The White House and Its Thirty-three Families.* New York: McGraw-Hill, 1962.

Johannsen, Robert W. (ed.). *Democracy on Trial: 1845-1877,* Vol. 4 *A Documentary History of American Life.* New York: McGraw-Hill, 1966.

Jones, Howard. *The Course of American Diplomacy.* New York: Franklin Watts Inc., 1985.

Jordan, Donaldson and Pratt, Edwin J. *Europe and the American Civil War.* Boston and New York: Houghton Mifflin Company, 1931.

Knightley, Philip. *The First Casualty: From Crimea to Vietnam.* New York and London: Harcourt Brace Jovanovich, 1975.

Lee, Richard M. *Mr. Lincoln's City: An Illustrated Guide to the Civil War Sites of Washington.* McLean, Virginia: EPM Publications, Inc., 1981.

Lee, Sir Sidney (ed.). "Sir William Howard Russell" *Dictionary of National Biography.* (Supp.), Oxford: Oxford University Press, 1966.

Leech, Margaret. *Reveille In Washington.* New York: Time Incorporated, 1962.

Mathews, Joseph J. *Reporting the Wars.* Connecticut: Greenwood Press, 1957.

McPherson, James. *Battle Cry of Freedom: The Civil War Era.* New York, Oxford: Oxford University Press, 1988.

_____. *Ordeal by Fire: The Civil War and Reconstruction.* New York: Alfred Knopf, 1982.

Nevins, Allen. *The War for the Union: The Improvised War 1861–1862.* New York: Charles Scribner's Sons, 1959.

_____. *The War for the Union: War Becomes Revolution: 1862–1863.* New York: Charles Scribner's Sons, 1960.

Rhodes, James Ford. *History of the Civil War 1861–1865.* New York: MacMillan Company, 1930.

Rogers, George C., Jr. *Charleston in the Age of the Pickneys.* Norman: University of Oklahoma Press, 1969

Seale, William. *The President's House: A History.* Washington, D.C.: White House Historical Association, 1986.

Sideman, Belle Becker and Friedman, Lillian (eds.). *Europe Looks at the Civil War.* New York: Orion Press, 1960.

Sifakis, Stewart. *Who Was Who in the Civil War.* New York, Oxford: Facts on File Publications, 1986.

Starr, Louis M. *Bohemian Brigade: Civil War Newsmen in Action.* New York: Alfred A. Knopf, 1954.

_____. *Reporting the Civil War.* Allan Nevins (intro.) New York: Collier Books, 1962.

Truman, Margaret. *First Ladies.* New York: Random House, 1995.

Wallace, Richard and Carr, Marie Pinak. *The Willard Hotel: An Illustrated History.* Washington, D.C.: Dicmar Publishing, 1986.

Weintraub, Stanley. *Uncrowned King: The Life of Prince Albert.* New York: The Free Press, 1997.

Weisberger, Bernard. *Reporters for the Union.* Boston: Little Brown and Company, 1953.

Wilkinson-Latham, R. J. *From Our Special Correspondent: Victorian War Correspondents and Their Campaigns.* London: Hodder and Stoughton, 1979.

Woods, Oliver and Bishop, James. *The Story of the Times.* London: Michael Joseph, 1983.

Wright, Louis B. *South Carolina: A History.* New York: W.W. Norton and Company, Inc., 1976.

Periodicals

Beach, Stewart. "Exonerating Great Britain: a Review of *Great Britain and the American Civil War* by Ephriam Douglas Adams." *The Independent,* (July 4, 1925): 23.

Bellows, Donald. "A Study of British Conservative Reaction to the American Civil War" *Journal of Southern History,* 51 (4) (1985): 505-526.

Blumenthal, Henry. "Confederate Diplomacy: Popular Notions and International Realities" *Journal of Southern History,* 32 (1966): 151-171.

Crawford, Marian. "The Anglo-American Crisis of the Early 1860s: A Framework for Revision" *South Atlantic Quarterly,* 82 (4) (1983): 406-23.

Crawford, Martin. "William Howard Russell and the Confederacy" *Journal of American Studies,* 15 (2) (1981): 191-210.

Gardner, J.L. "Bull Run Russell" *American Heritage,* 13 (June 1962): 59-63.

Guelzo, Allen C. "The Gentleman from the Times" *Civil War Times Illustrated,* 18 (7) (1979): 4-11, 41-45.

Hernon, Joseph M. "British Sympathies in the American Civil War: A Reconsideration" *Journal of Southern History,* 33 (1967): 356-367.

Jones, Wilbur D. "The British Conservative and the American Civil War" *American Historical Review,* 58 (1953): 522-543.

Smith, G. "England and the War of Secession" *Atlantic Monthly,* 89 (March 1902): 303-311.

Smith, G. "Great Britain and the Civil War" *Nation,* 84 (January 31, 1907): 103.

Web pages

"The Terror of Submission", The Charleston Mercury, October 11, 1860, http://members.aol.com/jfepperson/mercury.html.

The Times, www.britannica.com

The Times, www.spartacus.schoolnet.co.uk/PRtimes.htm.

"The War Begins! Fort Sumter", Confederate Military History, Volume 5, Chapter I, www.civilwarhome.com/CMHsumter.htm.

Index

Lawrence, Kansas — July 24, 2004 — #848